Miami

TEMPTING TROPICAL TASTES FOR

HOME COOKS EVERYWHERE

Miami

*Tempting Tropical Tastes
for Home Cooks Everywhere*

Carole Kotkin and
Kathy Martin

HENRY HOLT AND COMPANY   NEW YORK

Henry Holt and Company, Inc.
Publishers since 1866
115 West 18th Street
New York, New York 10011

Henry Holt is a registered trademark of Henry Holt and Company, Inc.

Published in Canada by Fitzhenry & Whiteside Ltd.,
195 Allstate Parkway, Markham, Ontario L3R 4T8.

Library of Congress Cataloging-in-Publication Data
Kotkin, Carole.
Mmmmiami : tempting tropical tastes for home cooks everywhere /
Carole Kotkin and Kathy Martin.—1st ed.
p.   cm.
Includes bibliographical references and index.
ISBN 0-8050-5673-4 (hb : alk. paper)
1. Cookery, American.   2. Cookery—Florida—Miami.   3. Cookery,
Cuban.   4. Cookery, Caribbean.   5. Cookery, Latin American.
I. Martin, Kathy, 1952–   .   II. Title.
TX715.K749   1998
641.59759′381—dc21   97-43884

Henry Holt books are available for special promotions and
premiums. For details contact: Director, Special Markets.

First Edition 1998

DESIGNED BY KATE NICHOLS

For my mother, Edna Martin, who taught me to cook,
and in memory of my father, Alex Martin,
who taught me what joy there can be in cooking for others.

—K.M.

For my husband, Sidney, with love and gratitude,
and for our wonderful children, Linda, Laura, and David.
In loving memory of my parents, Dorothy and Sol Freedland,
who always thought I could do anything,
and my mother-in-law, Ida Kotkin, a woman before her time.

—C.K.

Contents

Preface

Mmmmiami.

Even the name of the place is exotic and alluring. It's America's subtropical outpost, its gateway to the Caribbean and Latin America. It's a place where Cuban, Jamaican, Salvadoran, Haitian, Peruvian, Bahamian, Colombian, and countless other cultures meet and meld. You can taste it in the food: the sensuous sweetness of a ripe mango, the fiery bite of a Scotch bonnet pepper, the addictive crunch of plantain chips, the homey comfort of black beans and rice.

Innovative Miami chefs put the city on the culinary map in the 1980s with their New World creations, and the word spread: Today you can order gourmet arepas and empanadas, jerk-seasoned pork, and yuca-crusted fish at fine restaurants throughout the country. Food industry giants have taken note, too: Gerber has a line of tropical baby foods, the folks who make Thomas' English muffins are marketing Cuban bread, and Knorr has a line of Latin soup and seasoning mixes.

There is no need, though, to settle for restaurant-priced or processed versions of tropical tastes. Propelled by the burgeoning Latin population in the United States, fresh tropical produce is finding its way into mainstream supermarkets. Brooks Tropicals of Homestead, Florida, one of the nation's leading wholesalers of tropical fruits and vegetables, is shipping mangos, papayas, malanga, and much more to cities large and small across the country.

The aim of this cookbook is to expand your culinary horizons—to teach you how to enjoy these new ingredients and to use more familiar Miami mainstays such as citrus fruit, bananas, rice, and beans in fresh and exciting ways. The recipes represent our interpretations of those ingredients, as well as standards such as Arroz con Pollo (Chicken with Yellow Rice) and Key Lime Pie that you'd be sure to sample if you visited here. Along the way we hope to show you Miami as we know it—a vibrant, everchanging place filled with warmth, vitality, and wonderful food.

Miami has always been a city of immigrants and adventurers, culinary and otherwise. In the late 1800s, settlers bartered with the Seminole Indians for wild turkey and venison, kept sea turtles in cages near the water's edge for eggs and meat, and turned guavas and Surinam cherries into preserves. Scavenging was another source of sustenance, some of it surprisingly sophisticated: A virtual holiday was declared on the south Florida coast in the late 1880s after a ship en route from Bordeaux, France, to Havana wrecked on the reef, strewing barrels of wine along the beach. In 1896, the year the city was incorporated, a menu at the Hotel Miami hinted at cutting-edge things to come with dishes such as sea bass chowder, pineapple fritters, and Indian pudding with wine sauce.

The cultural mix that is so much a part of Miami has been here from the beginning, too. The 1,950 residents counted in the 1900 census of the city hailed from thirty-four of the forty-five states, as well as Great Britain, Germany, Sweden, Italy, Russia, Spain, Canada, the Bahamas, and China. The influx of new arrivals has never ceased. A wild land boom in the 1920s, a major Jewish migration from the Northeast in the 1930s, a wave of World War II veterans from the Midwest in the 1940s and '50s, and floods of refugees from strife-torn Cuba, Central America, and Haiti in the 1960s, '70s, and '80s have remade the face of Miami again and again. Today more than half of the two million people who live in metropolitan Miami speak Spanish at home.

Many of us have come here fleeing something—be it war, poverty, or brutal winters—but have stayed because of what we found here. Carole came to south Florida from upstate New York as a child more than forty years ago when Miami Beach was known for its New York–style Jewish delis rather than the chic South Beach night spots. She became a cooking teacher in the 1970s when fine cuisine had a French accent, and she has been part of the movement to explore and spotlight the tropical bounty in our own backyard. Kathy came here as a journalist twenty years ago, cooking the way her mom had taught her on the farm back in Wisconsin, and she embraced the spice of life so abundant in Miami.

We have both raised families here, sending children to schools where Haitian Flag Day is observed as well as George Washington's birthday, shopping in markets where the clerks are more likely to speak Spanish than English. Along the way we've learned that diversity doesn't always yield harmony, that cultural differences can be a source of friction as well as enrichment. But we've learned larger lessons, too: that the love of good food is universal, that there's no better place than the dinner table to explore and appreciate another culture, and that a good meal, lovingly prepared, breaks down barriers like nothing else. With that in mind, we invite you to join us at our table and to partake of this extraordinary place we call home.

Miami

TEMPTING TROPICAL TASTES FOR

HOME COOKS EVERYWHERE

Ingredients Guide

Supermarkets across the country have begun to tempt shoppers with seductive mango, shaggy malanga, and other tropical produce. These fruits and vegetables have long been staples of Caribbean and Latin cooking and are a foundation of Miami cuisine. This guide covers the produce you're most likely to find and tells you what you need to know to make it a part of your food repertoire.

Boniato (boh-nee-AH-toh)

This tropical tuber is also called Cuban sweet potato, camote, and batata dulce. The name *boniato* dates to sixteenth-century Cuba and is thought to come from the Spanish for good (*bueno*) or pretty (*bonito*), though there's nothing pretty about the boniato's scruffy reddish exterior. It is related to but quite different from the more familiar orange sweet potato. It has a drier, denser texture, a more subtly sweet flavor (it reminds some people of chestnuts), and an off-white or cream-colored flesh. A native of the tropical Americas, it was introduced to Spain by Columbus and gained popularity in Europe until it was supplanted by the white potato, a New World import that, unlike the boniato, can be grown in cooler climes. Boniato has about 115 calories per half-cup serving and is a good source of potassium.

SELECTION AND STORAGE: Boniato is available year-round. Choose rock-hard tubers with no bruising, mold, sprouting, or other blemishes. Store them in a cool, dry, well-ventilated spot for no more than a few days.

USES: Although it's used in some Latin desserts, boniato is most often served as a vegetable. It can be cooked like a white potato or orange sweet potato—baked, boiled, mashed, or fried—and can be substituted for them in virtually any recipe. Because of its dry texture, boniato requires more liquid than regular potatoes when mashed or pureed (see page 218). And because of its delicate sweetness, it is best not to season it too heavily.

PREPARATION: Boniato oxidizes quickly, so cover it with water as soon as it's peeled (you may even want to peel it under running water) and keep it submerged in the cooking liquid when adding it to soups and stews.

Calabaza (cah-lah-BAH-zah)

This large squash (it averages 8 to 15 pounds) is also called West Indian pumpkin, Cuban squash, and, in Jamaica, big mama squash. It's popular throughout Latin America and the Caribbean, and is not entirely new to North America: Early Florida settlers learned to use a related wild squash from Native Americans. Calabaza's tough outer skin is orange, tan, and/or green, and its moist flesh is bright orange. It tastes like pumpkin but is sweeter and milder. It has fewer than 20 calories per half-cup serving and is high in potassium and vitamin A.

SELECTION AND STORAGE: Calabaza is available year-round. Because it's so big, it's usually sold in chunks. Choose pieces that are heavy for their size, with hard, unblemished skin and firm, moist flesh. They can be stored, tightly wrapped, in the refrigerator for up to a week. A whole one will keep for up to a month in a cool, dry spot.

USES: On its own, calabaza can be watery and fibrous. It adds a nice taste and texture, though, when combined with other ingredients in soups, cakes, and Calabaza Gratin (page 219).

PREPARATION: Scrape out the seeds and fibers, and cook the calabaza using one of the following methods. It's done when you can pierce the flesh easily with the tines of a fork. When the squash is cool enough to handle, scrape the flesh from the skin and chop, mash, or puree it as directed in your recipe.

Steaming: This is an ideal method, especially for large amounts. Cut the squash into manageable chunks and steam it over simmering water. Begin testing for doneness after 15 minutes.

Microwaving: This is a quick way to cook a small amount. Cut the calabaza into 4-inch pieces and arrange them, skin side down, in a glass baking dish or pie plate. Cover tightly with plastic wrap and microwave on high power. One pound cooks in about 10 minutes.

Carambola (care-um-BOLL-ah)

Also called star fruit, the yellow, waxy-skinned carambola is Asian in origin, and its name is Hindu. It has a crisp, juicy texture and citrusy flavor that can be sweet or tart depending upon the variety. A carambola looks like a pleated oval, 4 to 6 inches long, and it forms star-shaped slices when cut crosswise. Its popularity with restaurant chefs and gourmet cooks has made it a valuable crop in the farming region south of Miami. The fruit is delicate and can easily be blown off the tree, so growers sometimes surround their carambola groves with windbreaks of taller, sturdier trees. Carambola is rich in vitamins A and C, and has only 60 calories per cup.

SELECTION AND STORAGE: Choose partly or fully yellow fruit with no brown spots or shriveling. Carambola bruises easily, so handle it with care. It ripens at room temperature and is ready when it no longer has any green and has developed a pleasant fragrance. It will keep well for a week or more in the refrigerator.

USES: Carambola doesn't discolor when sliced and makes a delightful garnish or an addition to salads. When cooked, it develops a more assertive, quincelike flavor.

PREPARATION: Carambola doesn't require peeling, but any browning along its ridges should be trimmed away. Then slice or dice it as desired, discarding the seeds.

Chayote (chy-YOH-tay)

A soft-skinned member of the squash family, chayote is called cho-cho in Jamaica, christophene in the French-speaking Caribbean, mirliton in Louisiana, and vegetable pear elsewhere. It was an important food crop for the Aztecs and Mayas, and was introduced to the Caribbean from Mexico in the 1700s. It is shaped like a large, slightly flattened pear and has apple-green skin and a furrow on the bottom that looks like a puckered mouth. It has a very mild (some would say bland) flavor and a firm, crisp texture. It has about 20 calories per half-cup serving and is a good source of potassium.

SELECTION AND STORAGE: Chayote is available year-round but is most abundant in winter. Choose firm, smooth ones with no blemishes. Store them in an unsealed plastic bag in the refrigerator; they'll keep for up to two weeks.

USES: Chayote may not have a lot of flavor, but it's highly versatile. It can be sautéed, steamed, grilled, or added to stir-fries and soups. It can substitute for zucchini and other summer squash in most recipes, but requires a longer cooking time. It can be sliced or grated and used in place of cucumbers or cabbage in salads. It can be pickled or used in chutneys and is ideal for stuffing.

PREPARATION: Chayote doesn't require peeling unless you get a large, tough one. Here's a trick we learned from Tony Merola, former marketing director of Brooks

Tropicals: If you're going to grate chayote for use in a salad, split it in half first and parboil it in lightly salted water for a few minutes. That will prevent it from "weeping" and making the salad watery. When chopping, remember that the soft almond-flavored seed is edible and can be used along with the flesh.

Coconuts

Carried by ocean currents, the coconut spread widely through the tropical world so long ago that its origins are unknown. Considered one of the world's most useful trees, the coconut palm provides shelter through its fronds and wood, and sustenance through its seeds—the largest of any seed we eat. The pre-Columbian Indians of South America used coconuts for food and drink, and African slaves in the region relied on them as well. Many south Florida beaches and streets were once lined with coconut palms, but the trees were devastated by a lethal yellow blight in the 1970s and have only slowly been replanted with blight-resistant varieties. One-half cup of loosely packed shredded coconut meat yields about 150 calories, much of it in the form of highly saturated fat, but its inimitable taste is well worth the occasional indulgence.

SELECTION AND STORAGE: Coconut meat is surrounded by a hairy brown shell, which in turn is covered by a large green or tan husk. The husk must be removed with a machete or hatchet, a task that's been done by the time a coconut reaches the supermarket. Choose a fresh coconut that is heavy and unblemished, not wet around the "eyes"—the small, dark spots on one end. Shake it to make sure it's full of liquid, which keeps the meat moist. (The liquid is coconut water, not coconut milk, which is a steeped and strained mixture of water and grated coconut meat.) A fresh coconut will keep at room temperature for up to four weeks, and longer if refrigerated.

PREPARATION: Once you get the coconut home, pierce two or three of the eyes with an ice pick or screwdriver and drain the coconut water into a container. Or chill the coconut first and suck out the sweet, refreshing water through a straw. (You can buy coconut drinks in the shell as well as iced chunks of coconut meat at Latin markets and roadside stands in Miami.)

To get at the meat, heat the drained coconut in a 400-degree oven for ten or fifteen minutes. Wrap it in a towel, and crack the shell all over with a hammer; the white meat will fall away from the shell. Use a vegetable peeler to remove the brown skin that clings to the meat. A medium-size coconut will yield about 3½ cups of grated meat. Whole or grated, the meat will keep in the refrigerator for several weeks and in the freezer for months.

Malanga (mah-LANG-gah)

Also known as yautia or tannier, malanga is the cormel (an underground stem similar to a tuber) of a large-leafed tropical plant. It's known in West Africa as the cocoyam, which has prompted speculation that it came to the New World with African slaves, but according to culinary historian Maricel Presilla, malanga was eaten by the native Arawak Indians long before Europeans and Africans arrived in the Caribbean. It is shaped like a knobby sweet potato and has shaggy, mottled brown skin. There are more than forty types, but for commercial purposes it is categorized by the color of its moist, starchy flesh—white (*malanga blanca*), pink (*malanga lila*), or yellow (*malanga amarilla*). It has a slippery feel when raw, and when cooked it has a potatolike texture and a mildly sweet, nutty flavor. It has about 135 calories per half-cup serving and is a pretty good source of thiamine and riboflavin.

SELECTION AND STORAGE: Malanga is available year-round. It should be firm and dry, with no soft spots, mold, or shriveling. Prick it with your fingernail to make sure that it's juicy and crisp, not dry or soft. Store it, uncovered, in a cool, dry place for no more than a few days.

USES: Malanga can be served boiled with mojo sauce like yuca (page 229), mashed like potatoes, added to soups and stews, or whipped into a savory soufflé (page 222). Its starchiness makes it an excellent coating for fried foods (page 186), and it fries up into crisp chips (see Tropical Chips, page 228). It's too waxy, though, to be baked in its skin like a potato.

PREPARATION: Peel malanga like a potato. For soups or stews, cut it into chunks and add it to the pot, allowing about twenty minutes of cooking time. To serve it as a side dish, cut the peeled malanga into thick slices and boil it in lightly salted water until tender, about fifteen minutes. To mash, moisten the hot cooked malanga with olive oil and cooking water or butter and hot milk, and mash it by hand. Cooked malanga hardens as it cools and should be served immediately.

Mango

Sweet, juicy mango is leading the tropical produce charge into mainstream America. It is showing up in everything from designer ice tea to canned fruit cocktail to baby food and is available fresh in grocery stores large and small throughout the country. (Kathy has bought it in her hometown, Frederic, Wisconsin; population 1,124.) Mango has been cultivated in India for thousands of years and was introduced to Florida more than 150 years ago. South Florida has a thriving mango industry and is an important developer of varieties (there are hundreds). Most mangos sold in the United States, though, are imported from Latin America and the Caribbean. The mango is a member of the same plant family as poison ivy and can cause allergic reactions. (The sap, foliage, and skin are most often the problem, but a few poor souls can't tolerate the flesh, either.) Mango has about 100 calories per cup, sliced, and is rich in vitamins A and C.

SELECTION AND STORAGE: Mango is available year-round but is most abundant in summer. Choose unblemished fruit that has at least some fruity fragrance (sniff the stem end) and red-orange color. (A few varieties remain green when ripe, but you don't often find them in stores.) Mango will ripen at room temperature and is ready when it gives to slight pressure, like a ripe peach, and has filled out in the "shoulders" around the stem end. Once ripe, it will keep at room temperature for several days and in the refrigerator for a week or more. Sliced, chopped, or pureed mango flesh freezes well.

USES: Ripe mango is marvelous on its own and in salads, salsas, sauces, and desserts of many kinds. Raw green (unripe) mango can be grated into salads and cooked into chutney.

PREPARATION: A ripe mango is so juicy and its skin so leathery that peeling it is a messy proposition. Here's the best way: Stand the mango on its stem end and cut straight down with a large knife on either side of the large, flat pit, slicing off the two rounded sides. Use a paring knife to remove and peel the flesh that clings to the pit. Peel the two rounds with a paring knife or by slipping a spoon under the skin and working it off. Or for instant cubes, cut a grid pattern down to but not through the skin on each of the rounds. Turn the round inside out so that the small squares of flesh stick out, and cut them away.

Papaya (pah-PIE-yah)

This avocado-shaped fruit, also called pawpaw, can be as small as a large pear or as large as a melon. The skin ranges from green when unripe to yellow-orange when ripe. The black seeds taste something like a radish and are sometimes used in salad dressings. When ripe, the pulp is orange or pink, softer than a ripe cantaloupe but similar in texture, with a sweet, perfumy taste and scent. Green papaya has a bland but pleasant taste. Papaya contains an enzyme, papain, that can break down protein and is widely used as a meat tenderizer. Botanically a berry, the papaya is a good source of vitamins A and C and potassium and has 55 calories per cup.

SELECTION AND STORAGE: Papaya is available year-round. Choose fruit with firm, unblemished skin and no soft patches. A ripe one will give slightly when pressed. It can be stored in the refrigerator for up to four days. To ripen a green one, leave it on the counter for a day or two.

USES: Ripe papaya is great on its own with a squeeze of lime juice or as an addition to fruit or green salads or salsas. Pureed, it's an excellent base for sorbets and salad dressings. Sliced ripe papaya is delicious when wrapped with prosciutto as an appetizer. Green papaya can be made into chutneys, used in soups or stews, or shredded raw for salads.

PREPARATION: Cut the papaya in half lengthwise and scoop out the seeds. Pare the thin skin and cut the fruit into slices or chunks. You can also use the halved papaya as a bowl for a fruit salad. To cook green papaya, simmer peeled chunks in water to cover for about twenty minutes, until tender; test by piercing with a fork.

Plantain (PLAN-tuhn)

Called *platano* in Spanish, the plantain is a big, starchy, firm member of the banana family that is virtually always cooked and is usually served as a vegetable. Portuguese explorers brought plantains from Africa to the Canary Islands in 1402, and a century later a Dominican friar took them from the Canaries to Hispaniola, the island shared today by Haiti and the Dominican Republic. They are widely grown and used in the Caribbean and Latin America. Plantains are about twice the size of bananas, and their taste and preparation change with the degree of ripeness, as described below. They have about 90 calories per half-cup serving and are an excellent source of vitamin A and potassium.

SELECTION AND STORAGE: Plantains are available year-round. Choose ones that are free of cracks, cuts, or mold, in the degree of ripeness that suits your recipe. If you need medium-ripe or ripe plantains and can find only green ones, you can speed up the ripening process by putting them in a paper bag (check them daily). Otherwise, they're best stored, like bananas, in a cool, dry, unrefrigerated spot where they will ripen slowly. If they've ripened to your liking before you're ready to use them, you can hold them in the refrigerator for a day or two, or peel and freeze them for several months.

Green: These plantains are very hard to the touch and green in color, with little banana flavor or sweetness. When cooked they have a bland but pleasant taste and a starchy texture.

Medium-ripe: These look and feel like just-ripe bananas. They have a slight banana flavor and sweetness when cooked and are quite starchy.

Ripe: These have an intensely sweet bananalike flavor and texture, and hold their shape when cooked. Plantains are considered ripe when the skin turns black; if they were bananas, you would be ready to throw them out or turn them into banana bread.

USES: In Miami, plantains are most often served fried as *tostones* (page 227), *maduros* (page 226), or chips (*mariquitas*, page 228), but are also good boiled, baked, and grilled, as described below.

PREPARATION: You can peel a ripe plantain like a banana, but not a green or medium-ripe one. Here's how to handle it: Cut off the ends of the plantain and cut three or four lengthwise slits in the skin along the ribs. Soak the plantain in cold water for 10 minutes, pull off the skin in strips, and dry the plantain with paper towels.

Boiling: Green or medium-ripe plantains can be peeled, cut into chunks, and simmered in water, as you would potatoes, for fifteen to twenty minutes, until tender. Then mash and season them for an interesting side dish, or chop and add them to soup or stew.

Baking or grilling: Ripe plantains are especially good with roasted meats, and baking or grilling lets you enjoy them without the fat of frying. To bake, slit the skin down the middle, put the plantains in a baking dish, and bake them at 350 degrees for about thirty-five minutes. Or prick the skin and microwave them on high power for about five minutes. To grill, prick the skin and cook them over medium, indirect heat for about thirty minutes. Cut them in half (one plantain yields two servings) and let your guests eat them out of the skin.

Yuca (YOU-cah)

You sometimes see it spelled *yucca*, but a single "c" is preferred. Also called cassava or manioc, yuca is a root vegetable with a barklike cover and a hard, bright white interior. When cooked it has a mild, potatolike flavor and a slightly glutinous texture. (Tapioca is made from yuca.) Yuca is a South American native and was cultivated by the Arawak Indians who inhabited Cuba, Puerto Rico, and Hispaniola (modern-day Haiti and the Dominican Republic) at the time of the Spanish conquest. Columbus was served casabe, a flat bread made from cassava flour, when he feasted with an Arawak chief on Hispaniola on December 26, 1492. (Spiny lobster and root vegetables completed the menu.) Casabe, as well as the West Indian condiment cassareep, is made from bitter cassava, which is poisonous when raw. Don't worry; it's quite different from the sweet variety sold as yuca in this country. In Miami, YUCA was adopted as an acronym by Young, Upscale, Cuban Americans, and that play on words was behind the naming of Yuca, a new-wave Cuban restaurant on South Beach. Yuca has about 135 calories per half-cup serving and is rich in potassium and carbohydrates.

SELECTION AND STORAGE: Yuca is available year-round. Choose roots that are firm and unblemished outside and snowy white inside, with no gray fibers or darkening next to the peel. Ask a produce clerk to cut one in half so you can check the interior. It's not a great keeper; store it in the refrigerator and use it within three days.

USES: Use yuca as you would a potato. It's a popular side dish in Miami when boiled and then drizzled with mojo or olive oil. You can also deep-fry it as fries or chips (see Tropical Chips, page 228), shred it and use it to coat chicken or fish, substitute it for potatoes in potato salad, or puree it and use it in breads, cakes, and fritters. It doesn't work well on its own as a puree, though; the texture is too sticky.

PREPARATION: To prepare yuca for cooking, rinse and cut it into 4-inch chunks. Slit the peel lengthwise, slip a paring knife under the pink inner layer, and pull off both layers of peel. Cut each section in half lengthwise and remove and discard the fibrous cord that runs down the center. Rinse well and cover with cold water. Frozen, peeled yuca, available in supermarkets with a Hispanic clientele, is a good shortcut.

Simmer yuca in water to cover and begin testing for doneness after 20 minutes by piercing it with a fork; when it's tender, it's done. Leftovers are good sliced and sautéed in olive oil with a little onion and garlic.

You can also bake yuca in its skin and serve it with salt, pepper, and butter. Allow forty minutes to one hour in a 350-degree oven depending on the size of the yuca.

Or if you're adept at deep-frying, cut it into ½-inch slices or strips and fry it up crisp and brown. Season it with salt or Jerk Seasoning (page 99) and serve it hot.

A dish can be only as good as the ingredients that go into it. Here are our preferences for a number of staples in this book:

Broth

Homemade chicken broth is best (if you need a recipe, check any general-purpose cookbook), but low-sodium canned broth is an acceptable substitute. Campbell's Healthy Request is one especially good brand. If you have a few minutes, simmer a little carrot, celery, parsley, and onion in the canned broth for made-from-scratch flavor. Canned beef and vegetable broths, on the other hand, don't measure up; if you don't have homemade beef or vegetable broth, substitute chicken broth. Even water is preferable.

Citrus juices

Freshly-squeezed is best. Refrigerated not-from-concentrate brands of orange juice are okay. Bottled lemon and lime juice aren't. Substitute fresh lemons if you can't get good limes, and vice versa.

Olive oil

Oil labeled "pure" has a higher smoking point than extra-virgin and is a better and more economical choice for sautéing. We prefer Spanish brands such as Carbonell, Musa, Sensat, and Goya for Spanish-style dishes, but other widely available brands such as Berio, Bertolli, and Colavita are good, too. Use high-quality extra-virgin oil for dressing vegetables and salads. Though expensive, Castello di Cacchiano, Badia a Coltibuono, Poggio al Sole, Lungarotti, and Sciabica are well worth it.

Pepper

Use good-quality whole black peppercorns—Tellicherry, Lampong, and Malabar are three excellent ones—and grind them as needed. Muntok white peppercorns (actually ripe black peppercorns with the skin removed) are the best kind to use when you don't want specks of black in a white dish. If you're in the market for a peppermill, the Peppermate brand has an excellent adjustable grinder and a removable measuring cup.

Roasted peppers

If you don't have time to roast your own, substitute jarred roasted peppers.

Salt

We use table salt for baking but kosher salt for just about everything else. It has a purer taste (it's not iodized), and its large crystals make it easier to control the saltiness of a dish. Keep a small bowl of it next to the stove and pick it up between your fingers to sprinkle on food. Because it doesn't penetrate meat, poultry, and fish as quickly, it doesn't deplete their juices the way table salt can. And because of its large crystals, a teaspoon of kosher salt has about half the saltiness of a teaspoon of table salt.

Tomatoes

In cooked dishes, good canned tomatoes are preferable to mediocre fresh ones. We prefer Italian plum tomatoes or, for diced, Del Monte Fresh Cut.

Vegetable oil

We prefer canola and safflower oil. They're monounsaturated (as is olive oil), which is the best choice when it comes to cholesterol control. They're also light, almost tasteless, and have a high smoking point.

Appetizers
and
First Courses

Guacamole with Papaya

Hot and Tangy Black Bean Dip

Basic Black Beans

Corn, Chile, and Cheese Quesadillas

Crispy Corn Pancakes

Potato and Black Bean Pancakes with Cilantro–Goat Cheese Sauce

Jamaican-Style Beef Patties

Yuca Puffs

Conch Fritters

Salt Cod Accras (Fritters)

Coconut Shrimp in Island-Spiced Batter

Scallop Seviche

Caribbean-Style Crab Cakes

 Whether you're serving a first course at dinner in the dining room or setting out snacks for a casual gathering in the family room, Miami offers plenty of appetizing possibilities. The following recipes showcase tropical delights such as papaya and mango, give a Latin accent to latkes (potato pancakes), and explore the delectable possibilities of seafood ranging from salt cod to shrimp, to mention just a few morsels.

A smart host knows the value of making a great first impression and of picking her or his shots. Schedules and budgets being what they are, it's not often practical to make every dish a showstopper, and putting extra effort into a sensational first course can make a dinner party. The main course may be simple grilled fish or long-simmered stew, but your friends will go home remembering those extraordinary Caribbean-Style Crab Cakes or the savory Jamaican-Style Beef Patties with the flaky, turmeric-tinted crust. Or you can start the meal with one of the mouth-watering recipes in the soup and salad chapters. (We like to leave a great last impression with dessert, but that's another chapter.)

For those around-the-coffee-table occasions, break out the chips and whip up our papaya-accented guacamole, Hot and Tangy Black Bean Dip, and a scintillating salsa or two. Add Yuca Puffs, Coconut Shrimp in Island-Spiced Batter, and a platter of crudités, and you won't have to set the dining table at all. The point is not to feel confined by categories. Many of these starters can be turned into lunch or supper entrees by making them in larger portions or bigger batches—and they're so good, we bet you'll want to do just that.

Guacamole with Papaya

[ABOUT 2½ CUPS]

Replacing some of the avocado with papaya gives this guacamole a hint of sweetness—a nice counterpoint to the tartness of the lime and the heat of the jalapeño. As a bonus, the papaya helps the dip keep its bright green color. (If papaya isn't available, use an additional avocado half and don't leave any leftovers!) Serve it with tortilla chips or, for a totally tropical presentation, homemade plantain or yuca chips (see Tropical Chips, page 228).

1 medium tomato, seeded and cut into chunks

½ medium red onion, peeled and cut into chunks

½ to 1 jalapeño pepper, seeded and cut into chunks

1 garlic clove, peeled

1 avocado (about 1 pound), peeled and cut into chunks

½ small papaya (about ½ pound), peeled, seeded, and cut into chunks

½ tablespoon chopped fresh cilantro

1 tablespoon fresh lime juice

½ teaspoon grated lime zest

½ teaspoon ground cumin

½ teaspoon kosher salt

¼ teaspoon freshly ground pepper

Combine the tomato, onion, jalapeño, and garlic in a food processor and pulse until finely chopped. Add the avocado, papaya, cilantro, lime juice, zest, cumin, salt, and pepper, and pulse to form a chunky puree. (Or mash the avocado and papaya with a potato masher, finely chop the other solid ingredients, and combine all of them.) Cover with plastic wrap and refrigerate for 1 hour for the flavors to blend. Taste and adjust the seasonings before serving.

The avocado is an ancient fruit that is known to have grown in Peru as early as 2000 B.C. and in Mexico as early as 8000 B.C. It gets its name from the Aztec word *ahuacatl*, "fruit of the testicle tree"—presumably because of its shape and the fact that it often grows in pairs—and it was once thought to be an aphrodisiac.

Horticulturalist Henry Perrine is credited with introducing avocados, as well as limes, to south Florida in the 1830s. (He was later killed in a Seminole attack on the aptly named Indian Key, between Key West and modern-day Miami.) Florida avocados are available from July through March, and most are grown in the Miami area. Their smooth skins stay bright green when ripe, and they are larger, milder tasting, and as much as 50 percent lower in fat than the bumpy, greenish-black–skinned Haas avocados grown in California.

Here's the best way to prepare an avocado: Cut around it lengthwise and twist the halves to separate them. To remove the seed, tap it firmly with the heel of a heavy knife blade, twist the knife, and lift. Dislodge the seed from the blade. Slip a spoon under the skin of each half and scoop out the flesh in one piece. Or cut the avocado in quarters, and pull off the skin with the tip of a paring knife.

Hot and Tangy Black Bean Dip

[ABOUT 2⅔ CUPS]

Hot pepper sauce and lemon give this dip its zing. Tabasco works fine, but you might enjoy expanding your arsenal of fire power with a Caribbean brand. Matouk's, a papaya-based sauce made in Trinidad, is a good one and is sold throughout the United States. As lively as the dip tastes, it is dull looking on its own, so don't skip the garnishes.

3 cups Basic Black Beans (recipe follows) or 2 15½-ounce cans black beans, rinsed and drained

½ cup sour cream

¼ cup fresh lemon juice

¼ cup coarsely chopped cilantro

2 garlic cloves, peeled

2 scallions, trimmed and chopped

½ teaspoon grated lemon zest

½ teaspoon hot pepper sauce

½ teaspoon ground cumin

Kosher salt and freshly ground pepper

Diced tomato and sliced scallions for garnish

Combine the beans, sour cream, lemon juice, cilantro, garlic, scallions, lemon zest, hot pepper sauce, and cumin in a food processor and process until smooth. Season to taste with salt and pepper.

Scrape the dip into a serving bowl and refrigerate it, covered, for at least 1 hour. Garnish with tomato and scallions, and serve with tortilla chips.

Basic Black Beans

[4 ½ TO 5 CUPS]

A number of our recipes call for cooked black beans, and cooking them from scratch is the best way to go. The beans stay firm and whole and don't break easily the way canned ones do. Cooked beans freeze well, too, and if you make a big batch and freeze them in 1-cup portions, they are more convenient than canned. For those inevitable times when you need a shortcut, see the Notes following the recipe below.

> 1 pound dried black beans
> 4 garlic cloves
> 1 bay leaf
> ½ teaspoon dry-leaf thyme, crumbled
> ¼ teaspoon dry-leaf oregano, crumbled
> ¼ teaspoon ground cumin
> 1 to 2 teaspoons kosher salt

Rinse the beans and discard any foreign matter. Put them in a pot with water to cover by about 2 inches and let them soak for at least 4 hours or as long as overnight. (Or boil the beans and water for 2 minutes and let them soak off the heat, covered, for 1 hour.)

Drain the beans and return them to the pot. Crush the garlic cloves with the flat side of a knife, discard the skin, and add them to the pot along with the bay leaf, thyme, oregano, and cumin. Add water to cover the beans by about 2 inches. Bring the water to a boil, lower the heat, and simmer the beans, uncovered, for 30 minutes. Add salt to taste and cook, covered, until the beans are tender but still firm, about 30 minutes longer.

Drain the beans and rinse them under cold water until the water runs clear. (This will keep them from muddying your salad or salsa.) Discard the bay leaf and, if still whole, the garlic.

NOTES:
- 1 pound dried black beans measures about 2¼ cups—a handy thing to know if your market sells them in 12-ounce bags.
- The cooking time will vary with the length of time the beans have been on the shelf. The longer it's been, the drier they'll be and the longer it will take them to rehydrate.

- Soaking and rinsing the beans is thought to remove some of the sugars that cause intestinal gas. If there's no time to soak, increase the cooking time by about 30 minutes.
- Some recipes warn that adding salt to the cooking water will toughen beans. We find that adding it during the last 30 minutes produces tender beans that are more flavorful than those salted after cooking.
- One 15½-ounce can of black beans contains about 1½ cups rinsed and drained beans. Three cans is the equivalent of 1 pound dried black beans, cooked.

Corn, Chile, and Cheese Quesadillas

[6 FIRST-COURSE SERVINGS OR 36 HORS D'OEUVRES]

These savory wedges combine two New World products, corn and hot chiles, with Muenster cheese, a South American favorite. For a simple side dish or dip, dispense with the tortillas, fold the cheese into the corn mixture, and heat it until the cheese has melted. Stir in the sour cream and cilantro, and serve hot.

6 6-inch flour tortillas

Vegetable oil

1 medium onion, peeled and chopped

1 jalapeño pepper, seeded and minced

4 cups fresh or frozen corn kernels (5 or 6 ears)

Kosher salt and freshly ground pepper

8 ounces Muenster cheese, grated

1 tablespoon chopped cilantro

1 egg, beaten

½ cup sour cream

½ cup Fresh Tomato Salsa (page 259) or your favorite brand

Preheat the oven to 300 degrees. Wrap the tortillas in foil and warm them in the oven for 5 minutes. (Or wrap them in damp paper towels and microwave on high for 45 seconds. Warming makes the tortillas more malleable.)

Meanwhile, heat 1 tablespoon of the oil in a skillet over medium heat and sauté the onion and jalapeño until soft, about 5 minutes. Stir in the corn and cook until heated through, about 3 minutes. Season to taste with salt and pepper.

Place the warm tortillas on a work surface in a single layer. Spoon an equal portion of the corn mixture onto each tortilla, mounding it to one side of the center. Top each with cheese and cilantro.

Working with 1 tortilla at a time, brush the edges with the egg and fold the bare half over the filling, pressing to seal the edges of the tortilla. Cover the finished quesadillas with a damp towel to keep them from drying out while you complete the rest.

Lightly coat a large nonstick skillet with oil and heat it over medium heat. Working in batches, sauté the quesadillas, turning once, until the cheese is melted and the tortillas are golden brown, about 4 minutes total.

Transfer the quesadillas to a cutting board. Cut each one into 3 wedges for first-course servings or 6 wedges for hors d'oeuvres. Arrange them on individual plates or a platter, garnish with sour cream and salsa, and serve warm.

Tips/Techniques: Sweet Corn

When buying fresh corn, choose ears with bright green, tight-fitting husks and fresh-looking, brownish gold silk. Already husked corn deteriorates faster, and it may have been husked in the first place because it was getting old.

The sugars that give the corn its sweetness begin turning to starches as soon as it's picked, so use it as soon as possible—preferably the day you buy it.

After stripping off the husk and silk, wipe the ears of corn with a damp paper towel to remove the last bits of silk.

An ear of fresh corn yields ½ to ¾ cup of kernels. A 10-ounce package of frozen corn contains 1¾ cups.

To do a neat job of cutting off fresh corn kernels, prop the husked ear in the tube of an angel food cake pan and slice straight down with a sharp knife. The kernels will fall into the pan rather than scattering on the counter.

Crispy Corn Pancakes

[16 PANCAKES]

These sweet golden rounds couldn't be easier or tastier, and you can mix the batter several hours ahead. Top the pancakes with Roasted Red Pepper Sauce (page 188), salsa, sour cream, or caviar, or serve them plain as a side dish with roast chicken or meat.

> 2½ cups fresh or frozen corn kernels
>
> 6 tablespoons flour
>
> 4 eggs
>
> 1 teaspoon kosher salt
>
> ¼ teaspoon freshly ground pepper
>
> ½ cup heavy cream or half-and-half
>
> 2 tablespoons melted butter or vegetable oil
>
> Vegetable oil for frying

Combine the corn and flour in a mixing bowl and stir to mix well.

In another bowl, beat together the eggs, salt, pepper, and cream.

Add the egg mixture and melted butter to the corn mixture and stir just to combine. (If making ahead, refrigerate the batter, covered, and let it come to room temperature before continuing.)

Lightly oil a large nonstick skillet or a griddle and heat it over medium-high heat. Spoon the batter into the pan, forming pancakes that are 2 to 3 inches across. Cook until lightly browned, 1 to 2 minutes. Turn and cook about 1 minute more, until the center is just firm. Serve hot.

Potato and Black Bean Pancakes with Cilantro–Goat Cheese Sauce

[8 APPETIZER SERVINGS]

This twist on Hanukkah latkes is an invention of Miami chef Carmen Gonzalez, founder of the Feeding the Mind Foundation, which provides culinary scholarships at Johnson & Wales University for abused women who are trying to put their lives back on track. Each year Carmen invites women chefs from around the country to Miami to prepare a gala dinner to benefit the foundation. Traditional latkes are served with sour cream or applesauce, but Carmen serves these with Green Mango Chutney (page 263) or with the pungent Cilantro–Goat Cheese Sauce. Served plain—and made bigger if you like—they're a fine accompaniment to roast chicken, pork, or rack of lamb.

3 baking potatoes (about 2 pounds), peeled

2 eggs, beaten

3 scallions, trimmed and thinly sliced

1 cup Basic Black Beans (page 19) or drained, canned black beans

2 tablespoons white vinegar

1 teaspoon kosher salt

½ teaspoon freshly ground pepper

¼ to ½ cup flour

Olive or vegetable oil for frying

Cilantro–Goat Cheese Sauce (recipe follows)

Cilantro sprigs for garnish

Grate the potatoes with a box grater or the shredding disk of a food processor (see Notes). Put them in a colander set over a large bowl and press to squeeze out as much liquid as possible.

Pour off the liquid, leaving the potato starch that has settled on the bottom. Add the potatoes, eggs, scallions, ¾ cup of the black beans, vinegar, salt, and pepper to the bowl, and stir to mix well. Add enough flour to make the batter hold together, and taste for seasoning.

Heat 2 tablespoons of oil in a large skillet over medium-high heat. Working in batches, fry sixteen 3-inch pancakes: Spoon a heaping tablespoon of batter into the pan for each pancake and flatten it with the back of the spoon. Fry, turning once, until golden brown and crisp, 2 to

3 minutes per side, and drain on paper towels. Add more oil to the pan and adjust the heat as needed.

To serve, overlap 2 pancakes on each plate and garnish with the sauce, a sprinkling of the reserved black beans, and a sprig of cilantro. Serve immediately.

NOTES:
- A combination of coarsely and finely grated potatoes gives the pancakes a creamy texture. If working by hand, grate half the potatoes on the fine side of a box grater and half on the coarse side. If using a food processor, grate all the potatoes with the medium shredding disk. Then insert the metal chopping blade and pulse half the shredded potatoes a couple of times.
- Adding white vinegar to the batter keeps the raw potatoes from discoloring. Use the same trick when making hash browns or regular latkes.

Cilantro—Goat Cheese Sauce

[1 CUP]

Pungent cilantro and earthy goat cheese are a delightful combination. Goat cheese (chèvre in French) was little known in this country until twenty years ago when adventurous American chefs began using it. Their interest spawned a domestic goat cheese industry, which includes south Florida's own Turtle Creek Dairy in Loxahatchee, near West Palm Beach. Goat cheese is lower in calories and easier to digest than many other cheeses and doesn't get stringy when heated. For this sauce we use Montrachet, a young, creamy, mild cheese sold in logs.

4 ounces goat cheese
½ bunch cilantro, minced
½ cup heavy cream

Combine the goat cheese, cilantro, and cream in a heavy saucepan over low heat and whisk until smooth, thick, and hot, about 5 minutes. Serve immediately.

Jamaican-Style Beef Patties

[ABOUT 15 PATTIES]

There is no better culinary example of "going native" than these highly spiced meat turnovers, which evolved from the staid Cornish pasties that British colonists brought to Jamaica. Cooks from the Spanish-speaking islands also know how to tuck a savory filling into a packet of dough; they call them empanadas. They're often fried, but we prefer to bake them. Miamian Steven Raichlen, author of Miami Spice, the High-Flavor Low-Fat series, *and many other creative cookbooks, bakes his slimmed-down empanadas in wonton or ravioli wrappers. Supermarkets with Hispanic or Caribbean clientele carry frozen, precut rounds of empanada dough—another good shortcut, though they lack the distinctive yellow hue that turmeric gives the Jamaican variety. Made larger, meat patties are ideal for lunch boxes and meals on the go.*

FOR THE DOUGH:

2 cups flour

½ teaspoon baking powder

½ teaspoon turmeric

½ teaspoon kosher salt

8 tablespoons (1 stick) unsalted butter, cut into small pieces and frozen

¼ cup ice water

FOR THE FILLING:

1 tablespoon vegetable oil

½ medium onion, peeled and finely chopped

1 garlic clove, peeled and minced

½ jalapeño pepper, seeded and minced

2 teaspoons curry powder

1 teaspoon dry-leaf thyme, crumbled

½ teaspoon ground cinnamon

¼ teaspoon ground cumin

¼ teaspoon ground allspice

½ pound lean ground beef

3 tablespoons dry bread crumbs (see Note)

1 cup tomato juice or chicken broth

½ cup raisins (optional)

Kosher salt and freshly ground pepper

To make the dough, place the flour, baking powder, tumeric, and salt in the bowl of a food processor and pulse to combine. With the machine running, drop the butter pieces down the feeding tube. Pulse several times until the largest pieces of butter are the size of small peas. Add the ice water 1 tablespoon at a time, pulsing between each addition, until the dough begins to clump. (Or mix by hand using a pastry blender.) Scrape the dough onto a piece of plastic wrap, form into a disc, and refrigerate for at least 1 hour.

To make the filling, heat the oil in a skillet over medium heat and sauté the onion, garlic, and jalapeño until soft, about 5 minutes. Add the curry powder, thyme, cinnamon, cumin, and allspice, and cook, stirring, for 1 minute more. Add the beef and cook, stirring to crumble it, until no longer pink.

Stir in the bread crumbs, tomato juice, raisins, and salt and pepper to taste. Simmer, uncovered, for 20 minutes, stirring often. The filling should be moist but not wet. Set aside to cool to room temperature. (If you use it hot, it will melt the dough.)

Preheat the oven to 400 degrees.

Roll out the dough on a floured surface to a thickness of about ⅛ inch and cut it into 4-inch circles. (If you don't have a cookie cutter that size, use a bowl or other container that's about 4 inches in diameter.) Roll out the dough scraps and cut again; you should have about 15 circles.

Place 1 tablespoon of the filling on each dough round, slightly off center. Moisten the edges of each round with a pastry brush dipped in water and fold the dough over the filling to form a half circle. Press the edges together with the tines of a fork to seal them. Poke the patty once or twice with the fork to make steam vents.

Arrange the patties on a baking sheet and bake until golden brown, about 20 minutes. Serve warm or at room temperature. Leftovers can be frozen, well wrapped, for up to a month and reheated straight from the freezer in a 425-degree oven for 10 minutes.

VARIATIONS:

For a shiny finish, brush the unbaked patties with an egg yolk beaten with 1 teaspoon of water.

Substitute ground pork, turkey, or chicken for the beef if you like.

Picadillo (page 148) makes an excellent patty filling.

NOTE: You'll never have to buy bread crumbs again if you save stale plain bread in the freezer. (French bread crumbs are best for deep-frying because they contain no sugar, which burns easily.) When you have enough to warrant dirtying the food processor, tear the frozen bread into chunks, process it into crumbs, and store the crumbs in a freezer bag. Use them straight from the freezer in recipes calling for fresh bread crumbs. For dry crumbs, spread them on a baking sheet and toast in a 350-degree oven for about 10 minutes.

People tend to associate deep-frying with greasiness, but if done properly, it produces beautifully crisp, browned foods that absorb a minimum of fat and deliver a maximum of flavor. Here's how to do it right:

· The best guarantee of success is to fry at the right temperature—hot enough to immediately sear the food but not so hot that the outside burns before the inside is cooked. The best temperature for most deep-frying is 370 to 375 degrees. The exceptions are foods such as onions and coconut that burn easily because of a high sugar content; they're best fried at about 360 degrees.

· Getting the oil hot enough is only half the job; you need to keep it hot once you begin frying. Adding too much uncooked food at one time will make the temperature plunge, so deep-fry in small batches and give the oil time to reheat between batches if necessary.

· It is well worth spending a few dollars on a deep-fry/candy thermometer so that you can measure the oil temperature accurately. If you're working without one, dip a wooden spoon into the oil; if brisk bubbles immediately form around it, the oil is hot enough for frying.

· The best oils for frying are the ones with the highest smoke point—the temperature at which they begin to break down and give off acrid odors and flavors. Peanut, safflower, and soybean oils are at the top of the list at about 450 degrees, with canola oil not far behind at 435 degrees. Neither corn nor olive oil (410 degrees) is a good choice for deep-frying.

· A deep fryer is a handy appliance, but if you don't have one, a deep, heavy saucepan, Dutch oven, or wok works well. To minimize the chances of spills, don't fill it more than half full.

· The oil should be deep enough so that the food is completely immersed—generally 2 inches or more.

· Moisture causes splatters, so dry unbattered items such as vegetable slices as much as possible before adding them to the oil. One good method is to spin them in a salad spinner and then blot with paper towels.

· Another way to minimize splatters is to ease food—not drop it—into the hot oil. For fritters, hold the spoonful of batter near the surface and use a second spoon to slide it in. Use tongs to lower vegetable slices, shrimp, and other solid items into the oil.

· Drain the fried food on a baking sheet lined with several layers of paper towels and keep it warm in a 200-degree oven while you fry the rest. Eat it as soon as you're done, or it will get soggy.

Yuca Puffs

[ABOUT 16 PUFFS]

You'll be amazed that starchy yuca (see page 10) can be turned into something as light as these tasty bites. Crisp on the outside and creamy on the inside, they can also be made with malanga (see page 7) or 1 cup of leftover mashed potatoes. Don't let yuca or malanga cool before pureeing, or it will harden. If you'd rather not deep-fry, the baked variation is also very good.

½ pound yuca

Kosher salt

1 egg, beaten

1 tablespoon fresh lime juice

2 tablespoons flour

½ teaspoon baking powder

3 scallions, trimmed and thinly sliced

½ red bell pepper, seeded and diced

1 small garlic clove, peeled and minced

Freshly ground pepper

Vegetable oil for frying

½ cup plain dry bread crumbs

Peel the yuca as directed on page 11. Cut in half lengthwise, discard the fibrous cord that runs down the center, and cut into chunks. Bring to a boil in lightly salted water to cover and simmer until tender, 15 to 20 minutes.

Drain the yuca well and transfer it to the food processor. Add the egg and lime juice, and process until pureed. Add the flour and baking powder, and pulse to mix. Add the scallions, bell pepper, and garlic, and pulse just to combine. (Or mash the yuca by hand and stir in the rest of the ingredients.) Add a little more flour if necessary to make a soft dough. Season to taste with salt and pepper. Chill the dough for at least 1 hour to firm it.

Spread the bread crumbs on a baking sheet. Form the dough into 1- to 1½-inch balls and roll them in the crumbs. The mixture will be soft and sticky, but rolling it in the crumbs will allow you to form neat balls. Refrigerate them on the baking sheet, covered, for at least 1 hour to firm them.

When ready to cook, heat 2 to 3 inches of oil to 375 degrees in a deep-fryer or a suitable pan (see page 28).

Working in batches, lower the balls into the oil with a slotted spoon. Fry them, turning several times, until golden brown on all sides, 2 to 3 minutes. Drain on paper towels and serve hot.

PLANNING AHEAD: You can make the batter and form it into balls up to 24 hours before cooking.

VARIATIONS:

➡ For heartier fare, add ¼ cup of diced ham to the batter.

➡ Instead of rolling the balls in the bread crumbs, a quicker method is to spoon heaping teaspoonsful of the chilled batter into the hot oil.

➡ Rather than frying, you can bake the puffs in a 400-degree oven until lightly browned, 10 to 12 minutes.

NOTE: Here's a smart solution to one of life's little vexations: When cleaning your food processor, remove the cover and blade, and cap the hollow shaft in the center of the bowl with a 35-millimeter film canister. That way you can fill the bowl to the brim with hot, soapy water instead of watching it drain out halfway.

Conch Fritters

[ABOUT 24 FRITTERS]

Miami's oldest black community, on the western side of Coconut Grove, was founded before the turn of the century by Bahamians. Each June the Grove hosts Goombay, a raucous celebration of Bahamian heritage that boasts whistle-blowing, drum-pounding junkanoo bands, and sizzling hot conch fritters. Scotch bonnet pepper gives these fritters a little extra sizzle, and beaten egg whites make them exceptionally light. If conch isn't available, substitute shrimp or crab, and chop it coarsely by hand rather than in the food processor.

1 pound conch, tenderized (see page 57)

3 scallions, trimmed and thinly sliced

1 garlic clove, peeled and minced

½ Scotch bonnet pepper or 2 to 3 jalapeño peppers, seeded and minced

¼ red bell pepper, seeded and diced

1 tablespoon minced cilantro

2 tablespoons fresh lime juice

Vegetable oil

1½ cups flour

¼ cup yellow cornmeal

1 tablespoon baking powder

1 teaspoon salt

1 teaspoon freshly ground pepper

4 eggs, separated

½ to ¾ cup milk

Cut the conch into chunks and pulse in a food processor until finely ground.

Scrape the conch into a large bowl and add the scallions, garlic, Scotch bonnet, bell pepper, cilantro, lime juice, and 2 tablespoons of oil. Toss to mix.

Sift the flour, cornmeal, baking powder, salt, and pepper into the bowl and stir to combine. Beat the egg yolks with ½ cup of the milk and stir into the conch mixture to form a soft dough. If it's too thick, add more milk.

Heat 2 to 3 inches of oil to 375 degrees in a deep-fryer or an appropriate pan (see page 28).

Meanwhile, beat the egg whites until they hold soft peaks. Stir about ⅓ of the whites into the conch mixture to lighten it, then fold in the rest.

Working in batches, spoon the batter into the hot oil by the heaping tablespoonful. Fry, turning several times, until golden brown on all sides, 2 to 3 minutes. Transfer to paper towels with a slotted spoon and serve hot with your favorite tartar sauce or salsa.

VARIATION: If you'd rather not deep-fry, thin the batter to the consistency of pancake batter and panfry it in 2- to 3-inch rounds.

Salt Cod Accras (Fritters)

[ABOUT 16 FRITTERS]

Dried, salted codfish may seem an anomaly in a region teeming with fresh fish, but it's a beloved part of many Caribbean cuisines. (It's also one of many "peasant" foods being given chic treatment these days by trend-setting chefs.) Called bacalao in Spanish and morue in French, salt cod sustained seafarers for hundreds of years and was so universally valuable, as culinary historian Jessica Harris writes in Sky Juice and Flying Fish, that it sometimes served as legal tender for slaves. In Jamaica, salt cod fritters are called Stamp and Go, perhaps because they can be fried up and packed off so quickly. These savory fritters don't take long to make, either, but you need to begin soaking the fish at least twelve hours ahead of time. Salt cod is sold in mainstream supermarkets in Miami and in Hispanic and Italian markets throughout the country. If you can't find it, substitute coarsely chopped shrimp or flaked, mild fish; the fritters won't be the same, but they will be delicious in their own way. Tropical Fruit Curry (page 262) is an excellent accompaniment.

8 ounces salt cod

1 cup flour

1 teaspoon salt

½ teaspoon baking powder

½ cup milk

2 eggs, beaten

3 scallions, trimmed and thinly sliced

½ Scotch bonnet pepper or 2 to 3 jalapeño peppers, seeded and minced

1 garlic clove, minced

1 tablespoon minced fresh parsley

2 teaspoons minced fresh thyme or ½ teaspoon dry-leaf thyme, crumbled

Salt and freshly ground pepper

Vegetable oil

Soak the cod in water to cover for at least 12 hours or as long as 24 hours, changing the water at least once. Drain the cod and put it in a saucepan with water to cover. Bring to a boil, lower the heat, and simmer, covered, until tender, about 30 minutes. Drain the fish again, discard any skin or bones, and use 2 forks to break the meat into flakes. Set aside.

Sift the flour, salt, and baking powder into a mixing bowl. Make a well in the center, add the milk and eggs, and stir to form a smooth batter. Add the scallions, Scotch bonnet pepper, garlic, parsley, thyme, and reserved cod, and stir just to combine. Season to taste with salt and pepper. Refrigerate the batter for at least 1 hour to firm it.

Heat 2 to 3 inches of oil to 375 degrees in a deep-fryer or an appropriate pan (see page 28).

Working in batches, spoon the batter into the hot oil by the heaping tablespoonful. Fry, turning several times, until golden brown on all sides, about 3 minutes. Transfer to paper towels with a slotted spoon. Serve hot.

Coconut Shrimp in Island-Spiced Batter

[8 FIRST-COURSE SERVINGS]

Jamaican jerk seasoning and Trinidadian-inspired curry, two disparate elements of Caribbean cooking, come together beautifully in these flavor-packed shrimp. Butterflying keeps the shrimp from curling too much and allows them to cook faster. To cut down on last-minute preparations, you can butterfly the shrimp and mix the dry ingredients for the batter several hours ahead.

24 jumbo shrimp

1 cup flour

2 to 3 teaspoons curry powder

2 teaspoons Jerk Seasoning (page 99) or a commercial jerk blend

1 teaspoon kosher salt

½ teaspoon baking powder

1 egg, beaten

¾ cup coconut milk

Vegetable oil

1 cup shredded coconut (unsweetened or sweetened)

Shredded lettuce and orange slices for garnish

Hot Orange Sauce (page 269)

Shell the shrimp, leaving the tails intact. Use a sharp knife to make a slit along the curve of the shrimp's back, cutting about ¾ of the way through. Scrape out the exposed vein with the tip of the knife and wash it away under cold running water. Open the shrimp like a book along the slit and press it flat with the flat side of a large knife. Set the butterflied shrimp aside to drain on paper towels.

Stir ½ cup of the flour, the curry, jerk, salt, and baking powder together in a mixing bowl. Make a well in the middle, pour in the egg and coconut milk, and stir to form a smooth batter. It should have the consistency of pancake batter; if it's too thick, add milk.

Heat 2 to 3 inches of oil to 360 degrees in a deep-fryer or an appropriate pan (see page 28).

Spread the coconut on one plate and the remaining ½ cup of flour on another. Set them near the hot oil along with the batter.

Using tongs and working in batches, coat the shrimp with flour, batter, and then coconut, and lower into the hot oil. Cook, turning once, until golden brown all over, about 2 minutes. Drain on paper towels.

To serve, line eight plates with shredded lettuce and arrange 3 shrimp, tails up, on top of each. Garnish with orange slices and serve with Hot Orange Sauce on the side.

Scallop Seviche

[6 SERVINGS]

Seviche—seafood marinated in citrus juice—has Peruvian and Ecuadoran roots, but Miami chefs have made it their own, even serving seviche "sushi." Fish is most often the main ingredient, but nearly any kind of seafood can be made into seviche. We love the way sweet, tiny bay scallops look and taste in this zesty dish. If they're not available, substitute sea scallops or sea bass fillets cut into bite-size pieces. Although the seafood becomes firm and opaque when marinated, it remains raw, so use only the freshest seafood from a reliable source.

1½ pounds fresh bay scallops

½ cup fresh orange juice

¼ cup fresh lemon juice

¼ cup fresh lime juice

1 small red onion, peeled and diced

1 red bell pepper, seeded, cored, and diced

1 small tomato, seeded and diced

1 small ripe avocado, peeled, pitted, and diced

1 garlic clove, peeled and minced

½ Scotch bonnet pepper or 2 to 3 jalapeño peppers, seeded and minced

1 tablespoon chopped cilantro or flat-leaf parsley

2 teaspoons grated fresh ginger

½ teaspoon grated lemon zest

½ teaspoon grated lime zest

Kosher salt and freshly ground pepper

Lettuce leaves

Cilantro sprigs for garnish

Rinse the scallops well under cold running water and drain well. Combine them with the orange, lemon, and lime juices, onion, bell pepper, tomato, avocado, garlic, Scotch bonnet pepper, cilantro, ginger, and lemon and lime zests in a nonaluminum container. Stir to mix well and season to taste with salt and pepper. Chill for at least 2 hours or as long as overnight.

To serve, line 6 salad plates with lettuce leaves. Drain the seviche, spoon it onto the lettuce, and garnish with the cilantro sprigs.

VARIATION: To serve as an hors d'oeuvre, spoon the seviche onto *tostones* (Twice-Fried Green Plantains, page 227) or tortilla chips.

Caribbean-Style Crab Cakes

[4 SERVINGS]

You find crab cakes just about everywhere you find crabs, but few have as much personality as this jerk-spiked version. They're easy, too; if you can make hamburgers, you can make these. Crabmeat is sold as lump (pieces of white meat from the back fin of the body), flake (bits of white meat from the body), and brownish claw meat. Lump is the most expensive, but it makes the meatiest, tastiest crab cakes. To maintain that meaty texture, don't use any more bread crumbs than necessary. (And don't bother with imitation crabmeat—it's nothing like the real thing.)

2 tablespoons unsalted butter or vegetable oil

1 small onion, peeled and diced

2 scallions, trimmed and thinly sliced

2 garlic cloves, peeled and minced

1 tablespoon chopped fresh cilantro or flat-leaf parsley

1 egg

1 tablespoon mayonnaise

2 teaspoons Dijon-style mustard

1 tablespoon fresh lemon juice

1 tablespoon Jerk Seasoning (page 99) or a commercial blend

½ teaspoon kosher salt

1 teaspoon freshly ground pepper

1 pound fresh lump crabmeat (see Note)

½ to 1 cup plain, dry bread crumbs

Vegetable oil

1 cup Roasted Tomato Sauce (page 184), heated

Cilantro sprigs for garnish

Melt the butter in a skillet over medium heat and sauté the onion, scallions, and garlic until soft, about 5 minutes. Remove the pan from the heat and stir in the cilantro.

Beat the egg, mayonnaise, mustard, lemon juice, Jerk Seasoning, salt, and pepper together in a mixing bowl. Stir in the crabmeat, sautéed vegetables, and enough bread crumbs to hold the mixture together. Taste for seasoning. Form the mixture into 8 patties. Place them on a baking sheet lined with wax paper and refrigerate, uncovered, for 1 hour.

Heat a thin layer of oil in a large skillet over medium heat. Working in batches if necessary, fry the crab cakes until golden brown, 4 or 5 minutes per side. Drain on paper towels. To serve, ladle a pool of Roasted Tomato Sauce on each of 4 small plates and place 2 crab cakes in the center. Garnish with cilantro and serve immediately.

PLANNING AHEAD: Uncooked crab cakes can be frozen for several weeks and then thawed in the refrigerator. Because they may be a bit soggy, dredge them in plain, dry bread crumbs before frying.

NOTE: Lump crabmeat is sold canned and pasteurized, a process that preserves its flavor and texture. Keep it in the coldest part of your refrigerator and, to be on the safe side, use it within a week of purchase. Before using, remove any bits of shell or cartilage. Handle it as little as possible, though; you've paid for the best and don't want the lumps to become shreds.

Soups and Stews

Cold Avocado and Cucumber Soup

Cold Mango Soup with Raspberry Puree

Florida Orange and Tomato Gazpacho

Calabaza, Sweet Potato, and Apple Bisque

Ginger, Lime, and Calabaza Soup with Ginger Cream

Black Bean and White Corn Soup

Florida Fish Chowder

Florida Keys Conch Chowder

Ajiaco Santafereno (Bogotá-Style Chicken and Potato Stew)

Florida White Chili

 You probably don't think of Miami as a soup and stew kind of place, but it can get downright chilly in the winter. And when your heaviest outdoor gear is a raincoat, 35 or 40 degrees can feel positively frigid. One memorable Christmas some years ago, a massive cold front moved in, and Miamians by the tens of thousands switched on the heat, overwhelming electricity supplies and knocking out power for hours. So much for turning on the holiday lights, let alone cooking Christmas dinner.

No matter how cold it gets where you live, warming soups like Calabaza, Sweet Potato, and Apple Bisque or Florida Fish Chowder will take off the chill. But soup can be welcome in the heat of summer as well: A frosty bowl of Florida Orange and Tomato Gazpacho or Cold Mango Soup with Raspberry Puree is as refreshing as a tall, cold glass of lemonade. The possibilities don't end with the weather report. Whether you need an elegant starter for a dinner party or a hearty one-dish meal for lunch or supper, you'll find it in this chapter. And a pureed soup that's a first course one night can become a main course at lunch the next day with the addition of leftover cooked chicken or beans.

Most good soups begin with good stock or broth, and we encourage you to make your own (or use a quality substitute; see page 11). Don't overcook a hot soup; you want the ingredients to retain their individual texture and taste. But do make it a day ahead if you can so that the flavors can mellow and meld a bit in the refrigerator. While you're at it, make a double batch and freeze half. It will lighten your load and warm your heart at the end of a busy day to know that dinner is just a zap of the microwave away.

Cold Avocado and Cucumber Soup

[4 SERVINGS]

The cucumber adds lightness and the buttermilk a bit of tang to this rich, yet wonderfully refreshing soup. A velvety texture and soft green color add to the appeal. It would be a memorable starter for a warm-weather dinner party of Grilled Swordfish with Lime, Jalapeño, and Sour Cream Sauce (page 198), and Orange-Marinated Strawberries (page 315) for dessert. Or make it the centerpiece of a summer soup-and-sandwich supper. For a more substantial soup, add chilled sautéed scallops or shrimp to each bowl.

3 small or 2 large ripe avocados

1 large cucumber, peeled, halved, seeded, and cut into chunks (see Note)

1 scallion, trimmed and coarsely chopped

2 tablespoons fresh lemon juice

1 tablespoon fresh orange juice

1 cup buttermilk

1 cup milk or half-and-half

2 teaspoons kosher salt

½ teaspoon freshly ground pepper

Hot pepper sauce (optional)

2 tablespoons minced dill, chives, or cilantro

Peel and seed 2 of the small avocados and cut them into chunks. (If using large avocados, cut 1½ of them into chunks; rub lemon juice over the cut surface of the remaining half, cover it with plastic wrap, and refrigerate it.)

Combine the avocado chunks, cucumber, scallion, lemon and orange juices in a blender or food processor, and process until smooth.

Scrape this puree into a 2-quart container and stir in the buttermilk, milk, salt, pepper, and hot pepper sauce to taste. Refrigerate it, covered, for at least 2 hours, until well chilled. (Don't chill it for more than 4 hours, or it may discolor.)

To serve, peel and dice the remaining avocado. Taste the soup for seasoning and check the consistency; if you'd like it thinner, stir in up to ½ cup of milk. Divide the soup among 4 chilled bowls, place a mound of avocado in the center of each, and sprinkle with the minced herbs.

NOTE: Use a teaspoon to scrape the seeds out of the cucumber halves.

Cold Mango Soup with Raspberry Puree

[4 OR 5 SERVINGS]

This gorgeous, scrumptious soup is such a showstopper, it's hard to believe how easy it is to make. The deep pink raspberry puree contrasts beautifully with the peach-colored soup; the buttermilk and pineapple juice cut the sweetness of the mango; and the cinnamon, ginger, and cloves add a pumpkin pie–like accent. Don't tell your guests that all it took was a bit of cutting and a few whirls of the blender.

FOR THE SOUP:

4 medium mangos peeled, seeded, and cut into chunks, or 4 cups frozen mango puree, thawed

½ cup pineapple juice

2 tablespoons fresh lemon juice

2 teaspoons honey

½ teaspoon ground cinnamon

½ teaspoon ground ginger

1 pinch ground cloves

1½ cups buttermilk

Cold milk or half-and-half (optional)

FOR THE PUREE:

1 cup fresh or frozen raspberries

1 teaspoon fresh lemon juice

Combine the mangos in a blender or food processor with the pineapple juice, lemon juice, honey, cinnamon, ginger, and cloves. Process until smooth.

Scrape the mixture into a 2-quart container and stir in the buttermilk. Refrigerate for at least 2 hours, until thoroughly chilled.

To make the puree, process the raspberries and lemon juice in a blender or food processor until smooth. Strain it through a fine-mesh sieve to remove the seeds. Pour into a plastic squeeze bottle with a small tip or into a small plastic food storage bag, then refrigerate.

To serve, taste the soup for seasoning and check it for consistency; if you'd prefer it thinner, stir in up to 1 cup of milk. Divide the soup among 4 or 5 chilled bowls. If using a bottle, squeeze the raspberry puree over each serving in a decorative pattern. If using a plastic bag, twist the top closed, cut a tiny triangle from one corner, and do the same.

VARIATION: You can substitute papaya for the mango and use orange juice instead of pineapple juice.

NOTES:

- When straining the raspberry puree, tap the side of the sieve to help the job along. If you try to force it through with a spoon, you'll clog the strainer.
- The perfect tool for making stylish squiggles of puree on top of the soup is a plastic squeeze bottle sold at beauty-supply stores. You can also use it for a similar restaurant-style presentation of almost any dish with a smooth sauce.

Florida Orange and Tomato Gazpacho

[6 SERVINGS]

Spanish explorers brought home peppers—both sweet and hot—as well as tomatoes from the Americas, giving the Andalusians new ingredients for their traditional cold soup of bread, water, olive oil, and salt. Here we incorporate oranges, which crossed the Atlantic in the opposite direction when Columbus introduced them to the New World. Oranges and tomatoes are a sublime combination. Each flavor adds richness and depth to the other, and the bits of fresh orange add bursts of sweetness to every bite.

1 cup fresh orange juice

3 slices good-quality white bread, torn into chunks

2 medium cucumbers, peeled, seeded, and coarsely chopped

1 medium green bell pepper, cored, seeded, and coarsely chopped

½ medium red onion, peeled and coarsely chopped

2 pounds ripe tomatoes (about 6 medium), peeled and seeded

1 large garlic clove, peeled

½ to 1 small jalapeño pepper, seeded

3 tablespoons fresh lime juice

2 tablespoons extra-virgin olive oil

2 teaspoons kosher salt

1 teaspoon freshly ground pepper

1 large orange, peeled, sectioned, and cut into ½-inch pieces

1 cup tomato juice (optional)

Paper-thin orange slices for garnish

Combine the orange juice and bread in a blender or food processor and let it soak for a few minutes. Working in batches if necessary, add half of the cucumbers, half of the bell pepper, half of the onion, and all the tomatoes, garlic, jalapeño, lime juice, olive oil, salt, and pepper. Process until very smooth. If you have a food mill, strain the puree through the fine disc (see Note).

Pour the mixture into a 2-quart container and add the remaining cucumber, bell pepper, and onion, and the orange. Refrigerate the gazpacho for 6 hours or as long as 24 hours for the flavors to blend.

Before serving, taste for seasoning and check for consistency; add some or all of the tomato juice if you'd like it thinner. Ladle the soup into chilled bowls and float 1 or more orange slices on top.

VARIATIONS:

→ If fresh tomatoes aren't at their peak, substitute 1 drained 28-ounce can of peeled, diced tomatoes.

→ For a striking garnish, top each serving with a dollop of sour cream sprinkled with black caviar or with a spoonful of Scallop Seviche (page 37).

NOTE: If you enjoy pureed soups, a food mill is an excellent $15 investment. As the food is forced through the strainer disc (you have a choice of coarse, medium, or fine), any skin, seeds, and coarse fibers are left behind. An ordinary sieve would strain out all the pulp, leaving you with a thin soup, whereas the food mill gives you body as well as smoothness.

Tips/Techniques: Fresh Tomatoes

When using fresh tomatoes raw, as in gazpacho or salsa, you want to get rid of those unappetizing seeds first. The best way is to cut the tomato in half crosswise, hold it over the sink, cut side down, and squeeze it gently to dislodge the seeds and the gelatinous pulp.

In cooked dishes and when pureed as in gazpacho, you want to peel the tomato, too; otherwise, the skin will come loose and float around unappealingly in the dish. Here are two good methods:

When the recipe calls for just one or two chopped or diced tomatoes, seed them first as directed above. Then rub the cut surface against the coarsest side of a box grater until all the flesh is grated and discard the skin.

When you need a bigger batch, cut the core from each tomato, turn it over, and score the bottom with an X. Drop the tomatoes into boiling water for about 30 seconds, then use a slotted spoon to transfer them to a bowl of ice water. The skin will slip right off. Halve and seed them as directed above and chop or dice them as your recipe requires.

If your garden or farmer's market yields a bumper crop of fresh tomatoes, you can pop some into a freezer bag and freeze them whole. When you need them for cooking, drop the frozen tomatoes into hot water, slip off the skin, and set them aside in a colander to thaw.

In cooked dishes, a few teaspoons of tomato paste will boost the flavor of so-so fresh tomatoes. Look for it in a tube; it will keep in the refrigerator for up to a year.

Calabaza, Sweet Potato, and Apple Bisque

[6 TO 8 SERVINGS]

Calabaza, or West Indian pumpkin (see page 4), can be watery on its own, but it lends a mellow flavor to soups like this bisque. We combine it with north-of-the-border sweet potato and apple—though, in fact, the Granny Smiths you buy might come from Argentina or Chile—and warm the blend with cumin and coriander. A bit of cream or half-and-half softens and enriches the flavor. This is a perfect starter for a Thanksgiving feast and a welcome addition to any meal. Make it a day ahead if you can so that the flavors have time to develop fully. And remember that you can use acorn, butternut, or any hard-shelled squash if calabaza isn't available.

2 tablespoons unsalted butter or vegetable oil

1 medium onion, peeled and chopped

1 large leek, white part only, chopped

1 garlic clove, peeled and chopped

1 teaspoon ground cumin

¼ teaspoon ground coriander

2 medium Granny Smith apples, peeled, cored, and coarsely chopped

1 large sweet potato, peeled and coarsely chopped

1 pound calabaza, seeded, peeled, and coarsely chopped

4 to 5 cups chicken or vegetable broth

½ cup heavy cream or half-and-half, plus more for garnish

Kosher salt and freshly ground pepper

Hot pepper sauce

Cilantro or flat-leaf parsley leaves for garnish (optional)

Melt the butter in a soup pot over medium heat. Sauté the onion, leek, and garlic until soft, about 5 minutes. Stir in the cumin and coriander, and cook 1 minute more.

Add the apples, sweet potato, calabaza, and 4 cups of the broth. Bring to a boil over high heat, lower to a simmer, and cook, partially covered, until the vegetables are very soft, about 30 minutes.

Strain the broth into another container. (If you're working ahead, use the container in which you'll refrigerate the soup.) Working in batches if necessary, puree the remaining solids with a little of the broth in a blender or food processor. Whisk the puree back into the rest of the broth.

Just before serving, whisk in the cream and bring the soup to a simmer. Season to taste with salt, pepper, and hot sauce. Ladle into bowls and garnish each serving with a drizzle of cream and a sprinkling of cilantro.

PLANNING AHEAD: The soup can be made up to 2 days ahead and refrigerated, or up to 2 months ahead and frozen.

Tips/Techniques: Soup Pointers

Pureeing soup is one job that a blender handles better than a food processor. Fill the blender no more than two-thirds full with cold soup and one-third full with hot soup. Make sure the lid is on tight or your kitchen ceiling will look like a Jackson Pollock painting.

After adding cream, sour cream, or yogurt to a soup, don't let it boil, or it will curdle. If you slip up, you can eliminate the curdling by pureeing the soup.

If using canned broth (see page 11), be sure to taste the soup before adding salt. If you oversalt it, cook a peeled and halved potato with the soup and remove it before serving; it should absorb the excess salt.

Fresh herbs lose their flavor if cooked too long, so add them toward the end of the cooking time.

A handheld immersion blender can be immersed right into a pot of soup to puree the contents.

Ginger, Lime, and Calabaza Soup
with Ginger Cream

[6 SERVINGS]

Calabaza takes a solo turn in this golden yellow soup—and gets a little zing from fresh ginger and lime juice. Ginger Cream is an optional though elegant garnish. You can also marinate nine medium-size shrimp in Gingered Shrimp marinade (page 209), sauté them just until opaque, cut each in half lengthwise, and arrange three halves on each dollop of Ginger Cream. You'll have a first course fit for a king—a perfect prelude to Roast Chicken with Savory Guava Glaze (page 112).

2 tablespoons unsalted butter or
    vegetable oil

2 medium onions, peeled and
    chopped

1½ tablespoons minced fresh ginger

1 garlic clove, peeled and minced

3 pounds calabaza or other hard-
    shelled squash, peeled, seeded,
    and diced

2 cups chicken or vegetable broth

2 tablespoons fresh lime juice

Kosher salt and freshly ground
    pepper

½ cup heavy cream or half-and-half

FOR THE GINGER CREAM (OPTIONAL):

½ cup heavy cream

1 teaspoon minced candied ginger

Melt the butter in a soup pot over medium heat and sauté the onion, ginger, and garlic until the onion is soft, about 5 minutes. Stir in the squash and broth, and bring to a boil over high heat. Lower the heat to a simmer and cook, partly covered, for about 25 minutes, until the squash is very tender.

Strain the broth into another container. (If you're working ahead, use the container in which you'll refrigerate the soup.) Working in batches if necessary, puree the solids with a little of the broth in a blender or food processor. Whisk the puree back into the remaining broth.

Just before serving, whisk in the cream and bring the soup to a simmer. Add the lime juice, and salt and pepper to taste.

To make the Ginger Cream, beat the heavy cream until it holds soft peaks, then fold in the candied ginger.

Ladle the soup into bowls and top each portion with a spoonful of Ginger Cream.

PLANNING AHEAD: The soup can be made up to 2 days ahead and refrigerated, or up to 2 months ahead and frozen.

VARIATION: If you love the flavor of coconut, try using unsweetened coconut milk instead of heavy cream.

Black Bean and White Corn Soup

[6 TO 8 SERVINGS]

This soup—two soups, actually, served side by side in the same bowl—makes a knockout presentation. The contrast goes beyond the visual as the sweet white soup plays off against the more piquant black one. As you'll learn when you turn to the black bean recipe, no food is more steeped with tradition in Miami's Cuban community, which makes it especially fun to give it this updated treatment. Both soups are delightful when served on their own. Use fresh corn if you possibly can; if white corn is not available, use yellow, and think of it as Checker Cab Soup.

FOR THE CORN SOUP:

2 tablespoons unsalted butter or vegetable oil

1 medium onion, peeled and chopped

5 cups (5 large ears) fresh or frozen white sweet corn

2½ cups chicken or vegetable broth

½ cup heavy cream or half-and-half

Kosher salt and freshly ground pepper

1 to 2 teaspoons sugar (optional)

FOR THE BEAN SOUP:

4 cups Cuban-Style Black Beans (page 245), using the soup variation

Chicken or vegetable broth

Chopped cilantro or flat-leaf parsley for garnish

To make the corn soup, melt the butter in a soup pot over medium heat and sauté the onion until soft, about 5 minutes. Stir in the corn. Add the broth and bring to a boil over high heat. Lower to a simmer and cook for about 5 minutes, until the corn is cooked.

Working in batches if necessary, puree the soup in a blender or food processor. If you have a food mill, pass the puree through the coarse disc.

Return the soup to the pot and stir in the cream. Season to taste with salt, pepper, and sugar, and heat to a simmer.

Pass the black bean soup through the coarse disc of a food mill or puree it in a blender, and heat to a simmer.

Add broth to one or both of the soups if necessary to give them the consistency of heavy cream. (They must be the same thickness or they won't stay separate in the bowls.)

Using two ½-cup measures, scoop a portion of each soup and pour them simultaneously into opposite sides of each soup bowl. With the point of a paring knife, make decorative zigzags or swirls along the line where the two soups meet. Garnish with cilantro and serve.

VARIATION: Divide the black bean soup among 6 soup bowls and drizzle a ladleful of corn soup over the top in a decorative pattern.

Florida Fish Chowder

[6 TO 8 SERVINGS]

Jerk Seasoning and curry powder add island accents to this hearty dish. Like our gazpacho, it combines the surprisingly complementary flavors of tomato and orange. There are no potatoes in this chowder—just fish and lots of it. In Miami we'd use snapper, grouper, or sea bass, but any firm white-fleshed fish is fine. Lobster, shrimp, or other shellfish make nice additions.

2 tablespoons olive oil

1 medium onion, peeled and finely chopped

1 green bell pepper, cored, seeded, and cut into small dice

1 garlic clove, peeled and minced

2 teaspoons curry powder

½ teaspoon Jerk Seasoning (page 99) or a commercial jerk blend

1 28-ounce can peeled and diced tomatoes

3 8-ounce bottles clam juice

Grated zest of ½ orange

1 sprig fresh thyme or ½ teaspoon dry-leaf thyme, crumbled

1 teaspoon kosher salt

1 teaspoon freshly ground pepper

2 pounds firm white-fleshed fish fillets, cut into ½-inch cubes

4 scallions, trimmed and thinly sliced

Heat the oil in a large soup pot over medium heat and sauté the onion, bell pepper, garlic, and curry powder until the onion is soft, about 5 minutes. Stir in the jerk seasoning and dried thyme if using, and cook for 1 more minute.

Add the tomatoes and their liquid, clam juice, orange zest, fresh thyme if using, salt, and pepper. Bring to a boil over high heat, lower it to a simmer, and cook, uncovered, for 15 minutes. (The chowder can be prepared up to a day ahead to this point and refrigerated. Return to a simmer before proceeding.)

Add the fish and cook just until opaque and flaky, 2 or 3 minutes. Taste for seasoning. Ladle the chowder into bowls, garnish with scallions, and serve immediately.

About Chowder

Chowder is usually associated with New England, but the name originated with French fishermen who cooked fish and potato stew in a cauldron called a *chaudière*. A typical chowder consists of potatoes, onions, seafood, and sometimes corn. If the broth is milk- or cream-based, it's New England chowder; if it's tomato-based, it's Manhattan chowder (a term of disdain among New Englanders, who consider it a big-city affectation). With either version, the vegetables should remain separate and visible, not mushy, so don't overcook the chowder. It eases last-minute preparation and improves flavor if you prepare the chowder ahead except for the seafood. At serving time, reheat it, add and cook the seafood in the chowder, toss a green salad, slice a loaf of crusty bread, and call everybody to the table.

Conch: The Mollusk and the Republic

You may never have tasted the sweet meat of the conch (pronounced "conk"), but there's a good chance you've put a pink-tinged, spiral-shaped conch shell to your ear in hopes of hearing the ocean's roar. Conch were once so plentiful in south Florida waters and such a mainstay of pioneer diets that to this day natives of the Florida Keys proudly call themselves Conchs. In 1982, after the U.S. Border Patrol began trying to check all cars entering and leaving the Keys for drugs and illegal aliens, angry local activists announced their intention to secede from the Union and form the Conch Republic. Taking a cue from *The Mouse That Roared*, they declared war on the United States, promptly surrendered, and made a half-serious—and unsuccessful—bid for foreign aid. The secessionists celebrate the republic's birthday each April and still rally beneath their blue flag from time to time in protest of untoward government actions.

The marine conch population isn't nearly as robust and was so depleted by the mid-1980s that Florida outlawed conch harvesting. The fresh and frozen conch sold in the United States today comes from Turks and Caicos, a British colony southeast of the Bahamas, and elsewhere in the Caribbean. If aquaculturists have their way, though, we'll someday be able to buy farm-raised Keys conch for our chowder and fritters.

Florida Keys Conch Chowder

[8 SERVINGS]

Conch is as tough as it is tasty and must be tenderized and chopped before cooking. (And unlike most other seafood, it becomes tender with long, slow cooking.) Ask the fishmonger to run it through the tenderizer twice. If you can't get conch, substitute three 6½-ounce cans of minced clams, eliminate the soaking and chopping, and add the clams and their juice during the last few minutes of cooking. We've used tropical produce but have given more readily available alternatives for each item. If you can find yuca, be sure to use it because it holds its shape and texture beautifully, and doesn't disintegrate like potato, even after several reheatings.

1 pound tenderized fresh or frozen conch meat

½ cup fresh lime juice

2 tablespoons unsalted butter or vegetable oil

2 stalks celery, finely chopped

1 medium onion, peeled and finely chopped

1 green bell pepper, cored, seeded, and finely chopped

1 garlic clove, peeled and finely chopped

4 8-ounce bottles clam juice

4 cups water

1 14½-ounce can peeled and diced tomatoes

2 carrots, peeled and sliced

1 chayote or zucchini, diced

8 ounces calabaza or acorn squash, seeded, peeled, and diced

1 small yuca or medium potato, peeled and diced (about 1 cup)

1 medium boniato or sweet potato, peeled and diced (about 1 cup)

2 tablespoons tomato paste

1 sprig fresh thyme or ½ teaspoon dry-leaf thyme, crumbled

1 teaspoon kosher salt

1 teaspoon freshly ground pepper

Hot pepper sauce

2 tablespoons chopped fresh parsley

Put the conch in a shallow bowl, pour the lime juice over it, and refrigerate for 1 hour. Reserve the lime juice and chop the conch finely in a food processor or by hand.

Melt the butter over medium heat in a large soup pot. Sauté the celery, onion, bell pepper, and garlic until the onion is soft, about 5 minutes. (If using dried thyme, stir it in during the last minute.)

Add the clam juice, water, tomatoes, and their juice to the pot, and bring it to a boil over high heat. Add the carrots, chayote, calabaza, yuca, boniato, tomato paste, and fresh thyme if using. Add the conch and reserved lime juice. Let the mixture return to a boil, lower the heat, and simmer, uncovered, until the conch is tender, about 45 minutes.

Season the chowder with salt, pepper, and hot sauce to taste. Ladle into soup bowls and sprinkle each serving with parsley.

VARIATIONS:

➡ One cup of light cream and/or 2 tablespoons of dry sherry can be added during the last 5 minutes of cooking.

➡ For a thicker, richer chowder, mix together 2 tablespoons of softened butter and 2 tablespoons of flour with your fingertips and whisk it into the finished soup. Bring to a boil for a few minutes. (The mixture, called a *beurre manié*, or kneaded butter, can be used to thicken any soup or sauce.) To add thickness but not fat and calories, scoop out a cup or so of the finished soup, puree it in a blender or food processor, and stir it back into the pot.

Ajiaco Santafereno
(Bogotá-Style Chicken and
Potato Stew)

[8 SERVINGS]

Ajiaco (ah-he-AH-coh) is considered a national dish by both Cubans and Colombians, but their interpretations of it are vastly different. Meaty Cuban ajiaco evolved from a highly seasoned stew of wild game and tropical tubers that was a specialty of the native Arawak Indians in Columbus's time. (The same dish is considered the progenitor of the pepperpot soups and stews of the English-speaking Caribbean.) Colombian ajiaco is a delicate chicken stew made with several kinds of potatoes. Ours is the latter kind, shared by Ariana Kumpis, who grew up in Bogotá and now runs a Miami cooking school. The recipe originated with her mother-in-law, Irene, whose family owned a famous restaurant called Tres Casitas in Bogotá. (The Spanish name for the dish is derived from the full name of the city, Santa Fe de Bogotá.) The elder Mrs. Kumpis served her ajiaco at midday because she considered it too heavy for the evening meal. Ariana makes a dinner party dish of it, with rustic bread and beer or white wine. Half the potatoes are cooked so long that they disintegrate, giving the stew its thickness; the other half are added near the end. Use several kinds of potatoes if you can; Yukon Gold or Yellow Finn are great choices. If baking and boiling potatoes are your only choices, use the bakers for the first stage. The stew is served with capers, avocado, and cream on the side, and each guest uses them to embellish his own portion. It's considered perfectly acceptable to pick up the corn chunks and eat them out of hand.

1 3½-pound chicken, cut into
   serving pieces

2 carrots, peeled and cut in half

1 stalk celery, cut into chunks

1 large onion, peeled and
   quartered

1 bay leaf

4 cups chicken broth

4 cups water

1 tablespoon kosher salt

2 pounds assorted potatoes, peeled

3 ears sweet corn, cut in 2-inch
   pieces

1 cup fresh or frozen peas

4 sprigs cilantro, chopped

FOR SERVING:

1 ripe avocado

½ cup drained capers

4 hard-cooked eggs, chopped

1 cup heavy cream

Combine the chicken, carrots, celery, onion, bay leaf, broth, and water in a large soup pot. Bring to a boil and skim off any foam from the surface. Lower the heat, add the salt, and simmer, partially covered, for about 45 minutes, until the chicken is falling off the bone. As it cooks, continue skimming off any fat that rises to the top.

Meanwhile, cut half of the potatoes into thin slices and half into chunks. (Leave any small new or fingerling potatoes whole.)

Remove the chicken with a slotted spoon and strain the broth through a fine-mesh sieve into a large container. Reserve the carrots; discard the celery, onion, and bay leaf. Skim as much fat as you can from the broth and return the broth to the pot (see Note). Add the sliced potatoes, bring the broth to a boil, lower the heat, and simmer, partially covered, for 30 minutes.

Add the remaining potatoes and simmer just until tender, about 15 minutes.

If the sliced potatoes haven't dissolved, mash some of them against the side of the pot with a wooden spoon to thicken the stew.

Add the corn pieces and cook until tender, about 5 minutes. Add the peas, reserved carrots, and cilantro, and let the stew sit, covered, off the heat.

Peel and seed the avocado and cut it into chunks. Place the avocado, capers, and eggs in separate small bowls and pour the cream into a pitcher.

Ladle the soup into bowls, making sure that each portion has pieces of corn and potato. Pass the avocado, capers, eggs, and cream.

NOTE: One good trick for skimming fat from hot broth is to seal several ice cubes in a small plastic bag and drag the bag along the surface of the broth; the fat will harden onto the plastic.

Florida White Chili

[6 SERVINGS]

Don't let its mild-mannered appearance fool you; this chili can pack as much punch as the most fiery beef-and-red-bean kind. You can up the amount of cayenne and hot sauce to taste, and if you're a real pyromaniac, substitute a Scotch bonnet pepper for the jalapeños. Don't get carried away, though; too much heat will overpower the subtle flavors of the cumin and cloves.

You'll dirty only one pot making this chili and can fix it a day or two ahead. (Refrigerate the chicken separately and add it along with the cheese once you've reheated the cooked beans.)

This is a thick, meaty chili; if you'd like it less so, thin it with chicken broth and decrease the amount of chicken to 1 pound. Or leave the meat out altogether and substitute vegetable broth for a vegetarian dish.

1 pound dried Great Northern beans, rinsed and picked over (see Notes)

2 pounds skinless, boneless chicken breasts, trimmed of fat

2 cups chicken broth

1 tablespoon olive oil

2 medium onions, peeled and chopped

4 garlic cloves, peeled and minced

2 or more jalapeño peppers, seeded and minced

2 teaspoons ground cumin

2 teaspoons dry-leaf oregano, crumbled

¼ to ½ teaspoon cayenne

¼ teaspoon ground cloves

2 12-ounce bottles beer

1 or more dashes hot pepper sauce

8 ounces Monterey Jack cheese, shredded (about 2 cups)

Kosher salt and freshly ground pepper

Sliced scallions, chopped cilantro, salsa, and/or sour cream

Put the beans in a 4- to 5-quart Dutch oven and add water to cover by at least 3 inches. Let soak for at least 4 hours or as long as overnight. (Or boil for 2 minutes and let stand, covered, for 1 hour.)

Rinse and drain the beans, and wipe out the pot.

Put the chicken and broth in the pot, and bring just to a boil. Lower the heat and simmer, covered, just until the chicken is cooked through, about 15 minutes. Drain, reserving the broth. When the chicken is cool enough to handle, cut it into ½-inch cubes.

Wipe out the pot again and heat the oil over medium heat. Sauté the onions until translucent, about 10 minutes. Stir in the garlic, jalapeños, cumin, oregano, cayenne, and cloves, and cook for 2 more minutes.

Add the beans, broth, beer, and hot sauce, and bring to a boil over high heat. Turn the heat to low and simmer, uncovered, until the beans are very tender, about 2 hours. Stir occasionally and add more broth if it gets too dry.

When the beans are cooked, stir in the chicken and 1 cup of the cheese. Once the cheese has melted, taste for seasoning; add salt, pepper, and more cayenne and hot sauce if you like.

Ladle the chili into bowls and serve it with scallions, cilantro, salsa, and/or sour cream, and the remaining cheese on the side.

NOTES:

- Before using beans, wash them in a colander under cold running water. Pick through them and discard any broken beans or pebbles. See Basic Black Beans (page 19) for more on bean cookery.
- If you overdo the cayenne and hot sauce, cool the chili by adding rinsed and drained canned Great Northern or cannellini beans.

Salads and Dressings

Sunny Citrus Vinaigrette

Mango Vinaigrette

Orange-Cumin Vinaigrette

Orange-Raspberry Vinaigrette

Lime-Tamarind Vinaigrette

Gingery Fat-Free Banana–Poppy Seed Dressing

GREEN SALADS

Baby Greens and Arugula with Fat-Free Papaya-Mint Dressing

Romaine and Queso Blanco with Spicy Glazed Pecans and Walnut Vinaigrette

SIDE SALADS

Green Papaya and Red Pepper Slaw

Warm Yuca Salad

Rice, Bean, and Corn Salad with Jalapeño Dressing

MAIN DISH SALADS

Calypso Chicken Salad

Chicken, Orange, and Black Bean Salad

Grilled Gingered Shrimp and Spinach Salad

"Fresh from Florida." That's the motto of the state's agriculture department, but it's more than a promotional slogan, especially in Miami—and especially when it comes to salads. Fresh produce from local farms, fresh fruit from backyard trees, and fresh approaches to combining ingredients have inspired these recipes. And we hope that they in turn inspire you. There's no better outlet for your kitchen creativity than salads—as starters, on the side, or as meals in themselves. You may not be able to play fast and loose with the ingredients in a cake batter, but you can mix and match greens, fruits, vegetables, dressings, and more to your heart's content.

Begin by thinking about what's in season where you live. The best lettuce, for example, isn't necessarily the one listed in the recipe; it's the one that's freshest in your market today. And if the yellow bell peppers look better than the red ones, get them instead. Then open your refrigerator door and consider the possibilities: leftover chicken or rice, perhaps, or a nice wedge of cheese or a juicy orange. Finally, try one of our dressing recipes. They're so good we've put them front and center, at the beginning of the chapter. Their fresh flavor will more than repay your investment of time and may inspire you to create your own combinations. You'll find plenty of tips in the pages ahead to guide you on your way. Now have fun!

Begin with the freshest greens possible. Stems and core ends should look freshly cut, not dried out, wilted, or discolored. Discard any bruised, discolored, or tough outer leaves.

Separate the remaining leaves and submerge them in a sink or large basin filled with cold water. Swirl them around and let them rest for a few minutes so that any grit settles to the bottom.

Dry the greens well so the dressing will adhere to them. Lift them out of the sink, shake off the water, and pat them with paper towels or spin them in a salad spinner.

Make a point of washing greens as soon as you bring them home from the store, and you'll be able to put a salad together in no time. They'll keep in the crisper drawer for a few days if well wrapped. Layer the leaves with paper toweling to absorb moisture, and seal them in a plastic bag (perforated vegetable-storage bags are ideal).

It's a good idea to rinse and dry commercial "prewashed" salad mixes and spinach. It can't hurt, and, as your mother might have said, you don't know who handled them last.

Most greens should be torn, not cut, into bite-size pieces; they'll turn brown less quickly that way. Tougher varieties such as iceberg and romaine are an exception.

For the most interesting salads, vary the texture, flavor, shape, and color of the ingredients. Don't combine bitter greens such as endive, chicory, and arugula, for example. Instead, toss one of them with a soft, mild lettuce such as Boston or a crisp one such as romaine. Add radicchio or red oak to the mix for a touch of red.

Introduce color and crunch with bell pepper, cucumber, zucchini, tomato, carrots, celery, broccoli, or cauliflower. Add brightness and contrasting sweetness with tropical fruit such as cubed or sliced papaya or mango, sliced carambola (star fruit), pineapple chunks, or orange or grapefruit segments. And use a scattering of fresh basil, mint, tarragon, chives, cilantro, or other herbs for accent.

Don't overlook leftovers for inspiration. Cooked vegetables, rice, pasta, or potatoes can all be the basis for a salad. To make it a meal, add smoked or grilled turkey or chicken breast, roast beef, cooked shellfish, or, for a vegetarian dish, a rinsed and drained can of black or cannellini beans.

Dress the salad just before serving so the greens don't become soggy. Toss the ingredients in a large bowl with just enough dressing to coat them lightly. If excess dressing pools on the bottom of the bowl, you've added too much.

Meat and grains tend to sink to the bottom of the bowl, so if you're combining them with greens, you may want to arrange the salad on a platter. Drizzle on a little dressing at serving time and pass the rest.

Chilling reduces flavor as well as the temperature, so be sure to taste a cold salad—or any chilled, prepared food—for seasoning before serving.

For extra crispness chill the salad plates in the refrigerator before serving.

Think outside the box (of croutons) for garnishes; Grit Sticks (page 232) or a sprinkling of toasted nuts, salted seeds, grated Parmesan, or crumbled queso blanco cheese are fine finishing touches.

$\mathscr{D}$ressings

 A basic salad dressing—a vinaigrette, as the French would say—is simply a combination of oil, an acidic ingredient such as vinegar or citrus juice, and seasonings. The usual proportions are one part acid to three parts oil, but the formula can be altered depending on the specific ingredients and, most important, on your taste.

For a low-fat version you can replace up to two-thirds of the oil in most vinaigrettes with a complementary liquid such as broth, tomato juice, buttermilk, yogurt, or fruit juice. (Though it won't lower the fat content, mixing 1 cup of vinaigrette with a pureed avocado half makes a wonderfully creamy, flavorful dressing.)

To give a basic vinaigrette a fresh twist, replace half of the vegetable or olive oil with walnut, hazelnut, avocado, pumpkin seed, or another specialty oil, or add a teaspoon of toasted sesame oil. Using balsamic, wine, and other flavored vinegars is another option.

Eating a lettuce leaf dipped in the dressing is the best way to check the flavor.

Sunny Citrus Vinaigrette

[ABOUT 2 CUPS]

This sensational dressing is bursting with the bright, fresh flavors of lemon, lime, orange, and grapefruit. Toss it with red leaf lettuce and thinly sliced Vidalia onion, and top the salad with slivers of apple or pear for a little North-South fusion. The best way to remove the zest for this recipe is with a citrus zester; a vegetable peeler will work, too. If you use a light touch, you'll leave the bitter white pith behind.

> Zest of ¼ lemon, ¼ lime, ¼ orange, and ¼ grapefruit
>
> 1 small shallot, peeled
>
> ½ cup fresh orange juice
>
> ¼ cup white wine vinegar
>
> ¼ teaspoon cayenne
>
> 1 teaspoon kosher salt
>
> ½ teaspoon freshly ground pepper
>
> 1 cup vegetable oil

Blanch the citrus zests in a small pot of boiling water for 1 minute to mellow their flavor. Drain well and combine in a blender or food processor with the shallot, orange juice, vinegar, cayenne, salt, and pepper. Process until smooth. With the motor running, add the oil in a thin stream until incorporated. Taste for seasoning. The vinaigrette will keep in the refrigerator for 2 weeks.

Mango Vinaigrette

[ABOUT 1¼ CUPS]

Try this sweet, tangy dressing over a bed of lettuce and shredded cucumber, jicama, and carrots, and top the salad with mango slices and cooked shrimp.

1 ripe mango, peeled, seeded, and coarsely chopped, or 1 cup frozen mango puree

⅓ cup cider vinegar

⅔ cup vegetable oil

3 tablespoons honey

1 teaspoon kosher salt

1 teaspoon white pepper

¼ teaspoon cayenne

½ teaspoon vanilla extract

2 tablespoons thinly sliced scallion

Combine the mango, vinegar, oil, honey, salt, white pepper, cayenne, and vanilla extract in a blender or food processor and process until smooth. Stir in the scallions and taste for seasoning. If the dressing is too thick, thin with water. It will keep well in the refrigerator for up to 2 weeks.

VARIATION: To add a little more punch to the dressing, toss about ½ inch of fresh ginger into the food processor along with the mango.

Orange-Cumin Vinaigrette

[1½ CUPS]

Toasting accentuates the nutty flavor of the cumin—a wonderful partner to the sweet orange juice and tangy zest. It takes just a couple of minutes to toast the seeds in a dry skillet over medium heat, shaking the pan occasionally. When the seeds are fragrant, they're ready.

2 garlic cloves, peeled

1 tablespoon Dijon-style mustard

¼ cup sherry vinegar or red wine vinegar

2 tablespoons fresh lime juice

2 tablespoons orange juice concentrate

2 tablespoons toasted cumin seeds, ground, or 1 tablespoon ground cumin

¼ teaspoon each grated orange, lemon, and lime zests

½ teaspoon kosher salt

¼ teaspoon freshly grated pepper

1 cup extra-virgin olive oil

Drop the garlic through the feeding tube of a food processor with the motor running. (This keeps it from lodging under the blade.) Add the mustard, vinegar, lime juice, orange juice concentrate, cumin, citrus zests, salt, and pepper. Pulse to mix. With the motor running, add the oil in a thin stream through the feeding tube to create an emulsion. Taste for seasoning. The dressing will keep for up to 2 weeks in the refrigerator.

Orange-Raspberry Vinaigrette

[ABOUT 1¼ CUPS]

This simple dressing is lovely over Bibb lettuce, garnished with orange sections and chopped walnuts. Add slices of roast chicken, and you have an elegant main dish.

½ cup fresh orange juice

2 to 3 tablespoons raspberry vinegar (see Note)

½ teaspoon kosher salt

¼ teaspoon freshly ground pepper

½ cup vegetable oil

1 tablespoon snipped fresh chives

Combine the orange juice, 2 tablespoons of the vinegar, and the salt and pepper in a small bowl or a jar with a screw top. Add the oil, whisking or shaking until well combined. Stir in the chives and add the remaining tablespoon of vinegar if you want a more pronounced raspberry taste. Taste and adjust the seasoning. The dressing will keep well in the refrigerator for up to 2 weeks.

NOTE: Raspberry vinegar is one of those pricey gourmet items that have begun making their way onto supermarket shelves, but you can easily make an economical batch at home. Just combine 1 cup of washed fresh raspberries or thawed frozen ones with 3 cups of white wine vinegar in a quart jar. Refrigerate, tightly covered, for at least 1 week. The vinegar will keep indefinitely in the refrigerator and should be strained as it's used.

Lime-Tamarind Vinaigrette

[ABOUT 1½ CUPS]

Here's another full-flavored dressing that will make your taste buds sit up and take notice. Tamarind, the pod of a tropical tree and a major ingredient in Worcestershire sauce, has a deep sweet-tart taste.

Drizzle the dressing over sliced ripe tomatoes or toss it with thin strips of romaine lettuce, jicama, and ripe mango and papaya. Garnish with toasted sesame seeds.

½ cup balsamic vinegar

¼ cup frozen tamarind pulp (see Note)

¼ cup fresh lime juice

2 tablespoons honey

1 tablespoon grated fresh ginger

½ teaspoon kosher salt

¼ teaspoon freshly ground pepper

1 cup vegetable oil

Mix together the vinegar, tamarind, lime juice, honey, ginger, salt, and pepper in a small bowl or a jar with a screw top. Add the oil and whisk or shake to blend. Taste for seasoning. The dressing will keep for up to 2 weeks in the refrigerator.

NOTE: If frozen pulp isn't available, you can replicate it with equal amounts of fresh lime juice, molasses, and Worcestershire (in this case, 1 tablespoon plus 1 teaspoon each).

Gingery Fat-Free
Banana—Poppy Seed Dressing

[ABOUT 1¼ CUPS]

The vinegar and ginger give a nice edge to this yummy dressing, a winner over greens or fruit or as a sauce with grilled fish. Here's a serving idea: Line a platter with lettuce leaves, top them with alternating grapefruit sections and ripe mango and papaya slices, and drizzle with dressing.

1 large, ripe banana, peeled and
    cut into chunks

1 cup plain nonfat yogurt

¼ cup light brown sugar

¼ cup fresh orange juice

1 tablespoon raspberry or cider
    vinegar

½ teaspoon grated fresh ginger

½ teaspoon kosher salt

¼ teaspoon pepper

1 tablespoon poppy seeds

Combine the banana, yogurt, brown sugar, orange juice, vinegar, ginger, salt, and pepper in a food processor or blender. Process until smooth. Add the poppy seeds and pulse a few times just to mix. Add more orange juice if the dressing is too thick. It will keep well in the refrigerator for up to 2 weeks.

Yes, We Have . . . Bananas

Botanically, bananas are berries, and the plants on which they grow are classified as herbs. A bunch of bananas consists of seven to twelve hands, and a hand is made up of about a dozen bananas. In some Latin markets in Miami, hundred-pound bunches of bananas are hung from the ceiling, and the bananas are cut from them to order.

    The most popular of fruits, bananas outsell apples. There are more than three hundred kinds, and the familiar Cavendish has begun giving up shelf space in upscale markets to exotic varieties such as plump, coral-skinned red bananas; fragrant, diminutive lady fingers (chicaditas); chubby apple bananas (Manzanos); and pale "ice cream" bananas. Though unmistakably bananalike, their flavors are as distinctive and appealing as their appearance.

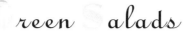

reen *Salads*

Baby Greens and Arugula with Fat-Free Papaya-Mint Dressing

[8 SERVINGS]

Mint complements the intense sweetness of the papaya, and papaya seeds add a peppery, radish-like accent to this pretty salad. The seeds are one of those love-'em-or-hate-'em ingredients. Taste one when you cut open the papaya; if you don't like it, substitute poppy seeds. (Proceed with caution if you have allergies, because papaya seeds cause allergic reactions in some people.) You'll have extra dressing; it will keep in the refrigerator for a week and is great on Bibb lettuce.

FOR THE DRESSING:

2 medium papayas

8 fresh mint leaves

1 tablespoon honey

5 drops Tabasco

1 tablespoon fresh lime juice

2 teaspoons cider vinegar

½ to 1 cup fresh orange juice

Kosher salt and freshly ground
 pepper

FOR THE SALAD:

2 bunches arugula

6 cups mesclun (mixed baby
 greens) or Bibb lettuce

2 red bell peppers, cored, seeded,
 and cut into thin strips

Cut the papayas in half. Remove the seeds, reserving 2 tablespoons of them. Cut the flesh from the peel and dice it. You should have about 3 cups.

To make the dressing, combine 2 cups of the papaya with the mint, honey, Tabasco, lime juice, vinegar, and ½ cup of the orange juice in a food processor and process until smooth. Add more orange juice if the mixture is too thick and season to taste with salt and pepper. Add 1 tablespoon of the reserved papaya seeds and pulse a few times until they are coarsely ground.

Wash and dry the arugula and mesclun, and tear into bite-size pieces. Toss the greens, bell peppers, and the remaining 1 cup of papaya with about ⅔ cup of the dressing. Sprinkle with the remaining 1 tablespoon of papaya seeds and serve.

Romaine and Queso Blanco with Spicy Glazed Pecans and Walnut Vinaigrette

[6 SERVINGS]

The spicy glazed pecans play off nicely against the saltiness of the cheese in this lively salad. Latin American queso blanco, also called queso fresco, has a texture similar to farmer cheese, goat cheese such as Montrachet, or sheep's milk feta, any of which can be substituted. Gorgonzola is another good stand-in if you like its assertive taste. Or press the glazed nuts into small wedges of Brie or rounds of goat cheese and use that as the garnish. The pecans are addictively good, so don't let yourself start munching or you won't have any left for the salad. The nuts alone make a great cocktail snack, and you can easily double or triple the recipe.

FOR THE PECANS:

2 teaspoons butter

1 tablespoon sugar

½ teaspoon kosher salt

½ teaspoon freshly ground pepper

¼ teaspoon cayenne

1 teaspoon water

⅔ cup pecans

FOR THE VINAIGRETTE:

2 tablespoons fresh lemon juice

1 tablespoon red wine vinegar

¾ teaspoon salt

½ teaspoon freshly cracked black pepper

¼ cup walnut oil

¼ cup olive oil

FOR THE SALAD:

1 head romaine lettuce, leaves separated, washed, and dried

6 ounces queso blanco cheese

To glaze the nuts, melt the butter in a skillet over medium heat. Stir in the sugar, salt, pepper, cayenne, and water. When the mixture begins to bubble, stir in the pecans. Cook, stirring constantly, until the nuts are well coated and the sugar has begun to caramelize, 3 to 5 minutes. Spread them on a parchment- or wax paper–lined baking sheet to cool.

To make the dressing, whisk the lemon juice, vinegar, salt, and pepper together in a small bowl. Slowly add the walnut and olive oils, whisking until blended.

To finish the salad, tear the lettuce into bite-size pieces and crumble or cube the cheese. Toss with the dressing in a large bowl and arrange on salad plates. Garnish with the pecans and serve.

PLANNING AHEAD: The nuts can be glazed several days ahead and stored in an airtight container. The lettuce can be washed, the cheese crumbled, and the vinaigrette made several hours ahead and refrigerated.

Green Papaya and Red Pepper Slaw

[4 TO 6 SERVINGS]

Like unripe plantain, green papaya is used as a vegetable rather than a fruit. It has a crisp, firm texture and a mild flavor that provides a backdrop here for fresh ginger and hot pepper. Even half a Scotch bonnet pepper makes a highly spiced salad, so if that's not your style, go with jalapeños in this colorful low-calorie salad. It's adapted from a dish we sampled at a Thai food booth at the Tropical Agriculture Fiesta, an annual celebration of the midsummer tropical harvest that's held under the sweltering July sun at the Fruit and Spice Park in the farming region south of Miami. Because papaya, mango, and carambola are grown throughout the tropical world, events like this are a magnet for our small Southeast Asian community. This salad would be great on a picnic (with no mayo in the dressing there's less danger of spoilage), and it's terrific as a condiment on roast beef or turkey sandwiches.

1 medium green papaya (about 1 pound; see Variations)

1 carrot, peeled

1 small onion, peeled

½ red bell pepper, seeded and cut in thin strips

½ to 1 Scotch bonnet pepper or 2 to 4 jalapeño peppers, seeded and minced

2 garlic cloves, minced

½ teaspoon grated fresh ginger

1 tablespoon sugar

1 tablespoon fresh lime juice

1 teaspoon kosher salt

1 teaspoon freshly ground pepper

Peel the papaya, cut it in half, and remove and discard the seeds. Rinse under cold running water and pat dry with paper towels. Shred the papaya, carrot, and onion using the largest holes on a box grater or the medium shredding disc of a food processor.

Toss the grated vegetables in a large bowl with the bell pepper and Scotch bonnet pepper, garlic, and ginger. Stir the sugar, lime juice, salt, and pepper together in a small bowl and toss with the vegetables. Refrigerate the salad, covered, for at least 1 hour. Taste for seasonings before serving.

VARIATIONS:

- You can use 1 pound of chayote (2 medium) instead of papaya. To prevent it from "weeping" and making the salad watery, cut the chayote in half and parboil for 1 minute. When cool enough to handle, grate the squash, seeds and all, and drain in a colander, pressing to remove the excess liquid.
- If you want to substitute cabbage for the papaya, use 3 cups, finely grated (half a small head).
- Although green mango may be no easier to find than green papaya, it can be substituted.

Warm Yuca Salad

[8 SERVINGS]

The firm, crumble-resistant texture of yuca (see page 10) makes it a great stand-in for potatoes in this salad. Yuca has a bland taste that puts the spotlight on the tart, creamy dressing; for contrasting sweetness you could substitute boniato (tropical sweet potatoes, page 3). If neither is available, you can, of course, use potatoes. Here's another twist: If you prefer an oil-based dressing, simply mix the warm tubers with 1⅓ cups of Chimichurri Sauce (page 138).

2 pounds yuca

Kosher salt

½ cup mayonnaise

½ cup sour cream

¼ cup fresh lemon juice

2 scallions, trimmed and thinly sliced

1 teaspoon celery seeds

2 tablespoons chopped fresh basil

2 tablespoons chopped fresh parsley

2 tablespoons drained capers (optional)

Freshly ground pepper

Cut the yuca into 4-inch sections, halve it lengthwise, and discard the fibrous cord running down the center. Insert the tip of a paring knife between the white flesh and the pale pink layer that surrounds it, and pull off the pink layer along with the barklike outer skin.

Combine the yuca, 1 teaspoon salt, and water to cover in a 2-quart saucepan. Bring to a boil, turn the heat to medium-low, and simmer until tender, 10 to 15 minutes. (Check it for doneness with the tip of a knife as you would potatoes.)

Meanwhile, stir together the mayonnaise, sour cream, lemon juice, scallions, celery seeds, basil, parsley, capers, and salt and pepper to taste.

Drain the yuca, and when it's just cool enough to handle, cut into ¾-inch cubes. Put in a large bowl and fold in the dressing. Serve immediately.

NOTE: Serving the salad warm brings out the most flavor in the dressing, but it's perfectly good cold, too. Chill in the refrigerator for at least 1 hour or up to 24 hours.

Rice, Bean, and Corn Salad with Jalapeño Dressing

[8 SERVINGS]

This eye-catching, palate-pleasing salad is adapted from a recipe by Bobbi Garber, Carole's former cooking school partner, who makes a big hit with it at parties. It uses converted (also called parboiled) rice, which is steamed and pressure-cooked before it's milled. This process makes it a bit more nutritious than regular white rice and, more to the point, allows it to cook up fluffy, with separate grains that don't harden or clump together when chilled. The salad keeps beautifully (it can be made up to two days ahead), and is fairly low in fat, too. Although we usually serve it as a side dish, it makes a great vegetarian entree.

FOR THE SALAD:

1½ cups converted rice

1½ teaspoons kosher salt

1½ to 2 cups Basic Black Beans (page 19) or drained, canned red or black beans

2 cups fresh, frozen, or drained, canned corn kernels

½ bunch scallions, trimmed and thinly sliced (about ½ cup)

FOR THE DRESSING:

2 jalapeño peppers, ribs and seeds removed

¼ cup fresh lime juice

2 tablespoons cider vinegar

1 tablespoon brown sugar

1 to 2 teaspoons chili powder

1 to 2 teaspoons ground cumin

2 to 4 tablespoons vegetable oil

½ teaspoon freshly ground pepper

TO FINISH THE DISH:

Red or green bell pepper strips for garnish

Cook the rice according to package directions, using ½ teaspoon of the salt. Combine the rice in a large bowl with the beans, corn, and scallions.

Combine the jalapeños, lime juice, vinegar, brown sugar, chili powder, cumin, oil, pepper, and the remaining 1 teaspoon of salt in a food processor or blender and process until the jalapeños are finely minced.

Pour the dressing over the salad and stir to mix well. Refrigerate, covered, for at least 3 hours (and up to 48 hours) for the flavors to blend. Let stand at room temperature for 30 minutes before serving, garnished with the bell pepper strips.

Main Dish Salads

Calypso Chicken Salad

[6 TO 8 SERVINGS]

Trinidad, half of the two-island nation of Trinidad and Tobago at the far eastern end of the West Indies, is home to calypso music. It's also home to the Caribbean's largest East Indian population, whose contributions to our melting pot are reflected by the curry in this flavorful chicken salad. Serve it on a bed of greens, in pita pockets, or, for a deliciously different presentation, in seeded papaya halves. For a taste of West Indian culture, visit Miami in early October for the annual Caribbean carnival when the streets are filled with the infectious sound of calypso, the sensual sight of sequined dancers, and the enticing scent of Trinidadian roti (page 124) and Jamaican curried goat.

1 cup mayonnaise

1 tablespoon fresh lime juice

2 to 3 teaspoons curry powder

1 teaspoon grated fresh ginger

Kosher salt

4 cups cubed cooked chicken breast (4 large or 6 small breast halves) (see Notes)

½ cup diced celery

½ cup coarsely chopped walnuts

½ cup raisins

1 8-ounce can pineapple chunks or tidbits, drained (1 cup), or ½ small fresh pineapple, grilled if desired and cut into chunks

Stir together the mayonnaise, lime juice, curry powder, ginger, and salt to taste in a bowl big enough to hold all the ingredients. Fold in the chicken, celery, walnuts, and raisins. Chill for at least 1 hour. Fold in the pineapple and taste for seasoning before serving.

VARIATIONS:

→ Use diced mango in place of the pineapple and replace ⅓ cup of the mayonnaise with mango chutney.

→ Substitute 2 pounds of peeled, cooked shrimp for the chicken.

NOTES:

• The pineapple is added just before serving so that it doesn't break down the mayonnaise.

• Using deli-roasted chicken is a good shortcut. To poach your own chicken breasts, simmer them in lightly salted water to cover for about 10 minutes. Be sure to save the cooking water for broth.

Chicken, Orange, and Black Bean Salad

[4 SERVINGS]

If you use the "cook once, eat twice" approach, this classy salad can be as easy to put together as it is pretty to look at. Just make a double recipe of Quick Caribbean Chicken Breasts (page 93), serve them hot off the grill one night, and make the salad from the leftovers a night or two later. Any mix of greens is fine, but we especially like a combination of watercress and red-tipped Boston lettuce.

Quick Caribbean Chicken Breasts (page 93)

1 cup Basic Black Beans (page 19) or drained,
    canned black beans

6 to 8 tablespoons Orange-Cumin Vinaigrette (page 71)

4 cups mixed greens

Kosher salt and freshly ground pepper

4 oranges, peeled and thinly sliced

2 scallions, trimmed and thinly sliced

After grilling or broiling the chicken, let stand for 5 minutes, then cut in thin diagonal slices across the grain.

Put the black beans in a small bowl with 3 tablespoons of the vinaigrette and toss to coat.

In a large bowl, toss the greens with enough of the remaining vinaigrette to coat lightly. Season to taste with salt and pepper. To serve, overlap the orange slices along the edge of four dinner plates (don't worry if they don't form a complete border). Mound a quarter of the greens in the center of each plate. Place a breast half on each, arranging the slices in a fan pattern. Spoon a ribbon of black beans across the chicken and sprinkle with scallion slices.

VARIATION: Use 2 ripe mangos in place of the orange and dress the salad with Mango Vinaigrette (page 70).

Grilled Gingered Shrimp
and Spinach Salad

[4 SERVINGS]

Here's another salad that gives you a start on a second meal—Gingered Shrimp and Star Fruit on a Stick—if you make a double batch of the marinade. The marinade will keep in the refrigerator for several weeks.

1 pound large shrimp, peeled and deveined

1 recipe Gingered Shrimp marinade (page 209)

1 red bell pepper, cored, seeded, and cut into 8 pieces

1 medium red onion, peeled and cut into 8 pieces

½ pineapple, peeled, cored, and cut into chunks

¼ cup vegetable oil

Kosher salt and freshly ground pepper

10 ounces fresh spinach, stemmed, washed, and dried

About ⅓ cup Orange-Raspberry Vinaigrette (page 72)

Combine the shrimp and marinade in a self-sealing food storage bag and let marinate for 20 minutes on the counter or up to 2 hours in the refrigerator.

Combine the bell pepper, onion, pineapple, and oil in a bowl. Season with salt and pepper, and toss to coat.

Build a medium fire in a charcoal grill (see page 100). With a gas grill, use indirect, medium heat. Coat the grill rack with oil and position it 4 to 6 inches from the heat source.

Thread the shrimp, pepper, pineapple, and onion onto skewers or enclose in a grill basket. Grill, turning frequently, for 6 to 8 minutes, until the shrimp are just opaque and the fruit and vegetables are nicely browned on the edges. Set aside to cool slightly.

Place the spinach in a large bowl with the grilled ingredients. Add enough vinaigrette to moisten the salad and toss to coat. Serve immediately.

The Main Course 1: Chicken and Other Poultry

Quick Caribbean Chicken Breasts

Triple Citrus Chicken Breasts

Spicy Pecan-Crusted Chicken Breasts

Jerk Seasoning

Grilled Island-Style Chicken with Jerk Marinade

Grilled Lemon-Garlic Chicken Quarters

Cuban-Style Braised Chicken

Jerk-Fried Chicken

Roast Chicken with Savory Guava Glaze

Arroz con Pollo (Chicken with Yellow Rice)

Chicken and Black Bean Pot Pie with Cornmeal Crust

Curried Chicken, Potato, and Calabaza with Roti (East Indian Flat Bread)

Grilled Whole Turkey with Mojo Marinade

Roast Duckling with Lime-Ginger-Mango Sauce

 The cultural fusion that makes Miami unique translates into an irresistible range of dinner possibilities—meat loaf infused with island spices, brisket simmered with tropical tubers, and simple chicken and fish dishes lifted out of the ordinary by tropical fruit salsas, Jamaican-style jerk seasoning, or Cuban-inspired marinades.

Although the cuisine is cutting edge, it's the product of an age-old process. The tropics have been transforming cooks since Columbus's time when explorers carried New World tomatoes, cocoa beans, and chili peppers to Europe, Africa, and Asia, and introduced cattle and citrus to this side of the globe. Each new wave of migration has given the tropical melting pot another stir. Cuban cuisine, for example, combines the food traditions of the island's indigenous Indians, Spanish conquerors, African slaves, and Chinese laborers. Elsewhere in the Caribbean, settlers from France, Britain, Holland, and the Indian subcontinent seasoned the pot. In Latin America, Spanish, Portuguese, and ancient Indian influences merged.

These far-flung foodways converge in Miami, where *arepas* (fried South American corn cakes) are sold alongside hot dogs at the baseball stadium, a bracing shot of Cuban coffee is as close as the corner cafe, and curry-filled Trinidadian roti (flat bread) is sold by street vendors. The poultry and meat dishes in this book capture the flavors of Miami in dishes as simple as lime-kissed Quick Caribbean Chicken Breasts, which is sure to become a weeknight favorite, and as elegant as herb-scented Leg of Lamb Florida Style, a stunning dinner party entree.

Grilling is an integral part of Miami cooking; in fact, we can claim it as our own: Centuries ago the Arawaks, a native people of the Caribbean, cooked their meat over open fires on grids made of green wood that the Spanish called *barbacoa*—the fore-runner of our barbecue grill. Grilling captures the essence of Miami entertaining, a relaxed and satisfying meal shared with friends amid balmy breezes and sunny skies. If it happens to be snowing where you are, don't despair; our grilled dishes come with indoor instructions, too!

SELECTION

Look for plump, full-breasted whole birds with smooth, unblemished skin. (Skin color varies depending on the chicken's diet.)

Choose tightly wrapped packages of chicken parts that are relatively free of liquid. Check the freshness date and look for a U.S. Department of Agriculture inspection sticker. A "Grade A" tag alongside the inspection seal indicates the highest quality.

Precut parts may cost more than whole chicken, but they save you from buying pieces you don't need—and cutting up the bird.

Ounce for ounce of edible meat, boned breasts and thighs are usually no more expensive than bone-in parts and are a time-saver.

Free-range chickens are raised with access to an outdoor yard, which some cooks think gives them better taste and texture.

Kosher chickens are raised and slaughtered in compliance with Jewish dietary laws and under the supervision of rabbinical inspectors. They're salted after slaughter to draw out the blood, which some cooks think makes them cleaner and more tender.

STORAGE AND HANDLING

Refrigerate uncooked chicken in its store wrapping; it will keep for up to two days. To store longer (up to six months), wrap the unopened package in freezer wrap, a freezer bag, or aluminum foil, and freeze it.

Defrost chicken in the refrigerator, never on the kitchen counter. Allow twelve to sixteen hours for a whole chicken, four to nine hours for parts. When pressed for time, thaw in the microwave following the manufacturer's directions.

When ready to use, rinse poultry under cold running water to wash away excess fat, bone chips, and/or skin.

SAFETY

Scrub your hands with hot soapy water before handling raw chicken. Scrub them again, along with the work surfaces and tools you've used, when you're done.

Marinate raw chicken in the refrigerator. If you want to serve leftover marinade, cook it first at a full rolling boil for at least three minutes.

To avoid contamination, transfer cooked chicken from the pan or grill to a clean plate, not the one that held it when it was raw.

THE SKINNY ON CHICKEN SKIN

Removing the skin eliminates most of the fat from chicken, but it also allows the meat to dry out more easily during cooking. If you're watching your fat intake, the solution is to cook chicken with the skin on and remove it before eating. The exceptions are breaded or coated chicken dishes, such as Jerk-Fried Chicken (page 110), in which you'd lose the flavorful coating along with the skin. (Don't worry; you'll find a nice skinless, oven-fried variation for that recipe.)

Quick Caribbean Chicken Breasts

[4 SERVINGS]

This marinade is loosely based on mojo, a blend of citrus juice, garlic, and oil that's an integral component of Cuban cuisine. If you put the chicken in the marinade in the morning, you can have dinner on the table in no time after work.

4 skinless, boneless chicken breast halves

2 tablespoons light soy sauce

1 tablespoon dry sherry

1 tablespoon vegetable oil

1 tablespoon fresh lime juice

1 teaspoon grated lime zest

1 garlic clove, peeled and minced

¼ teaspoon ground cinnamon

Trim and discard any excess fat from the breast halves. Rinse well under cold running water and pat dry with paper towels. Place between 2 layers of plastic wrap and pound with a meat mallet or the bottom of a heavy pan to an even thickness of about ½ inch (see Note).

Combine the soy sauce, sherry, oil, lime juice, lime zest, garlic, and cinnamon in a large, self-sealing plastic bag. Add the chicken breasts, seal the bag, and turn to coat well. Refrigerate for at least 2 hours or as long as overnight.

TO GRILL: Use indirect, medium heat (see page 100). If the grill rack is adjustable, place it about 4 inches from the heat source; close the cover if your grill has one. Grill the chicken for 4 to 6 minutes per side, turning once and basting with any remaining marinade. Cut into the meat to test for doneness; it should be fully white, with no trace of red.

TO BROIL: Adjust the rack so that the meat will be about 4 inches from the heat source and cook as directed above.

Serve immediately.

NOTE: Flattening chicken breasts allows them to cook evenly. Press down and out from the center as you pound for a uniform thickness.

Sautéing is simply the French word for frying. Although our collective fat phobia has pushed it out of favor, there is no substitute for the crisp texture and rich flavor and color that sautéing imparts. And if used occasionally and done correctly, it's a method that can fit comfortably into a health-conscious cook's repertoire. (Think of it this way: Sautéing six chicken breast halves in 2 tablespoons of oil adds 40 extra calories per serving at most, something you can burn off in ten minutes of brisk walking.) To minimize the amount of fat required, use a non-stick skillet. Keep in mind, though, that if you're going to deglaze the pan for a sauce, more of those succulent brown bits will form in a pan without a nonstick coating.

Here's how to achieve the crisp brown exterior and juicy interior that are the hallmarks of perfectly sautéed food:

• Heat the oil to just below the smoking point so that the food sizzles and browns as soon as it hits the pan. Using a really hot pan also minimizes the amount of oil the food absorbs. Once both sides are browned, lower the heat if necessary to finish cooking.

• To ensure that the food browns rather than steams, pat it dry with paper towels before adding it to the pan. For the same reason, use a pan that is large enough to hold the food without crowding. (Don't use too big a pan, though; if the food doesn't cover most of the bottom, the pan juices will burn.) A shallow pan with sloping sides is the best choice because it lets the steam escape easily.

• For a buttery flavor, use a fifty-fifty combination of cooking oil and unsalted butter. The oil stretches the butter's low smoking point, allowing the pan to get good and hot.

Triple Citrus Chicken Breasts

[6 SERVINGS]

Long before mangos and papayas appeared on the national scene, Florida was synonymous with citrus. This marinade bursts with the fresh flavors of lemon, lime, and orange. Honey—another Florida product—adds a hint of sweetness, and garlic and chives provide depth. A little cream pays big dividends in flavor and texture.

Like Quick Caribbean Chicken Breasts (page 93), this dish can be your salvation at dinnertime if you begin marinating the chicken in the morning or even the night before. We like to serve it with Tropical Couscous (page 234) and a green salad.

6 skinless, boneless chicken breast halves

1 teaspoon grated lemon zest (see Note)

1 teaspoon grated orange zest

1 garlic clove, peeled and minced

1 tablespoon snipped chives

1 teaspoon kosher salt

¼ teaspoon coarsely ground pepper

3 tablespoons fresh lime juice

2 tablespoons fresh lemon juice

1 tablespoon honey

1 teaspoon balsamic vinegar

2 tablespoons vegetable oil

2 tablespoons heavy cream

Paper-thin citrus slices and snipped chives for garnish

Trim and discard any excess fat from the chicken breasts. Rinse well under cold running water and pat dry with paper towels. Place between 2 layers of plastic wrap and pound with a meat mallet or the bottom of a heavy pan to an even thickness of about ½ inch. Put in a large, self-sealing plastic bag.

Whisk together the lemon and orange zests, garlic, chives, salt, pepper, lime juice, lemon juice, honey, and balsamic vinegar in a small bowl until the salt and honey dissolve. Pour over the chicken. Close the bag securely and turn to distribute the marinade. Refrigerate for at least 2 hours and as long as 24 hours, turning occasionally.

Remove the chicken from the bag. Shake the excess marinade into the bag and reserve. Pat the chicken dry with paper towels.

Heat the oil in a large, heavy, nonstick skillet over high heat until shimmering but not smoking. Sauté the chicken until browned, 2 or 3 minutes per side. Lower the heat to medium and continue cooking until the chicken is done, about 2 more minutes per side. The meat should have no trace of pink when you cut into it. Transfer to a serving platter and cover to keep it warm.

Pour the reserved marinade into the skillet and bring to a boil over high heat. Scrape the bottom of the pan with a wooden spatula or spoon to loosen any browned bits. Add any liquid that has collected around the chicken and let the mixture boil for about 2 minutes, until slightly thickened and reduced. Stir in the cream and let cook for another minute.

Pour the hot sauce over the chicken breasts. Garnish with citrus slices and chives, and serve immediately.

VARIATION: Half-inch-thick medallions of pork tenderloin are wonderful prepared this way, too.

NOTE: Cookbook author Giuliano Bugialli uses this trick for grating citrus zest: Spread a piece of parchment paper or plastic wrap over the teeth of the grater. Rub the citrus against it, turning the fruit as the peel is grated. The zest will cling to the paper when you pull it off, and the bitter white pith will stay behind on the teeth.

Spicy Pecan-Crusted Chicken Breasts

[4 SERVINGS]

The crunch of pecans, the bite of Jerk Seasoning, and the sweet heat of Pickapeppa Sauce (see page 98) make this a lively centerpiece for a casual, island-inspired meal with Grilled Pineapple and Avocado Salsa (page 257), Caribbean Rice (page 236), and a tossed salad on the side.

4 skinless, boneless chicken breast halves

1 cup all-purpose flour

2 to 4 tablespoons Jerk Seasoning (recipe follows) or a commercial jerk blend

½ teaspoon kosher salt

1 cup finely ground pecans (about 4 ounces)

1 cup fresh bread crumbs (2 slices) (see Notes)

2 or 3 egg whites (see Notes)

2 to 4 tablespoons Pickapeppa Sauce (or a 50-50 mixture of Worcestershire sauce and ketchup)

2 tablespoons vegetable oil

Trim and discard any excess fat from the chicken breasts. Rinse well under cold running water and pat dry with paper towels. Place between 2 layers of plastic wrap and pound with a meat mallet or the bottom of a heavy pan to an even thickness of about ½ inch.

Mix the flour, Jerk Seasoning, and salt in a shallow dish. In another shallow dish, mix the pecans and bread crumbs. In a third dish, beat the egg whites and Pickapeppa with a fork until frothy. Set a wire rack atop a baking sheet.

Dredge each breast half in the seasoned flour, then in the egg mixture, and finally in the pecan mixture, coating completely. Place on the rack and refrigerate for at least 10 minutes. (See Notes.)

Heat the oil in a large skillet over medium-high heat. Sauté the chicken for about 3 minutes per side, lowering the heat if necessary to keep the nuts from burning. The chicken should be lightly browned outside and cooked through but still juicy inside. Serve immediately or keep warm in a 200-degree oven for up to 15 minutes.

PLANNING AHEAD: You can bread the chicken up to a day ahead and refrigerate it, covered.

VARIATIONS:

➡ You can use almonds, cashews, hazelnuts, macadamia nuts, or walnuts instead of pecans.

➡ Firm white-fleshed fish such as snapper or grouper is also great prepared this way.

NOTES:

• Two tablespoons each of Jerk Seasoning and Pickapeppa make the chicken moderately spicy; 4 tablespoons produce a definite burst of heat. If you use the smaller amount of Pickapeppa, you'll need 3 egg whites in order to have enough liquid.

• To make fast work of the bread crumbs, tear the bread into chunks and process in the food processor with the whole nuts.

• Refrigerating the chicken—or any breaded ingredient—before frying helps the crumbs stick to the food rather than the skillet. To make a neat job of breading, use just one hand or tongs. That way you'll be able to answer the phone!

Jamaican Jerk and Pickapeppa Sauce

Strictly speaking, "jerk" refers not only to a seasoning blend but to a cooking method—slow-roasting in a pit over an allspice wood fire as practiced in the jerk huts of Jamaica. It's a three-hundred-year-old technique developed by the maroons, escaped slaves who lived in the island's desolate interior. Bands of maroons used hot spices and slow cooking to preserve the wild boar that sustained them as they eluded capture by British soldiers. And they in turn may have learned to use hot peppers and other indigenous seasonings from the native Arawak Indians.

We have heard it said that the name "jerk" comes from the way the seasoned meat is jerked around on the grills that cover modern-day Jamaican jerk pits. Given its original purpose as a preservative, though, it more likely derives from the Spanish word *charqui*, which means dried meat and is also the source of the word "jerky."

Pickapeppa, a tomato-based Jamaican condiment spiked with cane vinegar, mangos, raisins, tamarind, and hot spices, is widely sold in U.S. supermarkets and specialty stores. (Look for the brown bottle with the red and green parrot on the label. For the store nearest you, call the importer, Warbac Sales of New Orleans, at 504-834-1395.) You can approximate the taste with a fifty-fifty mixture of Worcestershire sauce and ketchup.

Jerk Seasoning

[ABOUT 4 TABLESPOONS]

Jerk seasoning can be dry, like this version, or wet, like the marinade on page 103, and a good recipe is so highly prized that Jamaican cooks have been known to keep theirs under lock and key. This dry rub is very good indeed. We'd describe the heat level as medium-high; you can adjust it by increasing (or decreasing) the cayenne by up to half a teaspoon. Commercial jerk seasoning is available but can lose its zing before you use the whole bottle. By making your own in small batches, you will ensure freshness. If you plan to use this often, double the recipe.

1 tablespoon onion powder

1 tablespoon garlic powder

1 teaspoon ground cayenne

½ teaspoon sugar

½ teaspoon dry-leaf thyme, crumbled

½ teaspoon dry-leaf oregano, crumbled

½ teaspoon kosher salt

½ teaspoon red pepper flakes

½ teaspoon ground allspice

½ teaspoon ground cinnamon

½ teaspoon ground cumin

Combine the onion powder, garlic powder, cayenne, sugar, thyme, oregano, salt, red pepper flakes, allspice, cinnamon, and cumin in a small jar. Rub the mixture between your fingers to release the full flavor of the thyme and oregano leaves. Shake to mix well. Store in a cool, dry place for up to 3 months.

There are lots of different types and brands of grills, and the best source of information about yours is the owner's manual. It's a good idea to review it when you take your grill out for the season. Here are some general grilling tips and guidelines:

The key to successful grilling is the same as that for stovetop cooking: a powerful, even source of heat. With a gas or electric grill, you simply select the heat level and let the grill preheat according to the manufacturer's instructions (generally 10 or 15 minutes).

With a charcoal grill, briquettes need twenty-five or thirty minutes to ignite thoroughly and may need to be replenished as you cook if the fire begins to fade.

- For a hot fire, let the coals burn down until they're red and glowing, and have a light layer of gray ash. You'll be able to hold the palm of your hand 6 inches above them for only 2 or 3 seconds.
- For a medium fire, let the coals burn down until they have a light layer of gray ash with a red glow occasionally visible underneath. You won't be able to hold your hand 6 inches above them for more than 4 or 5 seconds.
- For a slow fire, let the coals burn until they have a thick layer of ash with almost no red visible. You'll be able to hold your hand 6 inches above them for 6 or 7 seconds.

Before heating the grill, brush or spray the grill rack with oil to prevent sticking and make cleanup easier. A spray bottle filled with cooking oil is an inexpensive alternative to aerosol spray. A spray bottle filled with water comes in handy for putting out flare-ups.

Before setting the grill rack in place, arrange the coals according to the cooking method you're using:

- For direct heat, spread the coals in a single layer.
- For indirect heat, bank the coals on either side of the grill, leaving the center open. Place a disposable aluminum pan in the center to catch drips and, if you like, fill it with water for extra moisture. (Use juice or beer if you want to add flavor, too.) Indirect heat allows food to cook through without charring or drying out. It's the best choice for just about everything except extremely quick-cooking items like hot dogs and our thin Gaucho Grill steaks (page 137). (For indirect heat on a gas grill, consult your owner's manual.)

If your grill has a cover, use it unless you're fixing something that cooks very quickly. The lid holds in heat and smoke that would otherwise escape, allowing the food to cook more evenly and quickly, and producing more flavor. It's also more difficult to control flare-ups—one of the main causes of burned food—on an open grill.

Remember that outdoor cooking times are always approximate. Every fire is different, and weather conditions can speed or slow cooking, so you need to watch the food carefully and judge for yourself when it's done.

You can add extra flavor to grilled foods by tossing hickory or mesquite chips, bay leaves, or sprigs of rosemary or thyme on the coals during the last few minutes of cooking. For a Miami accent, use orange, lemon, lime, or grapefruit peels the same way.

After you remove the food from the grill, put the lid on if you have one, and let the fire burn the cooking residue off the grate. With a gas or electric grill, burn it off on high heat for ten to fifteen minutes. When the grate is cool enough to handle, scrub it with a metal brush or a wad of aluminum foil and wipe it clean with paper towels.

Grilled Island-Style Chicken
with Jerk Marinade

[4 SERVINGS]

This flavor-packed chicken gets its punch from the Scotch bonnet peppers in the Jerk Marinade. Closely akin to habanero peppers, they're among the world's hottest.

This is a great do-ahead party dish and will taste its very best if you begin marinating the chicken a day ahead. Then fire up the grill, put on some reggae music, aim the stereo speakers out a back window, and serve it on the patio with rice, Black Bean–Mango Salsa (page 194), and a cooling green salad.

> 1 3½-pound broiler-fryer, cut into serving pieces (or 3 pounds precut breast, leg, and thigh pieces)
> ¾ cup Jerk Marinade (recipe follows)

Rinse the chicken well, trim and discard any excess fat, and put in a large self-sealing food storage bag. Pour the marinade over the chicken and rub it in, lifting the skin and rubbing directly on the meat where possible. (If your skin is sensitive to hot peppers, wear rubber gloves.) Seal the bag and refrigerate for at least 2 hours and as long as 24 hours, turning occasionally to distribute the marinade.

When ready to cook, drain the chicken and pat dry with paper towels. Discard the marinade.

TO GRILL: Use indirect, medium heat (see page 100). If the grill rack is adjustable, place it 5 or 6 inches from the heat source. If it has a cover, use it.

Put the leg and thigh pieces on the grill 10 to 15 minutes before the breast and wing pieces, arranging the meat skin side down. Turn and baste the meat every 10 minutes and move it directly over the coals, skin side down, for the last 5 or 10 minutes. The chicken should cook in 30 to 40 minutes on a covered grill, and could take as much as 15 minutes longer on an open grill.

To check for doneness, cut into a thigh piece at its thickest point; the juices should be clear and the meat tender. Smaller pieces may be done sooner; push them to the side of the grill to stay warm.

If you don't want to watch the grill the whole time, start the chicken in a 375-degree oven for about 20 minutes and finish it on the grill—20 to 40 minutes, depending on grill type and conditions.

TO COOK INDOORS: Roast the chicken, uncovered, in a preheated 375-degree oven for about 50 minutes; the thigh should be fully cooked when cut at the thickest part. Baste every 10 minutes or so. If the finished chicken isn't as crisp as you'd like, run under the broiler for 1 or 2 minutes.

Serve immediately.

Jerk Marinade

[ABOUT 1½ CUPS]

2 tablespoons brown sugar
  (preferably dark)

1 tablespoon ground allspice

1 tablespoon dry-leaf thyme,
  crumbled

1 teaspoon ground cinnamon

1 teaspoon kosher salt

½ teaspoon cayenne

½ teaspoon freshly ground pepper

6 garlic cloves, peeled

2 inches fresh ginger, washed and
  cut into chunks (see page 104)

½ Scotch bonnet pepper or 3 or
  more jalapeños, seeded and
  coarsely chopped

1 small bunch scallions, trimmed
  and coarsely chopped

¼ cup vegetable oil

¼ cup red wine vinegar

2 tablespoons fresh lime juice

Combine the brown sugar, allspice, thyme, cinnamon, salt, cayenne, black pepper, garlic, ginger, fresh peppers, scallions, oil, vinegar, and lime juice in a food processor or blender. Process until smooth. Use immediately or refrigerate up to 2 weeks.

Tips/Techniques: Fresh Ginger

You may associate ginger with Asian cooking, but it's used widely in the Caribbean as well. It's grown commercially in Puerto Rico, Costa Rica, and Jamaica, and is the basis for Jamaica's famous ginger beer. Although it's sometimes referred to as gingerroot, it's actually a rhizome, a type of underground stem. With its pinkish brown skin and gangly, knobby appearance, a "hand" of ginger does indeed resemble a hand.

Look for plump, firm ginger with no shriveling. Uncut ginger will keep in a cool, dry place for up to a month. Once cut, it can be refrigerated for several weeks in a plastic bag with a piece of paper towel to absorb moisture. We like to store fresh ginger, well wrapped, in the freezer and grate it as needed; there is no need to thaw or peel it first. If you prefer to peel it, scrape off the skin with a spoon.

Tips/Techniques: Hot Peppers

Scotch bonnet peppers are so blazingly hot that you need only a very small amount in most recipes. Beneath the heat they have a fruity taste and are well worth trying if you can find them.

Jalapeños are more generally available but vary widely in firepower. We've heard it said that the hottest ones tend to be the smallest or the ones with pointy rather than rounded tips. The only sure way to gauge your batch, though, is to try it: Cut into a pepper, touch your fingertip to the cut surface, and taste it. Then adjust the quantity accordingly. If the peppers are too tame for your taste, include the membrane, which holds extra heat.

Jalapeño seeds are so hot that they can overpower the taste of the pepper. To remove them, cut off and discard both ends of the pepper, stand the pepper on one end, and slice straight down with a sharp knife, removing the flesh in four or five strips. Discard the membranes and seeds and julienne the flesh—cut it lengthwise into thin, matchstick-size pieces. Cut the strips crosswise into dice if that's what the recipe calls for.

You may want to wear latex gloves when handling hot peppers if your skin is sensitive. And you definitely don't want to touch your eyes—the tear-inducing pain of onion pales in comparison.

Grilled Lemon-Garlic Chicken Quarters

[8 SERVINGS]

Meaty chicken quarters are made to order for guests with big appetites. This garlicky marinade gives you the full flavor of the lemon, and you'll love the way the lemon slices look beneath the crispy skin. Top each finished piece with a generous spoonful of Corn and Black Bean Salsa (page 260) for an eye-catching presentation.

2 3½-pound broiler-fryers, quartered

1 teaspoon kosher salt

1 teaspoon coarsely ground pepper

½ teaspoon ground cumin

½ teaspoon dry-leaf oregano, crumbled

¼ teaspoon dry-leaf thyme, crumbled

12 garlic cloves, peeled and minced

½ cup olive oil

2 lemons, sliced paper-thin

Rinse the chicken well and trim and discard any excess fat. Pat dry with paper towels and put in a self-sealing food storage bag.

Combine the salt, pepper, cumin, oregano, and thyme in a small bowl. Rub the mixture between your fingers to release the full flavor of the herbs. Add the garlic and oil, and whisk to blend.

Pour the marinade over the chicken and rub it under the skin and into the meat. Add the lemon slices, tucking them under the skin wherever possible.

Refrigerate the chicken for at least 2 hours or as long as 24 hours, turning the bag several times to distribute the marinade.

Remove the chicken from the bag and pat dry with paper towels. Reserve the marinade and leave the lemon slices under the skin.

TO GRILL: Use indirect, medium heat (see page 100). If the grill rack is adjustable, place it 5 or 6 inches from the heat source. If it has a cover, use it.

Arrange the pieces on the grill skin side down, giving the leg quarters a 10-minute head start. Turn and baste the meat every 10 minutes and move it directly over the coals, skin side down, for the last 5 or 10 minutes. The chicken should cook in 30 to 40 minutes on a covered grill and could take as much as 15 minutes longer on an open grill.

To check for doneness, cut into a thigh piece at its thickest point; the juices should be clear and the meat tender.

If you don't want to watch the grill the whole time, start the chicken in a 375-degree oven for about 20 minutes and finish it on the grill—20 to 40 minutes depending on grill type and conditions.

TO COOK INDOORS: Roast the chicken, uncovered, in a preheated 375-degree oven for about 50 minutes; the thigh should be fully cooked when cut at the thickest part. Baste it every 10 minutes or so. If the finished chicken isn't as crisp as you'd like, run it under the broiler for 1 or 2 minutes.

Serve immediately.

Fresh garlic should have plump cloves that are dry and firm to the touch. Three kinds are generally available: strongly flavored white American; milder, light purple Mexican or Italian; and extremely mild elephant garlic (not really garlic at all but a member of the leek family).

Garlic is best stored uncovered in a cool spot away from the light. (Don't put it in the refrigerator, or it will dry out.) Stored properly, it will keep for two months. If a clove has begun to sprout, you can still use it, but discard the bitter green germ from the center.

To remove the papery skin, press down on the clove with the flat side of a large chef's knife until the skin splits and then slide it off with your fingers.

If you have a lot of garlic to peel, drop the cloves into boiling water for about a minute and then rinse them with cold water. Or put them in the microwave on high power for about fifteen seconds. Either way, the skins will slip right off.

To mince by hand, cut the peeled garlic in half lengthwise with a chef's knife and then place, cut side down, on a cutting board. (Sprinkle it with kosher salt so it won't stick to your knife as much, and reduce the amount of salt in your recipe accordingly.) Make several vertical and horizontal cuts in each clove, and finish by cutting it straight across into tiny pieces.

To puree, mash the garlic with the flat side of your knife and then mince it, pivoting the knife on its point. Or sprinkle the halved clove with kosher salt and mash it with the tines and back of a table fork.

A mini food processor makes quick work when you're chopping lots of garlic.

A food processor is also a good shortcut if you're combining the garlic with other chopped ingredients. Start the processor and drop the peeled garlic cloves down the feeding tube; that way they'll be chopped "on the fly" and won't stick to the blade. Scrape down the sides of the processor, add the other ingredients, and pulse to chop.

Take care not to burn garlic, or it will have an acrid taste. When â it with other ingredients, add the garlic to the pan last. When cooking it alone, start it in a cool pan and watch it carefully.

Cuban-Style Braised Chicken

[4 SERVINGS]

This savory dish is a Cuban classic that goes beautifully with Fried Ripe Plantains (page 226) and plenty of white rice for soaking up the rich onion-laced sauce. If you have enough time and skillets, make a double batch; it's even better the second day.

The marinade is based on a traditional Cuban adobo *made with the juice of the sour or Seville orange* (naranja agria *in Spanish). This seedy, wrinkly fruit is suitable only for cooking (it makes great marmalade) and is available in Latin markets and the produce section of some supermarkets. (When you stop at a traffic light in Miami's Little Havana neighborhood, a street corner vendor may come up to your car window offering bags of sour oranges and limes.) A fifty-fifty blend of lime and regular orange juice is a good substitute.*

1 3½-pound broiler-fryer, cut into serving pieces (or 3 pounds precut leg, thigh, and breast pieces)

¾ teaspoon kosher salt

½ teaspoon dry-leaf oregano, crumbled

½ teaspoon ground cumin

¼ teaspoon freshly ground pepper

2 garlic cloves, peeled and minced

½ cup sour orange juice (or ¼ cup each lime and regular orange juice)

1 medium onion, peeled and thinly sliced

2 tablespoons olive oil

Rinse the chicken well and trim and discard any excess fat. Pat dry with paper towels and put in a large self-sealing bag.

Combine the salt, oregano, cumin, and pepper in a small bowl and rub the spices between your fingertips to release the full flavor of the oregano. Stir in the garlic and sour orange juice.

Pour the marinade over the chicken and add the onion. Seal the bag and turn it several times to distribute the ingredients. Refrigerate for at least 2 hours or as long as 24 hours, turning the bag several times.

Remove the chicken from the bag and pat dry with paper towels; reserve the marinade.

Heat the oil over medium high heat in a heavy skillet that is large enough to hold the chicken without crowding. Brown the chicken well on all sides, about 10 minutes total. Turn the heat to medium-low and cook for 10 more minutes. Use tongs to transfer to a plate.

Pour the fat from the pan into a heat-proof container (discard it when it's cool). Add the reserved marinade with the onion to the pan. Bring just to a boil over high heat and lower to a simmer. Return the chicken to the pan along with any juices that have collected on the plate. Simmer, covered, for about 30 minutes, until the juices run clear when you cut into a thigh at its thickest part.

Transfer the chicken to a serving platter and cover with foil.

Turn the heat to high and boil the pan juices, scraping the bottom with a wooden spatula or spoon to loosen any browned bits. When the sauce has thickened slightly, pour it over the chicken or serve it on the side.

Jerk-Fried Chicken

[4 SERVINGS]

Many early Miamians came from Georgia and north Florida, and until the 1960s there was a strong southern element to the city. (You can still tell old-timers by the way they pronounce "Mi-a-muh.") Latin and Caribbean newcomers have transformed the city, and this delightfully spicy fried chicken—and the slimmed-down, oven-fried version in the Variation—blends a bit of the old and the new. Serve it with buttered mashed potatoes, à la Colonel Sanders, or Boniato Puree (page 218) for a Caribbean touch.

1 3½-pound broiler-fryer, cut into serving pieces (or 3 pounds
    precut thigh, leg, and breast pieces)

Salt and freshly ground pepper

1 cup flour

4 tablespoons Jerk Seasoning (page 99)

Vegetable oil

Remove and discard any excess fat from the chicken. Rinse well, pat dry with paper towels, and sprinkle liberally with salt and pepper.

Pour the flour and Jerk Seasoning into a food storage bag, twist or seal the top shut, and shake to combine. Drop in the chicken, 2 pieces at a time, close the bag, and shake to coat the pieces well. Lay the coated pieces on a baking sheet lined with wax paper.

Pour ¼ inch of oil into a heavy skillet (cast iron is best) that is big enough to hold the chicken without crowding. Heat over high heat until the oil begins to shimmer but not smoke, and lower the heat to medium-high.

Using tongs, add the chicken to the pan, skin side down; it should sizzle but not burn. Cook until golden brown on one side, about 10 minutes. Turn the chicken with tongs, let brown for a few minutes, and turn the heat to medium-low.

Discard the wax paper, and line the baking sheet with several layers of paper towels.

Continue frying until the chicken is golden brown and cooked through, 45 to 50 minutes total. Transfer it to the baking sheet to drain. Serve immediately or hold in a 200-degree oven for up to 20 minutes.

VARIATION: For moist, lower-fat chicken that is quite crisp, remove and discard the skin from as many pieces as possible. (The bony wing and back are almost impossible to skin, so chicken parts are the best choice.) Soak the chicken in buttermilk in the refrigerator for at least 1 hour. Drain the chicken (discard the milk) and coat it well with the seasoned flour. Place on a baking sheet that has been sprayed with vegetable oil and coat the chicken lightly with vegetable oil spray (this promotes browning and prevents white patches of flour on the finished pieces). Bake in a preheated 400-degree oven for about 50 minutes, until browned and cooked through.

Tips & Techniques: Fried Chicken

There are all sorts of tricks of the trade when it comes to frying chicken. Some cooks soak the chicken in buttermilk or milk and a little lemon juice first to make it more tender and juicy. Some insist on frying in lard, others in shortening flavored with bacon fat. Some say the skillet must be covered; others say never cover the skillet.

Our uncovered version produces chicken that is crisp and dry on the outside and moist inside. If you like a softer exterior, cover the pan after turning the heat to medium-low and uncover it for the last few minutes.

When panfrying, the oil is too shallow for a thermometer, but you can check for the right temperature by dipping the handle of a wooden spoon in it. If the oil immediately bubbles briskly around it, it's hot enough.

Roast Chicken with Savory Guava Glaze

[4 TO 6 SERVINGS]

This picture-perfect, deep-amber-colored chicken is one you'll be proud to bring to the table. The sweet, tangy glaze is resplendent with guava, a small tutti-frutti-scented tropical fruit that is most familiar, even in south Florida where it's grown, in paste and jelly form. (Pastries filled with guava paste are standard issue with a thimble-size cup of café cubano at Miami's countless Latin American coffeeshops.) If guava isn't available, apricot is a good alternative. (See Variations.)

The glaze is so rich and full flavored that you may want to double the recipe and refrigerate the extra for the next time you roast poultry or pork, anything from turkey and Cornish hens to tenderloins and spare ribs. Or make up an even bigger batch and bottle it for holiday giving. Your friends are sure to ask for the recipe.

The ingredient list may look long, but the marinade and glaze are simple to make. And once they're done, the chicken is a snap to finish. Baked potatoes (put them in the oven along with the bird) and a low-key green vegetable are all the accompaniment it needs.

1 3½- to 4-pound roasting chicken

1 teaspoon kosher salt

1 teaspoon ground cumin

½ teaspoon dry-leaf oregano, crumbled

½ teaspoon freshly ground pepper

2 large garlic cloves, peeled and minced

1 tablespoon olive oil

2 tablespoons fresh lime juice

TO FINISH THE DISH:

¼ cup chicken broth or water

FOR THE SAVORY GUAVA GLAZE:

¾ cup guava jelly

¾ cup guava nectar or juice (one 7-ounce can)

2 tablespoons guava puree (see Notes)

¼ cup fresh lime juice

1 tablespoon balsamic vinegar

1 tablespoon Dijon mustard

1½ teaspoons Worcestershire sauce

1 teaspoon paprika

½ teaspoon ground cumin

½ teaspoon salt

¼ teaspoon dry-leaf thyme, crumbled

¼ teaspoon freshly ground pepper

Remove and discard any excess fat from the chicken, rinse under cold running water, and pat dry with paper towels.

Combine the salt, cumin, oregano, and pepper in a small bowl and rub the spices between your fingertips to release the full flavor of the oregano. Stir in the garlic and olive oil to form a paste and rub it on the chicken, inside and out. Tie the legs together with kitchen string and tuck the wing tips under the back.

Set the chicken in a nonaluminum roasting pan and pour the lime juice over it (or squeeze it directly onto the chicken and save dirtying the juicer). Cover with plastic wrap and marinate in the refrigerator for at least 6 hours and up to 24 hours.

One hour before roasting, remove the chicken from the refrigerator.

Combine the guava jelly, nectar, and puree, and the lime juice, vinegar, mustard, Worcestershire sauce, paprika, cumin, salt, thyme, and pepper in a small saucepan. Bring to a boil, lower the heat, and simmer, stirring occasionally, for about 15 minutes, until the glaze has thickened and reduced to 1 cup. Remove from the heat.

Preheat the oven to 425 degrees.

Roast the chicken in the center of the oven for 15 minutes. Lower the heat to 375 degrees and continue roasting for 45 minutes to 1 hour. (If you forgot to take the chicken out of the refrigerator in time or it is on the big side, it could take up to 1 hour and 15 minutes.) Baste the chicken several times with the glaze during the last 15 minutes. The chicken is done if the juices run clear when the thigh is pierced and an instant meat thermometer inserted in the thigh registers 165 degrees.

Transfer the chicken to a warm platter and brush it with glaze one last time. Let it rest for 10 minutes before carving.

Meanwhile, pour off the pan juices and skim off and discard the fat. To deglaze the roasting pan, add the broth and bring it to a boil on top of the stove, scraping up the browned bits with a wooden spatula or spoon. Strain into the remaining glaze along with the reserved pan juices and heat through. Carve the chicken and serve it with the sauce on the side.

VARIATION: If guava products aren't available, substitute apricot preserves for the jelly, and apricot nectar for both the guava nectar and puree.

NOTES:

- If you don't want to dirty a juicer, insert the tines of a fork in half a lime and twist it as you squeeze. This works especially well with seedless Florida limes.
- Starting the chicken at 400 degrees helps to crisp the skin; finishing it at 375 degrees prevents the breast from drying out.

- A single ripe guava will yield all the puree you need for this recipe, but be prepared to strain out the myriad tiny seeds. Frozen guava puree, available in 12-ounce jars or 14-ounce bags in the freezer case of many supermarkets, is a good shortcut. You'll have more than a cup left over. Use it as a base for a batch of tropical fruit smoothies—*batidos*, as we say in Miami (see page 321); ripe banana or mango will soften its slightly astringent edge. Or whirl it in a blender with ice and rum to taste for a terrific daiquiri.

Arroz con Pollo
(Chicken with Yellow Rice)

[6 SERVINGS]

There are nearly as many renditions of arroz con pollo *as there are Latin American cooks in Miami. Puerto Ricans add capers and olives; Cubans stick to peas and pimientos. Purists color the rice with saffron, but most Miamians use ground orange annatto seeds or Bijol, a commercial blend of annatto, cumin, corn flour, and artificial coloring. Some soak the rice and coloring agent in water before cooking; others add them straight to the pot. The rice is served either dry or wet in Cuban households, but most Puerto Ricans like it* asopao *(soupy) and eat it with both fork and spoon.*

All of them start, though, with a traditional adobo *(marinade) and* sofrito *(sautéed onion, bell pepper, and garlic). This is a straightforward version, pared to the essential steps, but Variations lays out a host of options. It's an exceptionally hearty, full-flavored dish, a meal in itself with a simple green salad on the side.*

1 3½-pound chicken, cut into serving pieces (or 3 pounds precut thigh, leg, and breast pieces)

2 teaspoons dry-leaf oregano, crumbled

2 teaspoons kosher salt

1 teaspoon ground cumin

1 teaspoon freshly ground pepper

2 garlic cloves, peeled and minced

2 tablespoons fresh lime juice (see Variations)

TO FINISH THE DISH:

2 tablespoons olive oil

1 large onion, peeled and finely chopped

1 large green bell pepper, cored, seeded, and finely chopped

3 or 4 garlic cloves, peeled and minced

1 teaspoon ground annatto seeds or Bijol (see Variations)

1 teaspoon ground cumin

1 teaspoon dry-leaf oregano, crumbled

1 14-ounce package Valencia rice (about 2 cups; see Variations)

½ cup dry white wine (see Variations)

3 cups chicken broth (homemade or low-sodium canned; see Variations)

1 14½-ounce can crushed or diced
    tomatoes (about 2 cups)

1 bay leaf

1 tablespoon drained capers
    (optional)

12 small pimiento-stuffed olives
    (optional)

1 6½-ounce jar pimientos, drained
    and seeded

1 9-ounce package frozen baby
    green peas (about 2 cups)

Rinse the chicken well and trim and discard any excess fat. Pat dry with paper towels and put in a self-sealing food storage bag.

Combine the oregano, salt, cumin, and pepper in a small bowl and rub them between your fingertips to release the full flavor of the oregano. Stir in the garlic and rub this mixture into the chicken. Add the lime juice (you can squeeze it directly on the chicken), seal the bag, and turn it several times to distribute the marinade. Refrigerate for at least 2 hours and up to 24 hours, the longer the better.

About 1 hour before serving, heat the oil over medium-high heat in a large Dutch oven or a deep, heavy 12-inch skillet. (A paella pan is ideal if you have one, and it doubles as a serving container.)

Remove the chicken pieces from the marinade (reserve it) and pat dry with paper towels. Brown the chicken well on all sides, about 15 minutes total, and set aside on a plate.

Lower the heat to medium and sauté the onion, green pepper, and garlic until soft, about 5 minutes. Stir in the annatto, cumin, and oregano, and sauté for 1 or 2 minutes. Add the rice and stir well to coat it with oil and spices.

Add the wine, broth, tomatoes, bay leaf, and reserved marinade. Taste for seasoning; it should be slightly salty to flavor the rice. Bring the liquid just to a boil and turn the heat to low.

Return the chicken pieces to the pan, burying them in the rice.

Preheat the oven to 350 degrees.

Let the chicken and rice simmer gently, uncovered, until most of the liquid is absorbed, about 20 minutes.

Stir in the capers and olives, if using, and transfer the pan to the oven for 10 or 15 minutes, until the rice is tender and the chicken is cooked through.

Meanwhile, cut the pimientos into strips and thaw the peas in a colander under hot running water.

Remove the pan from the oven and stir in the peas. Transfer the chicken and rice to a serving dish, remove the bay leaf, and garnish with pimiento strips.

PLANNING AHEAD: Once the chicken is marinated, you can have this dish on the table in about 1 hour.

VARIATIONS:

- Sour orange juice—or a fifty-fifty blend of lime and sweet orange juices—would be more traditional, but we like the zing of the lime.
- In classic Spanish *arroz con pollo,* saffron is used to color and flavor the rice. You may substitute 4 or 5 strands of saffron for the annatto; toast it first in a dry skillet over medium heat for about 30 seconds and add to the pot with the other spices. Another method of coloring the rice is to soak it with 1 teaspoon of ground annatto or ½ teaspoon of Bijol in water to cover for 1 hour, and rinse and drain it well before adding it to the pot as directed. Or take a shortcut and buy already tinted yellow rice.
- Long-grain white rice will do, but short-grain Valencia is the better and more traditional choice because it cooks up moist and the grains stick together.
- If you like, skin the chicken pieces before marinating.
- For a soupier consistency, increase the amount of broth to 4 or 5 cups.
- For a malty flavor accent, omit the wine, and when the dish is done, pour 6 ounces of beer over the rice and let it stand, covered, for 5 or 10 minutes before serving.
- Some cooks add ½ cup of diced smoked ham to the sautéed onion, bell pepper, and garlic.
- For yet another layer of flavor, sprinkle on ¼ cup of freshly grated sharp cheese such as Parmesan just before serving.

Nothing's faster than a food processor for chopping onions and peppers, but hand chopping produces more uniform, attractive pieces. Here's how the pros do it, using a large, sharp, French chef's knife:

• Cut the onion in half vertically (stem end to root end) and peel off the skin, leaving the root intact. Place each half, cut side down, on a cutting board. With the knife parallel to the board and your fingers out of the way, make several horizontal slices, cutting to within ½ inch of the root. Then, holding the knife perpendicular to the board, make lengthwise cuts at the same intervals, again leaving the root end intact. Finally, slice straight down across the onion to produce perfect dice.

• Cut both ends off the bell pepper and save for another use. Stand the pepper on end and make one vertical cut along a rib. Spread it open, skin side down, flattening it as much as possible. (Keep it skin side down as you work; it's easier to cut through the porous interior.) Trim away and discard the seeds, membranes, and ribs. Cut the pepper lengthwise into strips, stack the strips together, and slice them crosswise into dice.

Chicken and Black Bean Pot Pie with Cornmeal Crust

[6 SERVINGS]

Black beans and leftover chicken (or turkey) have never had it so good as in this bold-tasting, festive-looking pot pie—a far cry from the bland, foil-wrapped kind that Baby Boomers ate from TV trays as they watched Ozzie and Harriet. Meat pies have been around since the time of the ancient Romans and are found around the world, from potato-crusted shepherd's pie in Britain to phyllo-covered bisteeya *in Morocco. Our version gets its flavor impact from a chili-spiked* sofrito *and a surprising hint of cinnamon, all set off by a mellow cornmeal crust. It's the kind of hearty, homey dish we love to make for a relaxing Sunday supper—perfect for Thanksgiving weekend when you've had your fill of fancy eating and your refrigerator is full of leftover turkey. Serve it with a tossed green salad and a simple dessert of Orange-Marinated Strawberries (page 315).*

Vegetable or olive oil spray

2 tablespoons olive oil

1 medium onion, peeled and diced

1 green bell pepper, cored, seeded, and diced

1 red bell pepper, cored, seeded, and diced

2 or more jalapeño peppers, seeded and minced

2 garlic cloves, peeled and minced

1 teaspoon ground cumin

½ teaspoon chili powder

½ teaspoon ground cinnamon

¼ teaspoon cayenne

5 tablespoons all-purpose flour

1 cup tomato juice

1 cup chicken broth

3 cups cubed cooked chicken or turkey (about 12 ounces)

1½ cups Basic Black Beans (page 19) or 1 15-ounce can black beans, drained and rinsed

1 cup fresh or frozen corn kernels

2 tablespoons chopped fresh cilantro or flat-leaf parsley

Kosher salt

Cornmeal Pastry Dough, chilled (recipe follows)

Coat an 8-by-12-inch or 9-by-11-inch baking dish with vegetable oil spray and set aside. Heat the oil in a large, heavy skillet over medium heat. Sauté the onion, bell peppers, jalapeños, and garlic until soft, about 5 minutes. Stir in the cumin, chili powder, cinnamon, and cayenne, and cook for another 1 or 2 minutes.

Add the flour and stir constantly with a wooden spoon until absorbed, about 1 minute. Add the tomato juice and broth. Bring to a simmer and cook, stirring, until the mixture thickens, about 2 minutes.

Remove the pan from the heat and stir in the chicken, black beans, corn, cilantro, and salt to taste (1 teaspoon of kosher salt seems about right, but it will depend on how salty your broth is).

Spoon the chicken mixture into the prepared baking dish and set aside. Preheat the oven to 400 degrees.

Roll out the dough into a rectangle about 1 inch larger all around than the baking dish (see Note). Center it over the filling, fold the overhanging dough into a decorative edge (even it off first with scissors if necessary), and cut several slashes in the crust to vent the steam.

Set the dish on a foil-lined baking sheet to catch any drips. Bake the pot pie in the center of the oven for about 25 minutes, until the pastry is golden and the filling is hot. Serve immediately.

PLANNING AHEAD: The pastry dough can be made 2 or 3 days ahead and the filling up to 1 day ahead and refrigerated.

NOTE: If you have trouble handling the dough, roll it out between 2 pieces of plastic wrap, then pull off the top piece of plastic, invert the dough over the filling, and pull off the second piece of plastic.

Cornmeal Pastry Dough

[1 POT PIE CRUST]

Cornmeal by itself would make too brittle a dough; you need the gluten of the flour to hold it together. This dough is on the fragile side, but rolling it out between sheets of plastic wrap (see Note, page 120) counteracts that problem.

1 cup all-purpose flour

½ cup yellow cornmeal

1 teaspoon salt

8 tablespoons (1 stick) unsalted butter, cut into 8 pieces and frozen

About ¼ cup cold water

TO MIX BY HAND: Stir together the flour, cornmeal, and salt in a medium-size bowl. Use a pastry cutter or 2 table knives crisscrossed scissors fashion to cut in the butter until the mixture resembles coarse crumbs. Sprinkle with cold water, 1 tablespoon at a time, tossing it lightly with fork after each addition until the dough is moist enough to hold together.

TO MIX IN A FOOD PROCESSOR: Combine the flour, cornmeal, and salt in the bowl of the processor and whirl to mix. Add the butter and pulse until the mixture resembles coarse crumbs; be careful not to overprocess. Add the water, 1 tablespoon at a time, pulsing between each addition until the dough just begins to pull together into a ball.

Shape the dough into a ball, flatten into a disc, and refrigerate, well wrapped, for at least 30 minutes before using.

Curried Chicken, Potato, and Calabaza with Roti (East Indian Flat Bread)

[4 TO 6 SERVINGS]

Columbus died believing he had found the spice-rich East Indies, and thanks to his misapprehension, "Indian" has endured as a name for the native peoples of the Americas. It wasn't until more than three hundred years later that true Indians—from India—enriched the Caribbean's cultural mix. After slavery was abolished in the nineteenth century, indentured workers from India (and, to a lesser extent, China) replaced slave labor on sugar and banana plantations. With the Indians came curry, called colombo *on French-speaking islands. The culinary legacy endures in dishes ranging from Jamaican curried goat to the curry-filled rotis that Trinidadian-born street vendors sell in Miami. Roti is an Indian flat bread, and if you'd like to try your hand at it, a recipe follows. This lively curry is wonderful over rice, too.*

2 tablespoons vegetable oil

1 large onion, peeled and diced

3 garlic cloves, peeled and minced

½ green bell pepper, cored, seeded, and diced

½ Scotch bonnet pepper or 2 jalapeño peppers, seeded and minced

2 teaspoons grated fresh ginger

2 to 3 teaspoons curry powder

1 teaspoon ground cumin

1 teaspoon tumeric

½ teaspoon dry-leaf thyme, crumbled

1 tablespoon tomato paste

1½ pounds skinless, boneless chicken, cubed (see Note)

2 cups peeled, diced calabaza or winter squash (about 1 pound)

2 cups peeled and diced potato (1 large baking potato)

½ teaspoon kosher salt

½ teaspoon freshly ground pepper

6 9-inch roti (recipe follows) or 3 to 4 cups hot cooked rice

Heat the oil in a large skillet over medium heat and sauté the onion, garlic, and peppers until the onion is soft, about 5 minutes. Add the ginger, curry powder, cumin, turmeric, and thyme, and cook, stirring, for 1 more minute. Stir in the tomato paste.

Add the chicken and stir to coat thoroughly with the spice mixture. Add the calabaza, potato, and enough water just to cover the chicken and vegetables. Bring to a boil, lower the heat, and simmer, uncovered, for about 30 minutes, stirring occasionally.

In the meantime, prepare the roti.

The finished curry should be slightly thick; if it is too thin, mash some of the vegetables against the side of the pan with a wooden spoon. For each portion, spoon about ½ cup of filling onto the center of a roti and fold it like an envelope—bottom up, sides in, top down. Or spoon it over rice. In either case, serve it hot.

NOTE: Put the chicken in the freezer for about 1 hour before cubing it; it is much easier to cut when partially frozen.

Roti (East Indian Flat Bread)

There are many kinds of roti, from simple flat bread like this one to a tricky and time-consuming version that contains a layer of dahl, a curried split pea puree. (Paula Delpech, a Trinidadian-born friend, says that unless she feels like spending a day in her Miami kitchen reconnecting with her roots, she buys that kind at a West Indian market.) Roti is traditionally made on a special griddle called a tawa, *but a cast-iron skillet produces the same crisp, delicate texture. If you enjoy playing with dough, you'll have a good time making these.*

2 cups flour
¼ teaspoon baking powder
¼ teaspoon salt
About 1 cup water
Vegetable oil

Sift the flour, baking powder, and salt into a mixing bowl and stir in enough water to make a stiff dough. Add more flour if it feels sticky.

Divide the dough into 6 pieces and roll each piece into a ball. Roll the balls out on a floured surface into circles about 9 inches across. Brush the tops with oil, dust with flour, and fold them back in on themselves to form balls again. (The layer of oil gives the roti its flakiness.) Let the dough rest for 30 to 45 minutes.

Roll one of the dough balls into a 9-inch circle. Heat a 10-inch cast-iron skillet over high heat and brush lightly with oil. Lift the rolled dough, stretch it into a 10-inch circle, and ease it onto the hot pan.

Cook the roti until the bottom is lightly browned and blistered, about 1½ minutes. Brush the top with oil and turn the roti with a spatula. Cook until the second side is lightly browned and blistered, about 1½ minutes more. Roll and cook the rest of the dough in the same way, stacking the finished rotis on paper towels. (Once you get the rhythm down, you can have the next roti ready for the pan when the first one is done; at first, though, you may need to pull the pan from the heat occasionally to keep it from smoking.)

Fill the roti and serve hot. If not using immediately, reheat briefly in a hot skillet before filling.

Grilled Whole Turkey
with Mojo Marinade

[10 TO 12 SERVINGS]

Roasting is the time-honored way to cook a turkey, but grilling takes about the same amount of time or even less, adds a smoky dimension to the taste, and frees up the oven for all those side dishes. The meat absorbs the flavor of the tangy marinade—a variation on the classic Cuban mojo (page 230)—and the skin crisps up to a rich mahogany brown.

You need a covered grill—either charcoal or gas—for this recipe. If the snow is too deep on your patio to fire up it up, the bird can be oven-roasted after it has been marinated. Either way, serve it with Carambola Cranberry Sauce (page 266) for a memorable Miami-style holiday feast.

FOR THE MARINADE:

8 garlic cloves, peeled

1 medium onion, peeled and coarsely
   chopped

2 teaspoons kosher salt

1 tablespoon ground cumin

1 tablespoon dry-leaf oregano,
   crumbled

1 cup sour orange juice (or ½ cup
   each lime and regular orange juice)

¼ cup vegetable oil

TO FINISH THE DISH:

1 10- to 12-pound turkey

Vegetable oil

The day before you plan to grill the turkey, puree the garlic, onion, salt, cumin, oregano, sour orange juice, and oil in a blender or food processor. Set aside.

Remove the giblets and neck from the turkey and save for another use (soup stock, giblet gravy, a treat for your cat). Rinse the turkey under cold running water. Drain well and pat dry with paper towels. Gently insert your fingers under the skin, loosening it as much as possible over the breast, thighs, and drumsticks. Be careful not to puncture the skin.

Set the turkey in a clean, sturdy plastic bag that is big enough to hold it easily (a fresh-from-the-box trash can liner works fine). Rub the marinade generously into the meat beneath the loosened skin and into the body and neck cavities.

Fasten the neck skin to the back with a skewer, tie the legs together, and tuck the wing tips under the thighs (see Note). Pour any extra marinade over the turkey and close the bag tightly. Refrigerate overnight, turning the turkey a few times to distribute the marinade.

ON A CHARCOAL GRILL: Remove the rack and open the vents in the top and base of the grill. Put a drip pan in the center of the base (an 8-by-12-inch disposable aluminum pan, available in supermarkets, is just the right size). Mound 25 to 30 briquettes on either side of the pan, and light them.

Let the coals burn down to a medium-hot fire (see page 100). Meanwhile, remove the turkey from the marinade, pat it dry with paper towels, and brush with vegetable oil. Place on a roasting rack (this will make it easier to remove from the grill).

When the coals are ready, fill the drip pan halfway with water. (This creates steam to help cook the bird and catches drips to prevent flare-ups.) Put the grill rack in place, 4 to 6 inches from the fire.

Place the roasting rack and turkey on the grill rack, directly over the drip pan, and cover the grill. Check the turkey after 1 hour and add a dozen or so briquettes to maintain the temperature. (Don't use quick-lighting briquettes at this stage, or your turkey will taste of lighter fluid.) If the turkey is still cooking after 2 hours, replenish the briquettes again.

A whole turkey can cook in as little as 10 to 12 minutes per pound, but the type of grill and briquettes and the weather conditions affect cooking time. That makes it especially important to use an instant-read meat thermometer. Begin checking the temperature—in the thickest part of the thigh near the body, avoiding the bone—after 1¾ hours for a 10-pound turkey and after 2 hours for a 12-pound turkey.

Remove the turkey from the grill when the thigh temperature reaches 165 degrees. (This is lower than generally recommended, but it keeps the breast meat moister; the temperature will rise to the desired 175 or 180 as the turkey rests.) Tent with foil and wait 30 minutes before carving.

ON A GAS GRILL: Use indirect, medium heat. Place the turkey on a roasting rack, put the rack inside a large foil pan, and place the pan on the grill. Pour a little water into the pan (don't let it touch the turkey), cover the grill, and proceed as directed above.

VARIATIONS:

➡ This marinade complements any poultry, as does the under-the-skin marinating method.

➡ You can degrease the drip pan contents just as you would pan juices from a roaster, cook them down on top of the stove, and use them as a sauce or to make gravy.

NOTES:

- For easier carving, cut out the wishbone—the V-shaped bone at the tip of the breast—before roasting the bird. Once it's out of the way, you can get larger, more even slices. (The same technique works for roast chicken or duck.)
- In *Roasting: A Simple Art,* Barbara Kafka makes a case for leaving the legs free because tying them slows down the cooking of the dark meat and increases the likelihood that the breast meat will dry out. Her method works fine with this recipe, though the presentation isn't as attractive.

Roast Duckling with
Lime-Ginger-Mango Sauce

[4 SERVINGS]

Lime and fresh ginger give the sweet mango sauce the edge it needs to stand up to the rich taste of duck. Allowing the skin to dry out in the refrigerator before roasting guarantees crispness—the hallmark of a well-roasted duck. If you buy the birds frozen, they can thaw and dry at the same time.

The recipe may look long, but that's because we provide plenty of detail for cooks who don't often make duck. Partially boning it, for instance, makes it much easier to eat, and pouring off the fat midway through roasting minimizes the oven mess.

It's not difficult, and because you can roast the duck and make the sauce well ahead of time, this makes a low-stress dinner party entree. Serve it with Wild Rice with Mango and Pecans (page 241).

2 3½- to 4-pound Long Island ducklings (see Notes)

3 tablespoons kosher salt

1 tablespoon ground coriander

1 tablespoon ground ginger

1 tablespoon paprika

2 teaspoons freshly ground pepper

1 teaspoon cayenne

Zest of 3 limes, grated (about 2 tablespoons)

3 garlic cloves, peeled and minced

1 tablespoon vegetable oil

FOR THE SAUCE:

½ cup chicken broth

⅓ cup sweet white wine, such as Riesling or sauterne

3 tablespoons fresh lime juice

1 tablespoon malt or cider vinegar

2 inches fresh ginger, grated (about 2 tablespoons)

1 cup mango puree (see Notes)

Zest of 1 lime, grated (about 2 teaspoons)

TO FINISH THE DISH:

Mango slices for garnish

Two days before serving, rinse the ducks under cold running water and pat dry with paper towels. Remove and discard the excess fat from the cavities and reserve the giblets and neck for another use. Place the ducks on a wire rack set inside a deep roasting pan and refrigerate, uncovered, for 2 days.

Early in the day you plan to serve the ducks (or the day before), position one of the racks in the lower third of the oven and preheat to 425 degrees.

Stir together the salt, coriander, ground ginger, paprika, pepper, cayenne, lime zest, garlic, and oil. Rub the ducks inside and out with this seasoning paste and tuck the wing tips under the back. Drain and wipe out the roasting pan and place the ducks in it, on the rack, breast-side up. Set the pan on the lower oven rack and reduce the heat to 350 degrees. Roast, uncovered, for 1 hour.

Remove the ducks, leaving the oven on. Lightly prick the skin (but not the meat) all over with a 2-tined fork to release the fat. Using wads of paper towels to protect your hands, transfer the ducks to a cutting board (preferably one with a well). Remove the rack from the roasting pan, carefully pour the fat and juices into a heat-proof container (a large fat-separating cup is ideal), and reserve.

Return the ducks to the rack and pan, and roast for about 45 minutes more. They're done if the juices run clear when a thigh is pierced and an instant-read thermometer registers 165 degrees in the thickest part of the thigh. (Don't let the thermometer touch the bone, which will be hotter than the meat.)

Using tongs or wads of paper towels, tip the ducks to drain the accumulated juices from the cavities into the pan. Set the ducks aside on the cutting board.

Remove the rack from the pan and add the pan juices to those reserved earlier. When the fat has risen to the top, drain and discard it. (Don't pour it down the sink unless you want to call the plumber.) Reserve the juices. (If the duck won't be served until the next day, refrigerate the unseparated pan drippings until the fat hardens, then peel it off.)

Put the roasting pan on top of the stove over medium heat. Add the broth, wine, lime juice, vinegar, and ginger. Stir with a wooden spoon to dissolve the brown bits on the bottom of the pan. (If you're working a day ahead, you can refrigerate this liquid and finish the sauce in a saucepan the next day.)

Add the reserved juices to the roasting pan, raise the heat to high, and boil for about 6 minutes, until the liquid is reduced to ½ cup. Pour it through a fine-mesh sieve into a saucepan, pressing the solids with the back of a spoon to extract as much liquid as possible. Discard the solids. Stir in the mango puree, lime zest, and any juices that have collected around the ducks. Taste, adjust the seasonings, and set aside.

When the ducks are cool enough to handle, bone them partially: Working with one duck at a time, use a kitchen shears or a large, sharp French chef's knife to cut all the way through the breastbone, opening up the cavity. With the duck still on its back, cut all the way through the ribs on both sides of the backbone and remove it. (You could save the backbone for stock along with the neck and giblets.) Working with half the duck at a time, peel the meat away from the rib cage. Remove and discard the rib cage (or save it for the stock pot, too), leaving the leg and wing bones in place. Repeat with the other duck. (If working a day ahead, wrap and refrigerate them at this point.)

Place the duck halves on a foil-lined baking sheet. Reheat in a preheated 350-degree oven until hot and crisp, about 15 minutes. If the skin isn't as crisp as you'd like, put it under the broiler for a couple of minutes.

Meanwhile, heat the reserved sauce and ladle it onto 4 dinner plates. Place a duck half on each plate and garnish with mango slices. Serve immediately.

PLANNING AHEAD: If you begin drying the duck skin 3 days before serving and roast it the day before, it will take only about 20 minutes to get the duck on the table. The sauce can be made a day ahead, too, and reheated just before serving.

VARIATION: Try the pungent spice rub on chicken, turkey, or Cornish hens, too.

NOTES:

- If you can't find ducklings, substitute a 5- to 6-pound duck, increase the roasting time by 30 to 45 minutes, and cut it into quarters for serving.
- You use more limes for zest than for juice; squeeze the extra limes and refrigerate or freeze the juice for future use.
- Beginning the roasting at 425 degrees helps the ducks' skin brown and crisp; finishing at 350 degrees keeps the skin from burning and the meat from drying out.
- Ducks render a great deal of fat that can catch fire if it overflows the roasting pan. Use a deep pan and check the duck frequently, removing the melted fat as necessary.
- Using frozen mango puree, available in many supermarkets, will save you time and mess. To peel fresh mango, see page 8.

The Main Course 2: Meat

Macho Steak

Caribbean Fajitas

Gaucho Grill with Chimichurri Sauce

Orange-Tamarind Brisket with Boniato and Carrots

Ropa Vieja (Shredded Beef in Savory Sauce)

Vaca Frita (Fried, Shredded Beef)

Miami Meat Loaf

Picadillo (Savory Ground Beef)

Fritas (Cuban-Style Hamburgers)

Veal Chops with Silken Mango-Lime Sauce

Roast Pork Little Havana with Adobo Seasoning

Roast Pork Loin and Bananas with Tropical Glaze

Garlicky Grilled Pork Tenderloin

Finger-Lickin' Red-Hot Jerk-Barbecued Ribs with Tropical Barbecue Sauce

Pork and Pineapple on a Stick with Passion Fruit Glaze

Griot (Haitian-Style Fried Pork Chunks)

Cuban Sandwich

Leg of Lamb Florida Style

Rack of Lamb with Coriander Marinade

Macho Steak

[4 SERVINGS]

With its large Latin population, Miami can be a muy *macho place, and this juicy, spicy steak reflects that facet of the city. If you don't eat red meat very often, you want it to be a real treat, and Macho Steak fits the bill. It takes only about 20 minutes to cook, but the key is to have all the ingredients measured and ready to add to the pan. Garnish each steak with a mound of Crispy Jerk-Fried Onion Rings (page 224) and listen to the macho men—and "macha" women—in your life roar with delight.*

2 jalapeño peppers, seeded and minced

3 garlic cloves, peeled and minced

1½ teaspoons ground cumin

½ cup dry white or red wine

½ cup beef broth

1 tomato, peeled, seeded, and chopped (see Variations)

2 tablespoons cold butter, cut into 4 pieces

2 tablespoons vegetable oil

4 8- to 10-ounce, 1-inch-thick New York strip steaks (see Notes)

1 tablespoon chopped cilantro or flat-leaf parsley

Kosher salt and freshly ground pepper

Stir the jalapeños, garlic, and cumin together in a small bowl and set near the stove. Place the wine, broth, tomato, and a large platter nearby, too; leave the cut butter in the refrigerator to keep cold.

Heat the oil in a large, heavy skillet over medium-high heat. Pat the steaks dry with paper towels to ensure even browning and season with salt and pepper.

Put 2 steaks in the skillet and cook to the desired doneness, about 4 minutes per side for medium rare. Transfer the steaks to a platter and cover loosely with foil to keep warm. Cook and cover the remaining steaks in the same way.

Pour off all but 1 tablespoon of drippings from the skillet and turn the heat to low. Add the jalapeños, garlic, and cumin, and cook, stirring, for 30 seconds. Turn the heat to high, stir in the wine, and bring to a boil, scraping up any browned bits with a wooden spoon. Boil, stirring constantly, until the liquid is reduced to 2 tablespoons, about 2 minutes.

Add the broth, return to a boil, and cook until reduced to ¼ cup, about 2 minutes.

Turn the heat to low, stir in the tomato, and simmer for 1 minute. Pour in any juices that have accumulated around the steaks and simmer for 1 more minute.

Add the butter, 2 pieces at a time, swirling the pan until it melts (see Notes).

Take the pan off the heat. Stir in the cilantro, taste for seasoning, and add salt and pepper to taste.

Transfer the steaks to dinner plates and spoon on the sauce.

PLANNING AHEAD: The peppers, garlic, cilantro, and tomato can be chopped and refrigerated up to several hours ahead of time.

VARIATIONS:

⇒ A 2-pound flank steak can be used instead of New York strip. Cook it for about 5 minutes per side for medium-rare and let it rest for a few minutes before slicing it diagonally across the grain.

⇒ If you can't get a good fresh tomato, use ½ cup of drained, chopped, canned tomatoes.

NOTES:

• The short loin lies next to the ribs. From this portion we get the Delmonico or club steak. If the filet portion is removed, the remaining section makes shell steaks, strip steaks, New York strips, or Kansas City strips. Any of these cuts can be used.

• Use a skillet just large enough to accommodate the steaks with about ½ inch between them. If the meat is too crowded, it will steam without browning; if there's too much room, the juices will burn. (For more on sautéing, see page 94.)

• If you use a splatter guard over the pan, you won't have a greasy cooktop to clean. They're available in department stores and cook shops.

• In his *Steak Lover's Cookbook*, William Rice recommends this "touch method" for judging the doneness of steak: At rare it should feel like the triangle of skin between your thumb and forefinger when your hand is limp; at medium-rare it should feel like the same spot when your fingers are extended; at medium, it should feel like that spot when your hand is closed into a fist.

• Swirling the pan rather than stirring to incorporate the butter allows it to melt slowly, forming an emulsion that thickens the sauce slightly.

Caribbean Fajitas

[6 SERVINGS]

Jerk Marinade adds a sweet-hot sizzle to this Miami remake of a southwestern classic, with avocado slices providing a mellow counterpoint. Ounce for ounce, Florida avocados have about one-third fewer calories and 50 percent less fat than their smaller California cousins; in fact, Brooks Tropicals, a major wholesaler, has begun marketing them as a "lite" alternative.

Fajitas are great for parties because once you've set out the tortillas and fixings, there is no serving to do. Add bowls of Cuban-Style Black Beans (page 245) and white rice, and let everyone help themselves.

2½ pounds skirt steak

½ cup Jerk Marinade (page 103)

½ cup fresh lime juice

1 tablespoon vegetable oil

1 or 2 large onions, peeled and
    thinly sliced

2 or 3 large green bell peppers,
    seeded, cored, and thinly sliced

1 ripe Florida avocado or 2 ripe
    California avocados

6 large flour tortillas

Kosher salt

6 tablespoons sour cream

Fresh Tomato Salsa (page 259)

Lime wedges

Cut the skirt steak with the grain into 4- to 5-inch strips and place in a large, self-sealing food storage bag.

Combine the Jerk Marinade with ¼ cup of the lime juice and pour over the meat. Seal the bag and turn it to distribute the marinade. Refrigerate for at least 2 hours or as long as 24 hours, turning occasionally. Remove from the refrigerator 1 hour before cooking.

Heat the oil in a skillet over high heat and sauté the onions and green peppers, stirring, until soft and slightly browned on the edges, about 3 minutes. Set aside, covered.

Peel and thinly slice the avocado and toss with the remaining ¼ cup of lime juice.

Wrap the tortillas tightly in foil.

TO GRILL: Use direct, medium heat (see page 100). Position the grill rack about 4 inches from the heat, and place the wrapped tortillas on the edge to warm.

Remove the meat strips from the marinade; discard the marinade. Pat dry with paper towels and season with salt. Grill 2 to 3 minutes per side for medium-rare, 4 to 5 minutes for medium.

TO COOK INDOORS: Sauté the meat in a large, lightly oiled skillet or grill in a pan over medium-high heat for 3 to 4 minutes per side for medium-rare.

Transfer the meat to a carving board and let rest a few minutes. Slice diagonally across the grain into ¼-inch strips.

Arrange the meat, avocado, peppers, and onions on a large platter. Serve the tortillas, sour cream, salsa, and lime wedges on the side.

VARIATIONS:

➤ If you're cooking indoors or your grill is crowded, warm the tortillas by placing them between 2 dampened paper towels and microwaving on full power for about 30 seconds. Or wrap them in foil and place in a 200-degree oven for about 15 minutes.

➤ Flank steak or boneless sirloin steak that is no more than ½ inch thick can be substituted for skirt steak.

➤ Chicken breast, pounded to a ½ inch thickness, or pork tenderloin, sliced ½ inch thick, is great prepared this way.

NOTES:

• According to Merle Ellis in *Cutting Up in the Kitchen,* "The skirt steak is actually the diaphragm muscle. There are only two skirts per beef. You may have seen them labeled 'London Broil' in some markets, but then in some markets you're likely to see most anything labeled 'London Broil.' "

• Tossing the avocado with lime (or lemon) juice prevents discoloration. If you don't want to add a citrus flavor to avocado, a quick rinse under cold running water will wash off some of the enzymes that cause discoloration and delay the process. Still, it's best to cut avocado as close to serving time as possible.

Gaucho Grill with Chimichurri Sauce

[4 SERVINGS]

You'll never reach for steak sauce again after you've tasted steak with fresh, zesty Chimichurri Sauce, another Miami legacy of revolution and refugee flight. Popular in Brazil and Argentina (thus the "gaucho" in our Gaucho Grill), chimichurri was introduced to Miami by Nicaraguans fleeing the Sandinista rebels who overthrew President Anastasio Somoza in 1979. Nephews of the deposed dictator founded Los Ranchos, a Nicaraguan steak house that now has five locations including Bayside, a festival marketplace on the downtown waterfront that is a magnet for visitors.

Chimichurri is served with Los Ranchos' signature dish, churrasco, *a marinated and grilled steak cut from the tenderloin (filet). In our version the steaks are marinated as well as served with garlic and parsley enriched chimichurri. Be sure to make the sauce several hours ahead so the flavors can meld.*

When you buy the meat, insist that it be cut from the solid center of the tenderloin rather than the end, which tapers and tends to separate. And when you're ready to cook it, make sure the fire is good and hot so the thin steaks don't dry out.

Yellow Rice with Corn (page 239) and a green salad would complete the meal nicely.

1 4-inch, center-cut beef tenderloin (about 2 pounds)
1⅓ cups Chimichurri Sauce (recipe follows)
Kosher salt

Trim the visible fat and membrane from the tenderloin. Pressing down with your free hand to steady the meat, cut it with the grain (not across it) into 4 lengthwise strips. Place the strips between sheets of plastic wrap and pound to an even thickness of about ¼ inch with a meat mallet (use the flat side, not the tenderizing side) or the bottom of a heavy pot.

Place the meat in a self-sealing food storage bag. Pour on ⅓ cup of unsalted Chimichurri Sauce and rub into the meat. Seal the bag and refrigerate for at least 4 hours or as long as 24 hours.

Remove from the refrigerator 1 hour before cooking. Build a hot fire in a charcoal grill (see page 100); with a gas grill, use direct, high heat.

Remove the steaks from the marinade; discard the marinade. Pat dry with paper towels and season with salt. Coat the grill rack with oil and position it about 4 inches from the fire.

Grill the steaks directly over the fire (don't cover them) to the desired degree of doneness. If your fire is really hot, it will take only about 1 minute per side for rare and 1½ minutes per side for medium-rare.

Serve immediately with the remaining Chimichurri Sauce on the side.

VARIATIONS:

➡ To cook indoors, broil the steak about 3 inches from the heat source or sauté it in a lightly oiled pan over high heat for the about same length of time as above. You'll get especially good results, complete with grill marks, from a ridged grill pan.

➡ For a more economical version, substitute four 8-ounce skirt steaks. (They don't need to be pounded.)

Chimichurri Sauce

[ABOUT 1⅓ CUPS]

This tangy sauce is essentially a vinaigrette and is great on salads, too. Hand-chopping and mixing gives it its classic, clear, green-flecked look. (It will turn green if you chop and mix it in a blender or food processor, though it will still taste fine.) The sauce will keep in the refrigerator for two or three days; let it come to room temperature and shake it well before using.

1 cup olive oil

¼ cup malt or cider vinegar

½ cup minced fresh parsley

6 garlic cloves, peeled and minced

2 teaspoons dry-leaf oregano, crumbled

1 teaspoon freshly ground pepper

½ teaspoon red pepper flakes

¾ teaspoon kosher salt

Combine the oil, vinegar, parsley, garlic, oregano, pepper, and pepper flakes in a glass jar with a tight-fitting lid. Let sit for at least 2 hours for the flavors to blend. Measure out ⅓ cup for the steak marinade and add the salt to the remaining sauce. Shake to mix before using.

Orange-Tamarind Brisket with Boniato and Carrots

[8 SERVINGS]

This flavor-packed pot roast is nothing like the onion soup–slathered version your mother might have made. The meat is marinated in a paste of garlic, spices, and tamarind pulp, from the seed pod of the tropical tamarind tree. A Cuban-born friend, Ileana Oroza, recalls picking and eating the fat brown pods as a child and delighting in their mouth-puckering power. The sweet-and-sour pulp (think of lime-spiked raisins) is a refreshing addition to smoothies, ices, and chutneys, and is an integral ingredient in Worcestershire sauce. Latin, Asian, and Indian markets sometimes carry fresh or dried pods, but they require soaking and straining. Frozen tamarind pulp is easier to find and use. If that's not available, substitute equal parts of fresh lime juice, molasses, and Worcestershire (in this case, 2 teaspoons each).

Once marinated, the meat cooks slowly in a sweet blend of orange juice and chicken broth, and gets a further bit of sweetness from the boniato (tropical sweet potato, page 3) and carrots that are added to the pot. A green salad is all you'll need to complete the meal.

FOR THE SEASONING PASTE:

2 tablespoons frozen tamarind pulp

3 garlic cloves, peeled and minced

1 teaspoon kosher salt

1 teaspoon freshly ground pepper

1 teaspoon paprika

½ teaspoon ground cumin

½ teaspoon ground cloves

½ teaspoon ground allspice

½ teaspoon dried, crushed red
    pepper flakes

TO FINISH THE DISH:

1 4-pound boneless, first-cut beef
    brisket

2 tablespoons vegetable oil

2 medium onions, peeled and
    chopped

2 large garlic cloves, peeled and
    chopped

2 bay leaves

1 cup fresh orange juice

2 to 4 cups chicken stock

2 pounds boniato, peeled and cut
    into 1½-inch chunks (see Notes
    and Variations)

1 pound carrots, peeled and cut into 1½-inch chunks	Kosher salt and freshly ground pepper
Orange slices and minced fresh parsley for garnish	

Stir the tamarind pulp, garlic, salt, pepper, paprika, cumin, cloves, allspice, and red pepper flakes together in a small bowl to form a paste. Set aside.

Use the point of a sharp knife to make ¼-inch-deep slits all over the surface of the brisket. Set in a large glass baking dish or a jumbo self-sealing food storage bag. Push as much of the seasoning paste as possible into the slits and spread the rest over the surface of the brisket. Cover with plastic wrap or seal the bag and refrigerate for at least 2 hours or as long as overnight.

Preheat the oven to 325 degrees.

Heat the oil over medium-high heat in a large, heavy Dutch oven. (If you don't have one large enough, use a roasting pan set over 2 burners.) Brown the brisket well, starting with the fatty side. Add the onions, garlic, bay leaves, orange juice, and enough chicken stock to come about halfway up the brisket.

Cover the pot tightly, put in the oven, and roast for 2 hours. Add the boniato and carrots, and more broth if necessary to keep the brisket covered halfway. Roast, covered, about 2 hours more, until the brisket is very tender when pierced with a fork.

Transfer the brisket to a cutting board and let rest for 10 minutes. (Keep the pot covered so the vegetables stay warm.)

Slice the brisket thinly across the grain and arrange the slices on a platter. Remove the vegetables from the pot with a slotted spoon and add them to the platter, along with a garnish of orange slices and parsley. Discard the bay leaves. Degrease the pan juices (see Notes), taste for seasoning, and add salt and pepper if needed. Spoon some of the juices over the meat and serve the rest on the side in a heated gravy boat.

PLANNING AHEAD: You can prepare the brisket completely up to 2 days ahead and refrigerate the meat, vegetables, and pan juices separately. When ready to serve, slice the meat, place it in a roasting pan with the vegetables, defat and add the pan juices, and reheat, covered, in a 325-degree oven for about 30 minutes.

VARIATIONS:
- You can substitute sweet potato for the boniato; if you do, use parsnips instead of carrots to vary the color of the vegetables.
- Dried apricots and prunes are a nice addition. Add them with the vegetables.

NOTES:
- A boniato is denser and more difficult to cut than a potato. To keep the knife from slipping and cutting you, take a small slice off the bottom of the boniato to steady it, slice it down the middle, and put the halves on the cutting board, cut side down, before slicing them into chunks. This is the safest way to cut any hard, round vegetable.
- Boniato oxidizes quickly, so cover it with water once peeled and immerse the chunks completely in the liquid when you add them to the pot.
- If you don't have a gravy separator, pour the pan juices into a 4-cup glass measure. When the fat rises to the top, immerse a bulb baster in the juices and suction them out in several batches, leaving the fat behind.

Ropa Vieja (Shredded Beef in Savory Sauce)

[6 TO 8 SERVINGS]

While American cowboys were turning skirt and flank steak into fajitas, Cuban cooks were poaching these flavorful but stringy cuts, shredding them into strands, and serving them as Ropa Vieja and Vaca Frita (page 144). (Some recipes call for brisket, but we prefer flank or skirt steak because the strands are thinner and easier to shred.) Ropa Vieja (rope-ah vee-A-ha) literally means "old clothes" in Spanish, perhaps because the strands of meat call to mind a threadbare garment. This set of old clothes, though, is dressed up in such a richly flavored sauce that you can take it anywhere. Serve it with white rice or pile it on crusty rolls for hot beef sandwiches with a Miami twist.

FOR THE BROTH:

2½ pounds skirt or flank steak

2 celery stalks with leaves, washed and cut into chunks

1 large onion, peeled and quartered

1 large carrot, scrubbed and cut into chunks

1 bay leaf

1 tablespoon kosher salt

FOR THE SAUCE:

2 tablespoons olive oil

2 large onions, peeled and thinly sliced

2 large bell peppers, seeded, cored, and thinly sliced

2 garlic cloves, peeled and minced

1 10¾-ounce can tomato puree (about 1¼ cups)

½ cup dry white wine

1 teaspoon dry-leaf oregano, crumbled

1 teaspoon ground cumin

¼ teaspoon ground cinnamon

¼ teaspoon ground cloves

¼ teaspoon cayenne

1 tablespoon drained capers

2 teaspoons fresh lime juice

Salt and freshly ground pepper

Cut the meat in half (with the grain of skirt steak but across the grain of flank steak) and place in a large soup pot. Add 2 quarts of water and bring to a boil over high heat. Skim off the foam and add the celery, onion, carrot, bay leaf, and salt. Turn the heat to low and simmer, covered, for about 1½ hours, until the meat is tender and the strands have begun to separate.

Remove from the heat and set aside to cool. Strain the broth; reserve 1 cup and store the rest for another use.

If using flank steak, cut it across the grain into 2- to 3-inch strips.

Pound the meat with a mallet (using the flat side) to separate the strands. Shred along the grain with your fingers. It will look like short lengths of spaghetti. Set aside.

Heat the oil in a large skillet over medium heat and sauté the onions, bell peppers, and garlic until soft, about 5 minutes. Stir in the tomato puree, wine, oregano, cumin, cinnamon, cloves, and cayenne. Lower the heat and simmer, stirring occasionally, until slightly thickened, about 5 minutes.

Stir in the capers, lime juice, reserved meat, and broth. Simmer for about 10 minutes, stirring occasionally, to blend the flavors. Taste the sauce and add salt and pepper if needed. Serve immediately or cover and keep warm over very low heat for up to 30 minutes.

PLANNING AHEAD: If you poach and shred the meat the day before, you can put this dish together in less than 30 minutes. Or make the whole dish ahead and reheat it; the flavors will meld and mellow in the refrigerator.

NOTE: Here's a neat way to freeze leftover broth: Pour it into self-sealing food storage bags. Seal the bags and lay them flat on a cookie sheet in the freezer until frozen. Remove the cookie sheet and stack the thin, flat bags of broth in the freezer. They'll take up much less room than the frozen blobs you'll get if you put the bags of broth straight into the freezer.

Vaca Frita (Fried, Shredded Beef)

[4 TO 6 SERVINGS]

Vaca Frita (vah-cah FREE-tah) means "fried cow" in Spanish, and Cubans consider it a humble dish—a way to get a meal out of meat that has been used to make beef soup stock. There is nothing humble, though, about its flavor and texture: The beef absorbs a pleasing sharpness from the salt and lime juice marinade and is fried up so brown and crisp that it almost crunches when you eat it. Serve it with smooth, sweet Boniato Puree (page 218) for dinner and use the flavorful stock in a batch of soup another day.

FOR THE BROTH:

2½ pounds skirt or flank steak

2 celery stalks with leaves, washed and cut into chunks

1 large onion, peeled and quartered

1 large carrot, scrubbed and cut into chunks

1 bay leaf

1 tablespoon kosher salt

TO FINISH THE DISH:

Kosher salt

½ cup fresh lime juice

Olive oil

1 large onion, peeled, halved, and thinly sliced

3 garlic cloves, peeled and minced

2 tablespoons finely chopped parsley

Cut the meat in half (with the grain of skirt steak but across the grain of flank steak) and place in a large soup pot. Add 2 quarts of water and bring to a boil over high heat. Skim off the foam and add the celery, onion, carrot, bay leaf, and salt. Turn the heat to low and simmer, covered, for about 1½ hours, until the meat is tender and the strands have begun to separate.

Remove from the heat, and set aside to cool. Strain the broth and reserve for another use.

If using flank steak, cut it across the grain into 2- to 3-inch strips.

Pound the meat with a mallet (using the flat side) to separate the strands. Shred it along the grain with your fingers. It will look like short lengths of spaghetti. Place in a nonaluminum container.

Stir 1 teaspoon of salt into the lime juice until dissolved and pour over the meat. Toss with your fingers to distribute the marinade. Cover and refrigerate for at least 1 hour or as long as overnight.

Drain the meat and squeeze it as dry as you can. Discard the marinade.

Heat ¼ inch of oil in a large skillet over medium-high heat. Spread the meat in an even layer in the bottom of the pan. Sauté it, turning once, until well browned and very crisp, 6 to 8 minutes total. Add the onion and garlic, toss with a spatula to combine the ingredients, and sauté until the onion is slightly softened, about 2 minutes.

Taste the meat for seasoning and add more salt if necessary. Stir in the parsley and serve immediately.

PLANNING AHEAD: If you poach and shred the meat the day before, you can finish the dish in under 15 minutes.

Miami Meat Loaf

[8 SERVINGS]

Meat loaf is one of those wonderfully adaptable dishes that readily absorbs the flavors of its sur-roundings. This one combines the mellowness of a Hispanic sofrito (sautéed onion, bell pepper, and garlic) with the sweet heat of Jamaican Pickapeppa sauce and jerk seasoning. Serve it with buttered Boniato Puree (page 218) or mashed potatoes and a steamed green vegetable.

1 tablespoon vegetable oil

1 medium onion, peeled and finely chopped

1 medium green bell pepper, cored, seeded, and finely chopped

3 garlic cloves, peeled and minced

2 eggs

¼ cup milk

3 tablespoons Pickapeppa sauce (see page 98) or 1½ tablespoons each ketchup and Worcester-shire sauce

1 tablespoon sharp mustard

½ teaspoon Jerk Seasoning (page 99) or a commercial jerk blend

1 teaspoon salt

½ teaspoon freshly ground pepper

1½ pounds lean ground beef

½ pound lean ground pork

2 cups fresh bread crumbs (about 4 bread slices) (see Note, page 27)

FOR THE TOPPING:

2 tablespoons ketchup

2 tablespoons Pickapeppa Sauce (or 1 tablespoon each ketchup and Worcestershire sauce)

Preheat the oven to 350 degrees.

Heat the oil in a large skillet over medium heat and sauté the onion, bell pepper, and gar-lic until soft, about 5 minutes. Set aside to cool.

Beat the eggs, milk, Pickapeppa, mustard, Jerk Seasoning, salt, and pepper together in a large bowl.

Add the ground beef and pork, and mix with your hands until well combined. Add the bread crumbs and sautéed vegetables, and mix well.

Pat the mixture into a 9-by-5-inch loaf pan, mounding it slightly in the middle. (Or form it into a free-standing loaf in a small roasting pan that has been coated with vegetable oil spray.) Stir together the ketchup and Pickapeppa, and spread it over the top of the loaf.

Bake for about 1½ hours, until the meat loaf has pulled slightly away from the pan. Let cool for 10 minutes, pour off the drippings, slice, and serve.

VARIATIONS:

- You can substitute ½ pound of ground veal or turkey or ¼ pound of chorizo for an equal amount of beef. Or use the "butcher's mix" of ground beef, pork, and veal that is available in many supermarkets.
- If you like your meat loaf hot, sauté a few seeded, minced jalapeños with the rest of the vegetables.

NOTES:

- Sautéing the vegetables before adding them to the meat mixture brings out their sweetness.
- Using fresh bread crumbs instead of dry makes for a moister, more tender loaf.
- If you make meat loaf often, look for a meat loaf pan with a perforated liner; it allows the fat to drain away easily.
- It's just as easy to make two meat loaves at once and freeze one for another day. Double the recipe and line a second loaf pan with aluminum foil, leaving a generous overhang on both long sides. Pat half of the meat mixture into the lined pan, bring the overlapping edges together, and roll them to make a secure seal (don't squish the meat mixture). Freeze the mixture in the pan and then transfer to a freezer bag. It will keep for up to 3 months. When ready to use, put it back in the pan and let thaw in the refrigerator. Roll back the foil and frost it with the ketchup mixture before baking. Increase the baking time by 10 minutes or so to compensate for the extra chilliness.

Picadillo (Savory Ground Beef)

[6 SERVINGS]

Picadillo (pick-ah-DEE-oh), a Cuban classic that is served over white rice, shows that there are as many tasty ways to stretch a pound of ground beef as there are imaginative cooks the world over. It has the consistency of sloppy joe filling and is just as easy and economical to make, but it has a much more sophisticated flavor. You'll love the way the saltiness of the capers and olives and the sweetness of the raisins play against the savory sofrito of sautéed onion, bell pepper, and garlic. Jalapeño is an unconventional addition—hot peppers aren't often used in Cuban cuisine— but we like the zing.

This is a great make-ahead dish for a Super Bowl party or graduation buffet. It won't break your budget and will keep beautifully—and actually improve in flavor—in the refrigerator or freezer. Fried Ripe Plantains (Maduros, page 226) and Cuban-Style Black Beans (page 245) are traditional accompaniments; we like to serve a green salad, too.

1 tablespoon olive oil

1 large onion, peeled and chopped

1 large green bell pepper, cored, seeded, and chopped

3 garlic cloves, peeled and minced

1 jalapeño pepper, seeded and minced (optional)

1 pound lean ground beef

½ pound lean ground pork

1 teaspoon ground cumin

1 cup canned crushed tomatoes

1 tablespoon drained capers

½ cup green olives with pimentos (preferably salad style)

½ cup raisins

1 tablespoon red wine vinegar

Kosher salt and freshly ground pepper

About 4 cups hot cooked white rice

Heat the oil in a large skillet over medium heat. Sauté the onion, green pepper, garlic, and jalapeño until soft, about 5 minutes.

Add the meat to the skillet and raise the heat to medium-high. Brown the meat, breaking it up well with a wooden spoon, until cooked through, about 10 minutes. Drain off the fat.

Stir in the cumin and tomatoes. Bring the mixture to a boil, turn the heat to low, and simmer, covered, for 15 minutes.

Stir in the capers, olives, raisins, and vinegar, and simmer, covered, for 5 minutes, until the raisins are plump. Season to taste with salt and pepper, and serve over the rice.

VARIATIONS:

- Use an additional ½ pound of ground beef in place of the ground pork.
- Use leftover picadillo as a stuffing for bell peppers or chayote squash (page 5) or a filling for empanadas or burritos.
- Turn the picadillo into Caribbean Chili by adding a rinsed and drained 16-ounce can of black beans and additional crushed tomatoes to taste.

Fritas (Cuban-Style Hamburgers)

[6 TO 8 SERVINGS]

Fast-food hamburgers are no modern-day invention. More than sixty years ago, street vendors in Cuba sold mini-burgers called fritas, which is pronounced FREE-tahs and literally means "frieds." They can be found today on some Cuban restaurant menus in Miami, most notably at El Rey de las Fritas (Hamburger King) on Southwest Eighth Street (Calle Ocho), the main thoroughfare of the Little Havana neighborhood. Each March The Little Havana Kiwanis hosts Calle Ocho Open House, a festival of Latin food and music that attracts nearly one million revelers.

From the outside, fritas look like all-American burgers in miniature, but they have a taste, color, and texture all their own. Chorizo, a paprika-rich Spanish pork sausage, gives the meat mixture its spicy flavor and reddish color, and shoestring potatoes tucked into the bun add a nice crunch.

Chorizo is widely available in supermarkets. You'll need half of a 5- to 6-ounce package for this recipe—a great excuse to make it twice. If your store has an accommodating meat department, ask the butcher to peel the sausage and run it through the grinder with the ground beef.

1 cup cubed stale bread (preferably Cuban, French, or Italian)	½ teaspoon kosher salt
	½ teaspoon freshly ground pepper
⅓ cup milk	1 small onion, peeled and cut in half
2½ to 3 ounces chorizo	
1 pound lean ground beef	Vegetable oil or vegetable-oil spray
1 egg, beaten	1 dozen dinner rolls (small, soft rolls), cut in half
Ketchup	
A few dashes of hot sauce	4 cups canned shoestring potatoes

Soak the bread in the milk in a small bowl.

Remove the casing from the chorizo. Cut it into chunks and process in a food processor until finely ground. (If you don't have a processor, put it through a hand-cranked meat grinder or mince by hand.) Put the chorizo in a large bowl with the ground beef and set aside.

Add the egg, 1 tablespoon of ketchup, the hot sauce, salt, and pepper to the soaked bread. Mix well with a fork and pour over the meat. Grate in the onion using a fine grater and mix all the ingredients well. (Your hands are your best utensils, so take off your rings and have at it.)

Lightly oil a large skillet and heat it over medium heat. Fry a tiny piece of the meat mixture and taste for seasoning; the saltiness of chorizo varies from brand to brand, so you may need to add more salt.

Shape the meat mixture into 12 balls and flatten them slightly into fat patties. (To ensure an even size, pat the meat into a rectangle first and cut into 12 equal pieces as though you were cutting a cake. Or measure out each portion with a ¼-cup ice-cream scoop.)

Preheat the oven to 200 degrees and place the dinner rolls on a baking sheet.

Reheat the skillet over medium heat. Add the patties, making sure they don't touch, and press down on them with a spatula to flatten them a little more. (A 12-inch skillet will hold all 12 comfortably; a 10-inch skillet may require 2 batches.)

Fry the burgers, turning once, until nicely browned and cooked through, 6 to 8 minutes total.

After you've flipped the burgers, warm the rolls in the oven for a few minutes. Put each finished burger on a roll bottom and top with a handful of shoestring potatoes and a squirt of ketchup. Put the roll tops in place and serve immediately.

PLANNING AHEAD: You can make and refrigerate the meat mixture up to a day ahead. If there's room in your refrigerator, form the patties, too, and store them, covered, on a baking sheet.

VARIATIONS:
- If you can't find chorizo, substitute any garlic sausage.
- The burgers can be made standard size, if you prefer, and served on hamburger buns.
- If you're adept at deep-frying, try making your own shoestring potatoes; you'll love their fresh flavor. Cut the potatoes with a mandoline slicer or use the same hand method or food processor blade you would to julienne vegetables. Here's one good technique, called reverse slicing: Fit the food processor with the slicing blade and set it to cut slices about ¼ inch thick. Peel 2 baking potatoes and push them the long way down the feeding tube and through the slicer. Remove the slices and put the top back on the food processor. Working in batches, stack the slices into bundles the same thickness as your feeding tube. Stack the bundles in the feeding tube perpendicular to the cutting blade. Start the processor and push the stacks through the slicer to produce matchstick-size pieces. Keep the cut potatoes

covered with cold water until you're ready to fry and then spin them in a salad spinner to remove the excess water.

→ Though they're not traditional, caramelized onions are a delicious substitute for shoestring potatoes. Here's how to make them: Peel and thinly slice two large onions. Melt ¼ cup of butter over medium heat in a large skillet (don't use a non-stick one—you want the onions to stick a bit in order to caramelize well). Add the onions, sprinkle them with 1 tablespoon of sugar, and turn the heat to medium-low. Let them cook, stirring occasionally, for about 25 minutes. Raise the heat to medium and cook until golden and caramelized, about 10 minutes more.

Veal Chops with Silken Mango-Lime Sauce

[4 SERVINGS]

This ethereal sauce is an adaptation of beurre blanc, *the classic French "white butter" sauce (though made with considerably less butter). It owes its wonderful texture to the emulsion that forms when cold butter is whisked into a reduction of wine vinegar, lime juice, shallots, and jalapeños. The butter also enhances the mango's rich flavor, and the lime juice adds just the right edge. It is well worth the expense of veal but would do wonders for pork chops, too.*

4 jalapeño peppers, seeded and minced

3 shallots, peeled and minced

¼ cup white wine vinegar

8 tablespoons fresh lime juice

4 tablespoons unsalted butter, chilled and cut into 4 pieces

1 cup mango puree (from 1 medium mango or use frozen puree)

4 tablespoons vegetable oil

4 veal rib chops, ¾ to 1 inch thick (about 2½ pounds total)

Salt and freshly ground pepper

Mango and lime wedges for garnish

Combine the jalapeños, shallots, vinegar, 6 tablespoons of the lime juice, and ¼ cup of water in a nonaluminum saucepan. Bring to a boil over high heat and boil for about 5 minutes, until the liquid is reduced to about 2½ tablespoons.

Turn the heat to low and whisk in the butter, 1 tablespoon at a time, adding the next piece as soon as the last one is incorporated.

Strain the sauce, pressing the solids to extract all the liquid. (Discard the solids.) Return the sauce to the pan and whisk in the mango puree. Taste for seasoning and set aside, covered.

Whisk the oil and the remaining 2 tablespoons of lime juice together in a small bowl and set aside.

Preheat the broiler.

Trim the excess fat from the chops and pat dry. Brush with the lime oil mixture, season with salt and pepper, and arrange the chops on a broiler pan.

Broil for about 4 to 6 minutes per side, brushing each side again with the lime oil. The chops are done when they're nicely browned outside and rosy pink near the bone.

Set the chops aside on a platter and cover loosely with foil.

Warm the sauce over very low heat (if it boils, the butter will separate). Whisk in any juices that have accumulated around the chops.

Garnish the chops with mango and lime wedges and serve with the sauce on the side.

PLANNING AHEAD: You can make the sauce up to 2 hours ahead of time and keep it at room temperature. Reheat it, adding the veal juices, as directed above.

VARIATION: You can grill the chops outdoors over a medium fire; they'll take about the same length of time.

Lechon Asado (Roast Suckling Pig) for Nochebuena

Centuries ago while observant Catholics in Europe were capping their meatless Advent season with a seafood meal, Spaniards in colonial Cuba were celebrating Christmas Eve (*Nochebuena*) with a feast of roast suckling pig. It was an example of the loosening effect that the distance from Rome—and from New World centers of church power such as Mexico—had on Catholic practices in Cuba, according to culinary historian Maricel Presilla. Ecclesiastic correspondence from the time, she says, documents frequent complaints about the Cuban colonists' free ways—marking saints' days, for example, with liquor-lubricated celebrations. The relaxing of religious mores aside, pork was a natural choice for Cubans: Pigs had arrived on the island with Columbus and had quickly thrived.

Five hundred years later, roast suckling pig (*lechon asado*) remains the centerpiece of a classic *Nochebuena* celebration in Miami. Traditionalists choose their pigs on the hoof at slaughterhouses such as Matadero Cabrera in Hialeah Gardens, which sells four thousand during a typical Christmas season. The pigs are butchered and ready for pickup on December 23 to allow time for long marinating in an *adobo* of garlic, oregano, salt, pepper, and sour orange juice, and slow roasting in backyard pits. Some Cuban bakeries will roast your pig in their big ovens and save you from the task of digging up the backyard.

Roast Pork Little Havana
with Adobo Seasoning

[8 TO 10 SERVINGS]

Tender, juicy pork roasts like this one are the main dish of choice for a small-scale Nochebuena
*(Christmas Eve dinner) and other celebrations in Cuban Miami. The meat marinates in the same
garlic-rich* adobo *as a* lechon asado *(see page 154) and roasts for hours in a slow oven until it
nearly falls apart when cut. Some recipes call for a fresh ham (leg), but we like Boston butt
(shoulder) because it is fatty enough to remain moist through the long cooking. Serve it with
Cuban-Style Black Beans (page 245), white rice, Yuca with Mojo (page 229), and a green salad
for an authentic Cuban feast.*

> 1 4- to 5-pound boneless Boston butt (pork shoulder)
>
> 3 garlic cloves, peeled and minced
>
> 1 teaspoon dry-leaf oregano, crumbled
>
> 1 teaspoon kosher salt
>
> ½ teaspoon freshly ground pepper
>
> Adobo Seasoning (recipe follows)
>
> 1 cup sour orange juice (or ½ cup each lime and regular orange juice)
>
> 1 onion, peeled and sliced into paper-thin rings

Rinse the pork and pat dry with paper towels. Poke it all over with the tip of a sharp knife,
cutting about ¼ inch deep.

Mash the garlic, oregano, salt, and pepper together in a small bowl to make a paste. (Or
chop the garlic coarsely and process it with the other seasonings in a mini food processor until
smooth.)

Rub the paste into the pork, pressing it into the slits. Place the pork in a large self-sealing
food storage bag. Mix the Adobo Seasoning with the sour orange juice and pour over the meat.
Seal the bag and refrigerate the pork overnight, turning several times to distribute the marinade.

Take the pork out 2 hours before roasting. Remove from the marinade and place in a roasting pan; reserve the marinade.

Heat the oven to 250 degrees. Roast the pork for 5 to 6 hours, basting it frequently with the reserved marinade. If the juices begin crusting on the pan bottom, pour in a little water. Test the meat by cutting into it; it should be very soft and loose, on the verge of falling apart. If it is not browned as deeply as you would like, raise the oven temperature to 400 degrees for the last 20 to 30 minutes.

Remove the roast from the oven and let it rest for about 20 minutes. Place the roasting pan on a burner over low heat, add ¼ cup of water, and stir with a wooden spoon to loosen the browned bits. Strain and degrease the pan juices.

Slice the pork thinly, arrange on a platter, and pour the juices over it. Place the onion slices on top and serve.

VARIATIONS:

- The pork can be grilled using the same method as Grilled Whole Turkey with Mojo Marinade (page 125). Allow about 5 hours but keep in mind that the time will vary depending on weather conditions and the temperature of your fire.
- For a Miami-meets-North-Carolina twist, use leftover pork to make a great southern-style barbecued pulled pork sandwich: Use two forks to pull the meat into shreds. Warm it and serve in buns topped with 1 tablespoon of Tropical Barbecue Sauce (page 162) and 2 tablespoons coleslaw.

Adobo Seasoning

[ABOUT ¼ CUP]

Adobo—a marinade of tart citrus juice, garlic, salt, pepper, and spices—is an essential element of Cuban cooking. Traditionally, the garlic and seasonings were mashed into a paste with a mortar and pestle, and the juice (usually sour orange) was whisked in. Thank goodness for food processors!

6 garlic cloves, peeled and coarsely chopped

2 tablespoons sour orange juice (or 1 tablespoon each lime and regular orange juice)

1 tablespoon chopped fresh cilantro or flat-leaf parsley

2 teaspoons kosher salt

1 teaspoon coarsely ground pepper

1½ teaspoons ground cumin

1 teaspoon dry-leaf oregano, crumbled

1 teaspoon dry-leaf thyme, crumbled

Combine the garlic, sour orange juice, cilantro, salt, pepper, cumin, oregano, and thyme in a blender or mini food processor. Process until smooth, scraping down the sides of the blender once or twice. Use immediately or refrigerate for up to 2 weeks.

Roast Pork Loin and Bananas
with Tropical Glaze

[4 TO 6 SERVINGS]

Bananas taste heavenly when coated with caramelized glaze, the Adobo-marinated meat stands up well to all the sweetness, and tamarind adds depth to the mix. Tamarind pulp is available frozen in supermarkets with a Latin clientele; keep a container of it in your freezer and scoop out what you need with a measuring spoon that has been dipped in hot water.

2 pounds boneless pork loin

Adobo Seasoning (page 157)

½ cup sour orange juice (or ¼ cup each lime and regular orange juice)

½ cup orange marmalade (preferably bitter orange)

½ cup pineapple juice

2 tablespoons fresh orange juice

2 tablespoons fresh lime juice

1 tablespoon tamarind pulp (see Notes)

4 firm small bananas or 2 medium-size bananas

Pat the pork dry with paper towels and poke it all over with the tip of a sharp knife, cutting about ¼-inch deep.

Place the meat in a self-sealing food storage bag. Add the Adobo Seasoning and rub it into the meat, pushing as much of it into the slits as possible. Add the sour orange juice, seal the bag, and turn to distribute the marinade. Refrigerate for at least 4 hours or as long as 24 hours, turning the bag a few times.

Remove the pork from the refrigerator 1 hour before roasting.

Preheat the oven to 350 degrees.

Remove the pork from the marinade and dry with paper towels. (Discard the marinade.) Place the meat in a small roasting pan and spread the marmalade over it.

Stir together the pineapple, orange, and lime juices, and the tamarind puree, and set aside.

Roast the pork for 1 hour, basting it frequently with the juice mixture.

Peel the bananas and cut them on the diagonal into 1-inch pieces.

Remove the pan from the oven (but leave the oven on). Pour in any remaining juice and stir with a wooden spoon to dissolve the juice that has caramelized on the bottom. (If necessary, add a few tablespoons of water.) Add the bananas and stir to coat them with the caramelized pan juices.

Return the pan to the oven for about 30 minutes more, until the center of the meat registers 160 degrees on an instant-read meat thermometer.

Transfer the meat to a cutting board, tent with foil, and let rest for 15 minutes. Use a slotted spoon to transfer the bananas to a platter. Set the roaster on a burner over medium heat, add ¼ cup of water, and stir gently to deglaze. Strain the pan juices.

Cut the meat across the grain into ½-inch slices. Arrange them on the platter and pour the pan juices over.

VARIATIONS:

Try the glaze and basting sauce on chicken quarters or brisket.

Bitter orange marmalade has a sharp edge that contrasts nicely with the sweet bananas, but regular orange marmalade or apricot jam will do.

NOTES:

- The pork, like any roasted or baked item, will continue to cook for a while after being removed from the oven. It will reach the desired 170 degrees by the time it is ready for carving.
- If you can't find tamarind pulp, substitute equal parts of lime juice, molasses, and Worcestershire sauce (in this case, 1 teaspoon each).

Garlicky Grilled Pork Tenderloin

Garlic, oregano, and cumin have a fairly subtle effect in traditional Cuban Adobo Seasoning (page 157); here they're combined with a healthy dose of chili powder to produce a lively, spice-crusted tenderloin. Papaya–Three Pepper Chutney (page 265) would make a sweet foil.

¼ cup chili powder

1 tablespoon dry-leaf oregano, crumbled

2½ teaspoons ground cumin

6 garlic cloves, peeled and minced

2 tablespoons vegetable oil

About 2 pounds pork tenderloin, fat and membrane trimmed (see Note)

Kosher salt and freshly ground pepper

Combine the chili powder, oregano, cumin, garlic, and oil in a small bowl to form a thick paste. Place the tenderloin in a self-sealing food storage bag and rub it with the seasoning paste, coating the meat well. Seal the bag and refrigerate for at least 4 hours or as long as 24 hours.

Remove the meat from the refrigerator 1 hour before cooking.

TO GRILL: Use indirect, medium heat (see page 100).

Remove the meat from the bag, season with salt and pepper, and grill, turning once. Smaller tenderloins (under 1½ inches thick) should be grilled uncovered and will take 12 to 15 minutes. Larger ones will cook more evenly if the grill is covered and will take 16 to 20 minutes. The meat is done when an instant-read meat thermometer registers 155 to 160 degrees. If you don't have a thermometer, cut into a piece to check; it should be cooked through but still have a hint of pink at the center.

TO COOK INDOORS: Roast the meat in a preheated 375-degree oven for 25 to 35 minutes, depending on the size of the tenderloins, until it tests done as described above.

Let the meat rest for 5 to 10 minutes before slicing across the grain.

NOTE: Six 5-ounce tenderloins—one for each person—are ideal; you may also use two 1-pound tenderloins or any other 2-pound combination your meat department has on hand.

Finger-Lickin' Red-Hot Jerk-Barbecued Ribs with Tropical Barbecue Sauce

[4 SERVINGS]

Abandon yourself to the glorious pig-out possibilities of these succulent ribs and pass out kitchen towels instead of napkins for wiping sauce-slathered chins and fingers. Serve plenty of cold beer, too, for dousing the Jamaican-inspired fire. After absorbing the flavors of the dry rub overnight, these ribs are hot, hot, hot! (We're told that milk is actually best for soothing singed palates, but these two-fisted ribs call for beer.) For a less incendiary effect, cut the amount of cayenne in the Jerk Seasoning or, if you're using a commercial jerk blend, reduce the amount of seasoning to ⅓ or ¼ cup.

If you're grilling, toss soaked hickory chips over the coals or lava rocks for a layer of smokiness. If you're using the indoor variation, you'll like the way the water in the roasting pan keeps the ribs nice and moist.

Tropical Barbecue Sauce is a quick and easy remake of bottled sauce that you'll want to use on grilled turkey breast or chicken, too.

> 2 racks spare ribs or 4 racks baby back ribs (about 3 pounds total)
> ½ cup Jerk Seasoning (page 99) or commercial jerk blend
> 2 cups Tropical Barbecue Sauce (recipe follows)

Rub the ribs thoroughly with the Jerk Seasoning and wrap each rack separately in 3 layers of heavy-duty foil, sealing tightly. Refrigerate overnight.

Remove the ribs and let stand at room temperature for about 1 hour before cooking.

TO GRILL: Use indirect, medium heat (see page 100).

Place the ribs, still wrapped in foil, on the grill. If your grill has a cover, use it, leaving the vents half open. Cook for 1 hour, turning once. (Add more coals if necessary after 45 minutes.)

Using tongs and pot holders to protect your hands, take the ribs off the grill and remove from the foil. Return to the grill and baste with barbecue sauce. Cook for 15 to 20 minutes more, basting and turning several times, until the ribs are crusty and cooked through.

TO COOK INDOORS: Season and marinate the ribs as directed above, wrapping them in a single layer of foil. Preheat the oven to 450 degrees. Unwrap the ribs and place on a rack in a roasting pan. Place the pan in the oven and pour in about ½ cup of water. Roast for 15 minutes. Lower the oven temperature to 350 degrees. Baste the ribs generously with barbecue sauce and roast for 20 minutes. Turn, baste the other side with sauce, and roast for about 45 minutes more, turning and basting with sauce once or twice more.

Serve with the remaining barbecue sauce on the side.

Tropical Barbecue Sauce

[ABOUT 2½ CUPS]

If you start with a hot barbecue sauce, taste it before you decide whether to add the hot sauce.

2 cups commercial barbecue sauce
⅓ cup fresh orange juice
2 tablespoons pineapple juice
2 tablespoons dark rum
½ to 1 teaspoon Caribbean hot sauce or Tabasco (optional)

Combine the barbecue sauce, orange juice, pineapple juice, rum, and hot sauce in a saucepan. Bring to a boil, lower the heat, and simmer for about 10 minutes. The sauce will keep in the refrigerator for months.

Pork and Pineapple on a Stick
with Passion Fruit Glaze

[4 TO 6 SERVINGS]

Pork and pineapple are a familiar combination, but our tangy-sweet marinade and ambrosial glaze lift it to new heights. Passion fruit's tart, honey-citrus flavor is a sensual delight, but its name actually has a religious connotation: One story attributes it to Jesuit missionaries who saw Christ's wounds, nails, crown of thorns, and Apostles represented in the parts of its flower. Passion fruit is sometimes available fresh, but for this recipe, frozen puree is a good shortcut. If you can't find it, substitute unreconstituted pineapple juice concentrate.

These tropical kebabs are so good and easy to prepare ahead that they're ideal for a backyard party. Serve them with Coconut-Orange Rice (page 237) and a crisp green salad dressed with Sunny Citrus Vinaigrette (page 69).

1½ pounds boneless pork tenderloin or lean loin

FOR THE MARINADE:

½ cup fresh orange juice

¼ cup fresh lime juice

¼ cup passion fruit puree

2 tablespoons dark rum

1 tablespoon brown sugar

½ teaspoon Caribbean hot sauce or
   Tabasco

2 garlic cloves, peeled and minced

¼ teaspoon ground cumin

TO FINISH THE DISH:

Kosher salt and freshly ground
   pepper

½ fresh pineapple, peeled and
   cored

Passion Fruit Glaze (recipe
   follows)

Trim the pork of any visible fat and cut into 1½-inch chunks.

To make the marinade, combine the orange juice, lime juice, passion fruit puree, rum, brown sugar, hot sauce, garlic, and cumin in a self-sealing food storage bag and shake to mix well.

Add the pork, seal the bag, and turn it to distribute the marinade. Refrigerate for at least 4 hours or as long as 24 hours, turning the bag occasionally.

Remove the meat from the refrigerator 1 hour before cooking.

Cut the pineapple into 1½-inch chunks. Drain the pork (discard the marinade) and season with salt and pepper. Thread the pork and pineapple chunks alternately on 6 metal skewers. (See page 208, Tips/Techniques: Cooking on Skewers.)

TO GRILL: Use direct, medium heat (see page 100).

Coat the grill rack lightly with oil and place the kebabs on it, directly over the heat source. Measure ⅓ cup of the Passion Fruit Glaze and brush it on the kebabs several times as they cook. Grill, turning carefully with tongs, for 10 to 12 minutes total, until all sides are nicely browned and the pork is barely pink in the center.

TO COOK INDOORS: Arrange the kebabs on a broiler pan and broil about 3 inches from the heat source, turning and basting several times, for 10 to 12 minutes, or until the meat is barely pink at the center.

Arrange the kebabs on a serving plate. Reheat the remaining glaze and serve on the side.

PLANNING AHEAD: You can make the glaze and assemble the skewers several hours ahead of time; remember to take the skewers out of the refrigerator 1 hour before grilling.

VARIATIONS: You can substitute chicken breast or shrimp for the pork, and mango, banana, or papaya chunks for the pineapple.

NOTES:

- To avoid contamination, don't put the grilled kebabs—or any meat—on the same plate that held them when raw. For the same reason pour off the glaze you need for basting rather than dipping your brush into the whole batch. (If you slip up, boil the remaining glaze for 3 or 4 minutes before serving it as a sauce.)
- Cutting all the pork chunks the same size ensures that they cook at the same rate.

Passion Fruit Glaze

[ABOUT 1⅓ CUPS]

This richly flavored glaze would be great on grilled chicken or pork chops, too, and would really jazz up a baked ham.

⅓ cup passion fruit puree

¼ cup dark rum

¼ cup fresh lime juice

½ cup brown sugar

1 tablespoon unsalted butter

Combine the passion fruit puree, rum, lime juice, sugar, and butter in a small, heavy saucepan. Bring to a boil over medium heat, stirring constantly. Turn the heat to low and simmer, stirring occasionally, until thickened, about 10 minutes. When cool, the glaze can be refrigerated, covered, for up to 1 week. Warm over low heat before using.

VARIATION: If passion fruit puree isn't available, use unreconstituted pineapple juice concentrate.

Griot (Haitian-Style Fried Pork Chunks)

[4 SERVINGS]

Marinated, braised, and finally fried, these flavor-packed pork chunks are crisp on the outside and tender on the inside—fabulous! Griot (GREE-oh) is a virtual national dish among Haitians and a mainstay on Haitian restaurant menus in Miami. We adapted this recipe from one shared by storyteller and cooking teacher Liliane Louis, who works to keep Haitian culture alive in Miami through cooking classes for Haitian-American children. Authentic griot—and the quite similar Cuban masas de puerco *(pork chunks)—is fried in rendered pork fat, but we've opted for vegetable oil. A tangy tomato salsa makes an unconventional but delightful accompaniment.*

2 pounds boneless pork shoulder, cut into 1½-inch cubes

1½ cups sour orange juice or ¾ cup each lime and regular orange juice

1 large onion, peeled and chopped

2 garlic cloves, peeled and minced

2 jalapeño peppers, seeded and minced

1 sprig fresh parsley

1 teaspoon kosher salt

½ teaspoon freshly ground black pepper

Vegetable oil

Combine the pork and ½ cup of the sour orange juice in a nonaluminum bowl and toss to cover the pork well. Drain in a colander.

Combine the pork, the remaining juice, onion, garlic, jalapeños, parsley, salt, and pepper in a self-sealing food storage bag. Refrigerate for at least 1 hour or as long as overnight.

Pour the pork and marinade into a large, heavy skillet and add just enough water to cover the meat. Bring to a boil, lower the heat, and simmer, uncovered, until the meat is very tender and the liquid has evaporated, about 1 hour.

Remove the meat with tongs and wipe out the pan, discarding the solids. Heat a thin layer of oil over medium-high heat. Fry the pork, stirring often, until browned and crisp on all sides. Serve hot.

Cuban Sandwich

[2 SERVINGS]

If your sandwich is flattened, it usually means somebody has made a mistake—unless it's a Cuban sandwich. At Miami lunch counters, this crisp-on-the-outside, soft-on-the-inside treat is made in a special press called a plancha, *but you can achieve much the same effect with an oven and a cast-iron skillet. Use soft supermarket-quality bread; baguettes are too crisp to flatten. The* media noche *variation, which literally means "midnight," is a favorite after-movie snack.*

> 1 loaf Cuban, French, or Italian bread, sliced lengthwise
>
> 2 tablespoons mayonnaise
>
> 12 small dill pickles, thinly sliced lengthwise
>
> 2 slices Swiss cheese
>
> ¼ pound sliced roast pork
>
> ¼ pound sliced boiled or baked ham
>
> 1 tablespoon butter, softened

Preheat the oven to 350 degrees.

Spread both cut surfaces of the bread with mayonnaise. Layer one half with pickle slices, cheese, pork, and ham, and cover with the second half. Slice the bread diagonally into 2 sandwiches.

Place the sandwiches side by side on a baking pan and spread the tops with butter. Shield the sandwiches with a piece of foil and place a cast-iron skillet on top of them, pressing down to flatten them.

Bake for 15 to 20 minutes, until the cheese melts and the sandwiches are crisp and piping hot. Serve immediately.

VARIATION: To make a *media noche*, substitute two long, soft rolls for the bread and spread mustard and softened butter on the roll along with the mayonnaise.

Fresh herbs will keep well for more than a week if you put them in a jar or glass, like a bouquet of flowers, add enough water to cover the stems by about an inch, cover the tops with a plastic bag, and refrigerate. (They're less likely to get knocked over if you put them in the door.) Change the water every couple of days and discard any slimy or yellowed stalks. Just before using them, wash the herbs under cold running water and dry with paper towels or, for a big batch, in a salad spinner.

Cilantro stems are so tender that they can be used along with the leaves, but you should remove the tough stems from basil and most other leafy herbs. (Save the stems in the freezer and toss them into the stockpot the next time you make broth.)

Dill and chives are best snipped with kitchen shears (they get watery if minced). Other fresh herbs can be minced in a food processor (use the pulse setting and be careful not to turn them into mush). You can control the consistency better if you cut them by hand with a large, sharp French chef's knife. Here are some pointers:

- Roll large leaves like basil into a tight bundle and slice the bundle crosswise into thin strips; to mince, cut across the strips.
- Twist the leaves and tender outer stems of curly parsley into a tight bundle and cut as described above.
- Stack small leaves like Italian parsley on a cutting board, place the tip of your knife on the board, and rock the handle up and down, moving the blade back and forth across the leaves until cut to the desired size.

For best flavor and color, add fresh herbs during the last twenty minutes of cooking.

Leg of Lamb Florida Style

[8 SERVINGS]

At Easter time, when winter is just loosening its grip on much of the country, Miami is reveling in its most glorious weather of the year—sunny 70-degree days, comfortably cool nights, and low humidity. (Don't get too jealous; while northerners are greeting summer with Memorial Day barbecues, chances are we're wading through a monsoonlike May deluge.)

We planned an al fresco Easter menu featuring this savory grilled lamb, Warm Yuca Salad (page 81), Gingered Banana Chutney (page 264), grilled spring vegetables, and tropical fruit sundaes. It's a festive meal you'll enjoy serving no matter the time of year. (The indoor version makes the lamb a cold weather option, too.) Use merlot or pinot noir in the marinade and serve the rest of the bottle with dinner.

FOR THE MARINADE:

¼ cup olive oil

⅓ cup red wine vinegar

⅓ cup dry red wine

4 jalapeño peppers, seeded and chopped

2 tablespoons Dijon-style mustard

¼ cup chopped fresh rosemary, basil, parsley, oregano, and/or thyme

4 garlic cloves, peeled and minced

⅓ cup fresh orange juice

½ teaspoon freshly ground pepper

TO FINISH THE DISH:

1 6-pound leg of lamb, boned and butterflied (see Note)

1 8-ounce can tomato sauce

3 tablespoons honey

Kosher salt

Fresh rosemary sprigs for garnish

Stir together the oil, vinegar, wine, jalapeños, mustard, fresh herbs, garlic, orange juice, and pepper in a small bowl.

Trim the fat and fell (the paper-thin, pinkish red layer) from the surface of the lamb. Place in a shallow nonaluminum pan or a jumbo self-sealing plastic bag. Reserve ½ cup of the marinade and pour the rest over the meat, turning to coat. Cover tightly or seal the bag and refrigerate for at least 8 hours and preferably overnight.

Combine the reserved marinade, tomato sauce, and honey in a small bowl to use for basting.

Let the meat stand at room temperature for 1 hour before cooking. Discard the marinade, pat the meat dry with paper towels, and season with salt.

TO GRILL: Use indirect, medium heat (see page 100).

Coat the grill rack lightly with vegetable oil. Grill the meat, turning once, for 40 to 45 minutes total. (If your grill has a cover, use it.) Begin checking the meat after 30 minutes. During the last 10 minutes, brush the meat frequently with the basting sauce. Check the meat at its thickest point with an instant-read thermometer; it should register 125 degrees for rare, 130 degrees for medium rare (it will continue cooking off the heat).

TO BROIL: Preheat the broiler to its highest setting. Place the meat, fat side down, on a rack in a broiler pan. (Line the pan with foil first for easier cleanup.) Place the meat about 5 inches from the heating element and broil for about 15 minutes, until well browned, basting it a few times. Turn it with a 2-pronged fork and broil for 15 to 20 minutes more, basting again, to the desired degree of doneness.

Let the meat rest for 10 to 15 minutes before carving it against the grain into diagonal slices. Arrange on a platter and garnish with rosemary sprigs.

In a small saucepan, heat any remaining basting sauce to a full boil and cook for about 3 minutes. Pass it with the meat.

VARIATION: You can use 1½ teaspoons each of dried rosemary, leaf oregano, basil, and thyme in place of the fresh herbs.

NOTE: A butterflied leg is a boned leg of lamb that has been split almost in half and spread open like a book for easy grilling. Ask your butcher to butterfly it for you. The meat is thicker in the center than at the edges, which gives you a range of doneness choices—medium-rare to medium—to offer your guests.

Rack of Lamb with Coriander Marinade

[4 SERVINGS]

The coriander plant grows where the sun is hot—Asia, Latin America, and the Mediterranean. Its aromatic seeds and pungent leaves are most often associated with Asian and Middle Eastern cooking, but cilantro leaves (their Spanish name) are widely used in the Caribbean, Latin America, and Mexico. The seeds and leaves work together beautifully in this marinade, and the lemon juice accentuates the lemony flavor of the seeds.

A well-trimmed rack of lamb makes a sophisticated and surprisingly easy dinner party entree. The lamb roasts at 450 degrees, rests briefly, and finishes at 400 degrees, giving it a rich brown color and preserving its tenderness. Put it in the oven when your guests arrive, and you'll be able to enjoy the cocktail hour with just a few brief trips to the kitchen. You'll need only 5 minutes to carve and present the lamb.

Cream of carrot soup, Baby Greens and Arugula with Fat-Free Papaya-Mint Dressing (page 75), Bogotá-Style Potatoes (page 248), and Individual Chocolate–Cuban Coffee Soufflés (page 312) would complete the menu beautifully.

MARINADE:

1½ teaspoons whole coriander seeds

1 teaspoon black peppercorns

¼ teaspoon cayenne

3 garlic cloves, peeled

2 tablespoons chopped fresh cilantro

1 tablespoon olive oil

2 tablespoons fresh lemon juice

TO FINISH THE DISH:

2 trimmed racks of lamb (about 6 ribs each; about 4 pounds total) (see Notes)

Kosher salt

Cilantro sprigs for garnish

To bring out the flavor of the coriander seeds, roast them in a dry skillet over medium heat until very aromatic, about 3 minutes. Combine in a mini-chopper or blender with the peppercorns, cayenne, garlic, cilantro, oil, and lemon juice, and process until smooth.

Place the racks of lamb in a self-sealing food storage bag and coat completely with the herb paste. Seal the bag and refrigerate for at least 6 hours or as long as 24 hours.

Remove the lamb from the refrigerator 1 hour before roasting.

Preheat the oven to 450 degrees. Remove the lamb from the marinade; discard the marinade. Pat the lamb dry with paper towels and season with salt.

Place the racks of lamb, meat side down, in a small, shallow roasting pan (a 9-inch cast-iron skillet works well) and interlace the ribs to form an arch.

Place the pan in the center of the oven and roast the lamb for 15 minutes. Remove from the oven and lower the temperature to 400 degrees.

When the oven has reached the lower temperature, about 10 minutes, return the lamb to the oven. (If you need a little extra time—guests are late or you're not quite ready—you could wait 20 minutes, but no more.) Roast the meat for about 15 minutes. It's done when it feels springy to the touch and registers 125 to 130 degrees for medium-rare on an instant-read thermometer. (The lamb will dry and toughen if cooked beyond that point.)

Let the meat rest on the counter for 10 minutes before serving. Meanwhile, warm 4 dinner plates in the turned-off oven.

Carve the racks into separate rib portions. Arrange 2 or 3 in an overlapping pattern on each warmed plate. Garnish with cilantro leaves and serve immediately.

VARIATION: This marinade is also wonderful with a pork rib roast.

NOTES:

- To simplify carving, ask the butcher to remove the chine bone from the racks of lamb and make ½-inch cuts between the ribs.
- For the most attractive presentation, "french" the racks of lamb: Trim all but a thin coating of fat from the meaty side of the racks. Turn them fat side down and score each rib about 2½ inches below the tip. Remove the fat and meat (there won't be much) above the cut and scrape the bones clean. (An accommodating butcher will do this for you.)

Ground spices and dried herbs lose their potency over time, so it's best to buy them in the small quantities and replace them after six months. (Write the purchase date on the package to keep track.) Store them in a cool, dry place (not next to the stove!) and keep red spices like paprika, chili powder, cayenne, and red pepper flakes in the refrigerator.

Buying and grinding whole spices—in a coffee mill reserved for that purpose—will give you the best possible flavor. Whole nutmeg, allspice, and cloves are sold in many supermarkets, and a whole host of others are available by mail order. (Penzeys in Muskego, Wisconsin, is one reputable source; call 414-574-0277 for a catalog.)

You can punch up the flavor of whole spices by toasting them. Spread on a baking sheet in a 350-degree oven or in a dry skillet over medium heat for a few minutes until they become aromatic.

Dry-leaf spices like oregano and thyme will impart more flavor to a dish if you rub them between your fingertips first to crumble them. (Another method, recommended by Mediterranean cooking expert Paula Wolfert, is to push the dried herbs through a mesh sieve.) When combining a lot of herbs and spices, it's easiest to measure them all into a small container like a custard cup and then rub to crumble and mix them at once.

The Main Course 3: Seafood

Jerk-Fried Snapper with Banana-Orange Rum Sauce

Oven-Steamed Yellowtail with Roasted Tomato Sauce

Grouper with Malanga-Pecan Crust

Mahi-mahi (Dolphin) with Cilantro Pesto and Roasted Red Pepper Sauce

Coconut Mahi-mahi with Passion Fruit Sauce

Cornmeal-Coated Catfish with Black Bean–Mango Salsa

Grilled Tuna Steaks with Avocado, Corn, and Tomato Salsa

Grilled Swordfish with Lime, Jalapeño, and Sour Cream Sauce

Grilled Ginger-Pepper Salmon with Boniato Puree and Shallot Sauce

Cashew-Crusted Pompano

Escovitch or Pescado en Escabeche (Pickled Fish)

Shrimp Creole

Gingered Shrimp and Star Fruit on a Stick

Paella Marina

Stone Crabs

South Florida is a seafood lover's paradise, and our rich harvest of recipes ranges from Cashew-Crusted Pompano to Shrimp Creole to Grilled Swordfish with Lime, Jalapeño, and Sour Cream Sauce. Throughout the country, fresh fish and shellfish are more readily available than ever. Packed on ice and shipped by air, they're often sold thousands of miles from where they were caught. Here in Miami, sushi-quality tuna is jetted off to Japan, and farm-raised salmon is imported from Chile. No matter where you live, you have a better chance than ever of finding Florida-caught seafood or a good alternative in your market. Here's a guide to the most popular of the sixty-plus species fished commercially here.

FLOUNDER: Gulf, southern, and summer flounder and southern fluke are the most popular Florida flatfish. They average three to five pounds but can weigh as much as twenty pounds. Smaller ones are sold whole, while larger flounders make excellent fillets and, occasionally, steaks. Their lean, firm, yet delicate flesh has a fine texture and mild flavor that make it good for baking, broiling, panfrying, or poaching.

Alternatives: sea bass, sea trout, gray sole, plaice, snapper.

GROUPER: Members of the sea bass family, groupers range in size from a few pounds to over one hundred pounds. Black, red, and yellow-edge are the most common South Florida varieties, and along with snappers they're a mainstay of commercial fishing—the "beef cattle" of Florida waters, as a fisherman friend puts it. The grouper has no intermuscular bones, which makes it ideal for filleting. Its firm, lean, mild-tasting white meat holds together well when cut into chunks for kebabs or chowder. It is well suited to nearly any cooking method but can get chewy if overdone. The strong-tasting skin should be removed before cooking.

Alternatives: tilefish, monkfish, dolphin (mahi-mahi), snapper, halibut, pike, sea bass, haddock, cod.

KING MACKEREL (KINGFISH): King mackerel ranges from five to twenty pounds but has been known to reach one hundred pounds. Because it is so large, it is one of the few mackerels that can be bought as steaks. It has a high oil content, blue-tinged flesh that whitens when cooked, and an intense flavor that is an acquired taste. It is often served *en escabeche* (page 204) or smoked.

Alternatives: bluefish and both freshwater and sea trout.

MAHI-MAHI (DOLPHIN): Increasingly labeled by its Hawaiian name to avoid confusion with the marine mammal, mahi-mahi ranges in size from three to forty-five pounds and is sold in steaks and fillets. It is a moderately fat fish with firm, sweet white meat that can be baked, fried, poached, or grilled. When cooking outdoors, leave the skin on to hold the meat together on the grill.

Alternatives: grouper, tilefish, snapper, cod, halibut, striped bass.

POMPANO: A member of the jack family, the Florida pompano is caught mainly in Gulf Coast waters and is widely considered the best-tasting commercial fish around. It is small, topping out at about eight pounds and typically weighing one or two pounds. Its tender, delicately flavored light meat has a relatively high oil content and is excellent sautéed, broiled, grilled, or baked—especially *en papillote* (in paper).

Alternatives: Although there is no substitute for pompano's distinctive flavor, snapper or salmon can be used in many of the same recipes.

SNAPPER: Red snapper—a gorgeous rose-colored fish with a silver-pink belly and red eyes—is the most highly prized local variety, but mangrove, mutton, hog, and yellowtail snapper are also popular. Depending on the type, snappers can weigh as much as forty pounds, but most of those caught commercially are under ten pounds. Smaller snappers are sold whole, and larger ones are cut into fillets and steaks. The firm, lean, mild white meat can be cooked almost any way.

Alternatives: flounder, ocean perch, orange roughy, cod.

SWORDFISH: Named for the long, slender bill that juts from its upper jaw, swordfish can weigh more than one thousand pounds and is popular with game and commercial fishermen alike. Its firm, dark meat has a surprisingly mild flavor and a relatively high oil content, and is well suited to grilling, broiling, smoking, and braising. Like tuna it is best cooked quickly on the grill to prevent drying.

Alternatives: shark, tuna, marlin, wahoo (ono).

TUNA: A member of the mackerel family, tuna is in a class of its own as far as cooks are concerned. The bulk of Florida's tuna catch is yellowfin, which weigh upwards of three hundred pounds and have relatively delicate-flavored pink meat, and blackfin, which range from eight to sixty pounds and have more assertive red flesh. Fresh tuna is sold in both fillets and steaks. Its firm meat and high oil content make it ideal for broiling or grilling, but it is best cooked quickly and not past medium-rare to preserve its moistness.

Alternatives: swordfish, shark, wahoo, or marlin can be substituted in most tuna recipes.

SHOPPING AND STORAGE

It is essential to start with truly fresh fish. That means you need to be flexible; if you set out looking for grouper and find that the flounder is fresher, buy it and adjust your menu accordingly.

Shop at a busy store that has a high turnover.

Make sure the fish is embedded in ice in the display case, not just sitting on top.

Take a good whiff of the fish; it should have a pleasant sea-brine aroma, not a "fishy" smell.

If possible, buy a whole fish and have it cut into steaks or fillets. You'll be much better able to judge its freshness that way. (Take the head and bones home, too, and use them to cook stock.)

In a whole fish, the eyes should be full and slightly bulging, not sunken. (Bright, clear eyes indicate freshness, but cloudy eyes don't necessarily mean the fish is old.) Eyes can get damaged in handling, so gills can be a more reliable indicator of freshness. They should be bright pink or red, not brownish or greenish. Unfortunately, some retailers cut out the gills so it's impossible to check.

• In fillets and steaks, look for shiny white or pink meat with no yellowing or black spots. It should be compact, with no separating along the crevices of the tissue.

• In both whole and cut fish, the flesh should be firm and elastic to the touch; if it remains dented when you remove your finger, it isn't fresh.

• As soon as you get home, rinse the fish in cold water and loosely wrap it in plastic wrap. Cover the bottom of a deep tray with ice, place the wrapped fish on top, and cover it with more ice. Store it in the coldest part of the refrigerator until you're ready to use it—ideally the same day, but never more than two days. If the ice melts, drain off the water and add fresh ice.

• If you're not able to serve the fish as soon as you had planned, cook and refrigerate it. It won't taste quite as good reheated as fresh-cooked, but it won't go to waste and will keep for two to three days in the refrigerator.

COOKING TIPS

• When coating fish with flour, do so just before sautéing it. If left to sit, the flour will get soggy and won't produce a crisp crust.

• When sautéing, broiling, or grilling, turn the fish just once; overhandling can make it fall apart.

• Whatever the cooking method, the easiest and worst mistake is overcooking. A long-standing and fairly reliable rule of thumb is to allow ten minutes per inch of thickness at the thickest point of the fish. Exceptions are tuna, which is best cooked medium-rare, and heavily coated fish, which may take longer.

• To test most fish for doneness, insert the tip of a sharp knife and take a look inside. Remove from the heat when the fish is opaque throughout but before it fully flakes. Like all foods, fish cooks a bit more off the heat.

Jerk-Fried Snapper with Banana-Orange Rum Sauce

[4 SERVINGS]

Snapper is a fish lover's favorite for its firm texture and delicate flavor, and any variety—red, mangrove, hog, or mutton snapper, for example—will work well here. A dusting of jerk-seasoned flour helps the fish hold its own with the sweet and tangy rum-based sauce—a delightfully rich-tasting concoction that would be wonderful served over vanilla or coconut ice cream, too.

Alternatives: mahi-mahi (dolphin), flounder, halibut, orange roughy, cod, or other firm white-fleshed fish.

2 oranges

2 firm, ripe bananas or 4 "finger" bananas

½ cup flour

1 tablespoon Jerk Seasoning (page 99) or commercial jerk blend

1 tablespoon vegetable oil

3 tablespoons unsalted butter

4 skinless 6-ounce snapper fillets

2 tablespoons brown sugar

¼ cup dark rum

2 tablespoons fresh lime juice

Kosher salt and freshly ground pepper

Lime wedges for garnish

Peel and section the oranges and cut the sections into ½-inch triangles (discard the seeds). Peel the bananas and cut them on the diagonal into 1-inch slices. Toss the orange and banana slices together, then set aside. (The orange juice will keep the bananas from browning.)

Mix the flour and Jerk Seasoning together well in a shallow plate.

Heat the oil and 1 tablespoon of the butter in a large skillet over medium-high heat.

Coat the fillets well with the flour mixture, shake off the excess, and sauté them, turning once, until just opaque, about 3 minutes per side for ½-inch-thick fillets. Transfer the fish to a warm platter and cover.

Wipe out the skillet with paper towels. Reduce the heat to medium, add the remaining 2 tablespoons of butter, and cook until nut brown and foaming.

Stir in the brown sugar until blended. Stir in the rum and lime juice, raise the heat to medium-high, and bring the mixture to a boil. Cook, stirring, for about 3 minutes, until slightly reduced and thickened.

Stir in the reserved orange and banana slices. Coat well with the sauce and cook for 1 minute. Taste for seasoning and add salt and pepper if you like.

Spoon the sauce over the fish, garnish with lime wedges, and serve immediately.

VARIATIONS:

- Sliced ripe plantain and cubed mango, papaya, and/or pineapple can be used in place of some or all of the bananas and oranges.
- Add 1 or 2 tablespoons of chopped pecans or macadamias with the fruit.

NOTE: When frying fish, be sure the fat is hot before adding the fish to the pan or it will stick. Butter alone burns easily; a combination of butter and oil eliminates that problem while still giving the fish a buttery flavor.

Oven-Steamed Yellowtail with Roasted Tomato Sauce

[6 SERVINGS]

Yellowtail is another popular variety of snapper, easy to spot by the yellow stripe that runs its length. In this recipe the thin fillets are steamed quickly in a hot oven to preserve their moistness and are served with a rich-tasting Roasted Tomato Sauce.

Alternatives: ¼-inch-thick red snapper, orange roughy, or flounder fillets, or salmon cut on the diagonal into thin slices.

Vegetable oil or vegetable oil spray
6 skinless 6-ounce yellowtail fillets, about ¼ inch thick
Kosher salt and freshly ground pepper
Roasted Tomato Sauce (recipe follows), warmed
Chopped cilantro or flat-leaf parsley for garnish

Place an oven rack in the bottom position and preheat the oven to 500 degrees. Lightly brush or spray a baking sheet with oil.

Arrange the fillets in a single layer on the baking sheet. Wet the palm of your hand under cold running water and pat the top of a fillet to moisten the fish slightly. Repeat with the rest of the fillets and season them well with salt and pepper.

Place the baking sheet on the bottom oven rack and bake the fish for 2 to 3 minutes, checking after 1½ minutes. Remove as soon as opaque throughout.

Spoon the warm sauce onto 6 dinner plates and top with the fish. Sprinkle with cilantro and serve immediately.

Roasted Tomato Sauce

[ABOUT 2 CUPS]

Roasting concentrates the mellow sweetness of the tomatoes. A hint of orange zest and balsamic vinegar gives the simple sauce a surprisingly complex flavor that you can enjoy on pasta, too.

> 5 tablespoons extra-virgin olive oil, plus more for the pan
>
> 4 large, ripe tomatoes (about 2 pounds), halved and seeded
>
> 1 garlic clove, peeled
>
> 1 teaspoon brown sugar
>
> 1 teaspoon grated orange zest
>
> 2 tablespoons balsamic vinegar
>
> ¼ teaspoon kosher salt
>
> ¼ teaspoon freshly ground pepper

Preheat the oven to 425 degrees.

Lightly brush or spray a baking sheet with oil and arrange the tomato halves on it, cut side down. Roast for 10 minutes.

Remove the tomatoes from the oven and use a fork or tongs to pull off the skins (they should come off easily). Drizzle the tomatoes with 3 tablespoons of the oil and roast for 25 to 30 minutes more, until very soft and dark red.

Scrape the tomatoes into the container of a blender or food processor. Add the garlic, brown sugar, orange zest, vinegar, and the remaining 2 tablespoons of oil. Process until smooth. Season with salt and pepper, and serve warm.

PLANNING AHEAD: You can roast the tomatoes 1 or 2 days in advance and refrigerate them, well covered, but for the best flavor, make the sauce no more than a couple of hours ahead.

VARIATION: Turn the sauce into a luscious vinaigrette by adding 3 additional tablespoons of olive oil and 2 additional tablespoons of balsamic vinegar.

When you try to imagine Italian or Spanish cuisine without tomatoes, you get a sense of the revolutionary impact that Columbus and company had on the world's eating habits. The tomato plant originated in the Andes, although the Incas didn't cultivate it. It was the Aztecs who named the plant *tomatl* and learned to cook with it. Conquistadors encountered it in Mexico and brought it back to Spain in the 1520s.

The tomato gradually caught on with continental cooks, but the English and their North American colonists resisted its charms, fearing that, like other members of the nightshade family, the tomato was poisonous. Although Thomas Jefferson grew tomatoes at Monticello, they weren't widely used in the United States until after the Civil War. Botanically the tomato is a fruit, but it was ruled a vegetable for trade purposes in 1893 by the U.S. Supreme Court.

The farming region south of Miami is a major producer of winter tomatoes, and we enjoy luscious vine-ripened tomatoes from November to May. Unfortunately, Florida tomatoes have a less-than-wonderful reputation in the rest of the country. Mishandling is a major reason: To withstand the trip north, tomatoes are usually shipped unripe, and many consumers make the mistake of refrigerating them that way. In fact, refrigeration prevents a tomato from ripening properly and kills its flavor. The solution is to leave unripe tomatoes at room temperature until they're a deep red, and then use them right away. Leftover ripe tomatoes can be refrigerated for a day or so but should be left at room temperature for an hour or two before serving to improve their flavor.

Grouper with Malanga-Pecan Crust

[4 SERVINGS]

Malanga is an especially starchy tropical tuber that provides plenty of sticking power to this nutty coating. Pickapeppa (page 98), our favorite Jamaican condiment, adds a dash of spice, and the fish fries up sweet and crisp. Use baking potatoes if malanga isn't available, and try this tropical treatment on flattened chicken breast halves, too.

Alternatives: snapper, mahi-mahi (dolphin), ocean perch, sea bass, halibut or any firm white-fleshed fish fillet.

> ⅓ cup pecan pieces
>
> 1½ pounds malanga
>
> Kosher salt and freshly ground pepper
>
> 4 skinless 6-ounce grouper fillets
>
> 2 tablespoons Pickapeppa sauce (or 1 tablespoon each ketchup and Worcestershire sauce)
>
> 8 tablespoons vegetable oil
>
> 4 tablespoons snipped fresh chives

Pulse the pecans in a food processor until finely ground but not pasty.

Peel the malanga and grate it on the large holes of a box grater or with the medium shredding disk of the food processor.

Mix the pecans and malanga well, and season to taste with salt and pepper.

Sprinkle the fillets with salt and pepper, and brush with Pickapeppa sauce.

Press a ¼-inch layer of the pecan-malanga mixture onto the side of each fillet opposite the skinned side.

Divide the oil between 2 nonstick skillets and heat over high until hot but not smoking.

Turn the heat down to medium-high and place 2 fillets, coating side down, in each pan. Sauté until golden brown, 4 or 5 minutes, lowering the heat if necessary to keep the crust from burning. Turn the fish and cook, skin side down, for 4 or 5 minutes more, just until opaque throughout.

Transfer the fish to dinner plates, crust side up. Garnish with chives and serve immediately.

PLANNING AHEAD: You can coat the fish and refrigerate it, covered, for up to 4 hours. If you sauté it straight from the refrigerator, allow an extra 1 or 2 minutes for it to cook.

Mahi-mahi (Dolphin) with Cilantro Pesto and Roasted Red Pepper Sauce

[4 SERVINGS]

Mahi-mahi is the Hawaiian name for dolphin, a firm-fleshed fish abundant in Florida's warm coastal waters. Though many locals find it a bit silly, mahi-mahi is becoming the name of choice here, too, in deference to diners who can't order dolphin without thinking of Flipper, the most famous of those other dolphins, the marine mammals.

Whatever you call it, it's a moist, flavorful fish with a tough skin that should be removed before cooking and dark-colored flesh that turns white when cooked. It is showcased in this recipe with a robust, bright green cilantro pesto and a mellow red bell pepper sauce—a feast for the eyes as well as the taste buds. If you adore cilantro, use the full amount for the pesto; if you like it in moderation, use a fifty-fifty blend of cilantro and flat-leaf parsley. If you don't like it at all, substitute the traditional basil or skip the pesto and simply serve the fish with the red pepper sauce.

Alternatives: any firm-fleshed fish such as cod or salmon cut 1 inch thick.

> 4 1-inch-thick mahi-mahi steaks or fillets, about 6 ounces each
> Olive oil
> Kosher salt and freshly ground pepper
> Roasted Red Pepper Sauce (recipe follows), warmed
> Cilantro Pesto (recipe follows)

Brush the fish with the oil and season with salt and pepper.

TO GRILL: Use direct, medium heat (see page 100). Coat the grill rack lightly with oil, and if adjustable, position it about 4 inches from the fire.

TO BROIL: Preheat the broiler, positioning a rack so the fish will be about 4 inches from the heat source.

Cook the fish, turning once, until nicely browned on both sides and just done in the center, 8 to 10 minutes total. The flesh will be white all the way through and will barely separate into flakes when pierced with the tip of a knife.

Spoon a pool of Roasted Red Pepper Sauce onto each of 4 dinner plates. Top the sauce with the fish, and top each piece of fish with a tablespoon of Cilantro Pesto. Serve immediately.

PLANNING AHEAD: If you make and refrigerate the sauces early in the day—or even the day before—you can put this dish together in less than 30 minutes. Let the pesto come to room temperature and reheat the roasted pepper sauce before serving.

VARIATIONS: Try this sauce and pesto combination with sautéed veal scallops or boneless chicken breasts. Or toss hot pasta with the pesto and top it with the sauce.

Roasted Red Pepper Sauce

[1½ CUPS]

4 large red bell peppers

¼ cup dry white wine

1 teaspoon minced shallots

1 tablespoon unsalted butter (optional)

Kosher salt and freshly ground pepper

Roast, core, and peel the peppers (see Roasting Peppers, page 190)

Combine the wine and shallots in a saucepan and boil over high heat until reduced by half, about 2 minutes.

Combine the wine reduction and peppers in a food processor or blender and process until smooth.

Return the puree to the saucepan and boil over high heat until reduced to 1½ cups, 6 to 8 minutes. Remove from the heat, whisk in the butter until melted, and season to taste with salt and pepper.

Cilantro Pesto

[ABOUT ¼ CUP]

This gorgeous green pesto has a pungent, peppery taste. For the best possible flavor, use Parmigiano-Reggiano cheese. Leftovers are superb on pasta. Use the larger measure of olive oil for a thinner pesto.

2 ounces Parmesan cheese, cut into chunks

3 medium garlic cloves, peeled

⅓ cup walnuts

½ to ¾ cup extra-virgin olive oil

2 cups coarsely chopped cilantro leaves and stems, slightly packed
   (or 1 cup each cilantro and flat-leaf parsley)

Kosher salt and freshly ground pepper

Process the cheese in a food processor until finely ground. With the motor running, add the garlic, then the walnuts and oil, processing until smooth. Stop the processor, add the cilantro, and pulse until smooth, scraping down the sides once or twice if necessary. Season to taste with salt and pepper. The pesto will keep, covered, for up to 2 weeks in the refrigerator. Pour a thin layer of olive oil over the surface to preserve the bright green color. Let it return to room temperature before using.

VARIATION: To make in a blender, grate the cheese before proceeding as described above.

Roasting peppers intensifies their flavor and adds a rich smokiness. Here are three good ways to do it:

- On a grill over a medium fire, about 4 inches from the heat, roast the peppers whole, turning several times, until they are blistered and lightly charred on all sides, 10 to 15 minutes.
- In the oven, place halved peppers, cut side down, on a baking sheet and put about 4 inches from a preheated broiler until roasted as described above.
- On the stovetop of a gas range, hold a pepper over the flame with tongs or a large two-tined fork and turn until roasted on all sides. (This works best if you need to roast just one pepper; protect your hand with a pot holder or oven mitt, or the tongs will get too hot to hold.)

Once roasted, put the peppers in a bowl and cover with plastic wrap. Let steam for 20 minutes to loosen the skin, then scrape it away with a table knife (it's okay if bits of charred skin remain). Resist the temptation to rinse them, or you'll wash away flavor. Core and seed the peppers, and cut them as your recipe directs.

Coconut Mahi-mahi
with Passion Fruit Sauce

[4 SERVINGS]

If you've never enjoyed the rich, subtle sweetness of coconut au naturel, *you're in for a treat. It has a much more interesting flavor than the heavily sweetened kind you sprinkle on cakes. You'll find unsweetened coconut in health food stores and some supermarkets, or if you're ambitious, you can buy a fresh coconut and grate your own (see page 6). Here the coconut forms a crisp yet moist coating for mahi-mahi fillets that are served with a rich, tangy-sweet passion fruit sauce. Gingery Fat-Free Banana–Poppy Seed Dressing (page 74) also makes an excellent sauce here.*

Alternatives: *Snapper, halibut, cod, or any firm, white-fleshed fish.*

1 cup shredded unsweetened coconut	4 6-ounce mahi-mahi fillets, about ½ inch thick
¾ cup flour	Freshly ground pepper
½ cup milk	2 tablespoons vegetable oil
2 eggs	2 tablespoons unsalted butter
Kosher salt	Passion Fruit Sauce (recipe follows)

Put the coconut, flour, milk, and eggs in separate shallow dishes. Beat the eggs well with 1 teaspoon of salt.

Set a wire rack over a cookie sheet.

Sprinkle the fillets with salt and pepper. Dip them one at a time in the milk, the flour, the egg mixture, and then the coconut, coating them well on both sides. Set the fillets on the rack and refrigerate for at least 10 minutes to help the coating adhere.

Heat the oil and butter in a 12-inch skillet over medium-high heat. Sauté the fillets, turning once, until the coconut is golden brown and the fish is opaque throughout, about 8 minutes total.

Transfer the fish to dinner plates, drizzle with Passion Fruit Sauce, and serve immediately.

PLANNING AHEAD: You can coat and refrigerate the fish, covered, for up to 3 or 4 hours before cooking.

NOTES:

- Butter alone burns easily at high temperatures; combining it with vegetable oil lets you get the pan hot enough for sautéing and still enjoy a buttery taste.
- It is important not to turn fish—especially coated fish—more than once while sautéing because it tends to fall apart.
- Beating the eggs with salt breaks up the whites and makes for a more even coating (no globs of white).

Passion Fruit Sauce

[ABOUT ½ CUP]

Look for passion fruit puree in the freezer case of supermarkets with a Hispanic clientele. If you can't find it, substitute unreconstituted pineapple juice concentrate.

> ½ cup dry white wine
> 2 shallots, peeled and minced
> 2 teaspoons fresh lime juice
> ¼ cup passion fruit puree
> 4 tablespoons unsalted butter

Bring the wine, shallots, lime juice, and passion fruit puree to a boil in a small, heavy saucepan. Let it cook down until it is reduced to ⅓ cup, about 5 minutes.

Remove the pan from the heat and whisk in the butter until melted and the sauce is slightly thickened. Serve immediately.

Cornmeal-Coated Catfish with Black Bean–Mango Salsa

[4 SERVINGS]

A sensational salsa adds a tropical twist to an old-time favorite that recalls Miami's southern roots. In days gone by, people elsewhere in the country considered wild catfish a "trash" fish that only southerners could love, probably because it absorbed the flavors of the muddy river and lake bottoms in which it wallowed. Aquaculture, a big industry in Florida, has changed all that. The farm-raised, grain-fed catfish sold today in markets nationwide has a mild, almost sweet flavor and firm texture that makes it suitable for nearly any cooking method. Here it is soaked in buttermilk for a bit of tang, coated in flour and cornmeal, and fried up crisp and moist.

Alternatives: grouper, halibut, red snapper, or flounder fillets; if thicker than ½ inch, allow extra cooking time.

4 8-ounce catfish fillets
1 cup buttermilk
⅓ cup cornmeal
⅓ cup flour
Kosher salt and freshly ground pepper
¼ cup vegetable oil
Black Bean–Mango Salsa (recipe follows)

Place the catfish in the buttermilk in a shallow dish and refrigerate for 30 minutes. Meanwhile, mix the cornmeal and flour well in a shallow dish.

Remove the catfish from the buttermilk, shake off the excess, and season the fish liberally with salt and pepper. Dip the fish in the cornmeal mixture, coating both sides well.

Heat the oil in a 12-inch nonstick skillet over medium-high heat. Add the fish and lower the heat to medium. Fry, turning once, until nicely browned and just cooked through, about 3 minutes per side. Transfer to plates and serve immediately with the Black Bean–Mango Salsa on the side.

Black Bean–Mango Salsa

[ABOUT 4 CUPS]

The pineapple's acidic edge is the perfect foil for the mango's luscious sweetness in this wonderfully full-flavored salsa. It's a welcome addition to any meal and makes a great cold salad mixed with an equal amount of cooked rice or orzo. Cut the fruit into ½-inch dice so the pieces are about the same size as the beans.

> 2 cups Basic Black Beans (page 19) or rinsed
>   and drained canned black beans
> 1 cup diced ripe mango
> 1 cup diced fresh pineapple
> 1 or 2 jalapeño peppers, seeded and minced
> ½ cup minced red onion
> 3 tablespoons fresh lime juice
> 1 tablespoon chopped cilantro or flat-leaf parsley
> Kosher salt and freshly ground pepper

Combine the beans, mango, pineapple, jalapeño, onion, lime juice, cilantro, and salt and pepper to taste in a nonaluminum bowl. Cover and chill for at least 1 hour.

VARIATIONS: There's nothing like the taste of fresh pineapple, but canned will do if the fresh fruit is not available. Papaya can be substituted for the mango.

If you haven't cooked fish on the grill, you're in for a treat. When done right, it imparts a hearty, smoky flavor that does as much for a meaty piece of fish as it does for a beefsteak.

The best cuts of fish for grilling are steaks, fillets, or kebabs at least 1 inch thick. Our favorites include swordfish, salmon, grouper, snapper, mahi-mahi (dolphin), whole pompano, tuna, halibut, and monkfish.

To prevent sticking, start with a clean grill rack, heat it over the coals or a fire, and brush or spray it with vegetable oil. To keep the fish from breaking apart, turn it just once and don't move it around. Or better yet, use an oiled grill basket.

Grill fish about 4 inches from the fire. If the fish is ½ inch thick or less, cook it on an open grill over a hot fire in order to sear the flesh quickly. Grill thicker fish on a covered grill over medium-hot coals to keep the outside from overcooking before the inside is done.

Timing, as they say, is everything. Food continues to cook after it is removed from the heat, so take your fish off just before it's cooked all the way through. To test, insert the tip of a metal skewer into the thickest part of the fish; if the skewer slides in easily and the flesh looks barely opaque, take it off the grill.

Grilled Tuna Steaks with Avocado, Corn, and Tomato Salsa

[6 SERVINGS]

Meaty fresh tuna, lightly charred on the outside and silky red on the inside, is sensational on the grill. A few years ago most restaurant diners would have sent back a tuna steak that had been cooked rare, but these days it's a popular and healthful alternative to beefsteak. It's worth the extra money to buy the best-quality tuna you can find—solid-colored meat with little or no connective tissue and no bruises. The brighter red the meat is, the higher its grade. We especially like yellowfin because of its delicate flavor, but blackfin, bluefin, or albacore work well, too.

In this recipe, grilled tuna is paired with a colorful salsa of buttery avocado, crisp corn, and juicy cherry tomatoes that can be made ahead except for adding the avocado. Peel and dice while the tuna is on the grill, and you'll be ready to dish up when the fish is done.

Alternatives: swordfish steaks cut 1¼ inches thick.

6 tuna steaks, preferably yellowfin, cut 1¼ inches thick
Olive oil
Cumin
Salt and freshly ground pepper
Avocado, Corn, and Tomato Salsa (recipe follows)

TO GRILL: Build a hot fire in a charcoal grill (see page 100) and use indirect heat. With a gas grill, use indirect, medium-high heat.

Lightly brush or spray the steaks with oil and sprinkle with cumin, salt, and pepper.

Grill the tuna, turning once, until charred outside and still rare at the center, 2 or 3 minutes per side.

TO COOK INDOORS: Broil the fish about 4 inches from the heat source for 3 to 4 minutes per side.

Transfer the steaks to dinner plates and spoon the salsa on the side.

Avocado, Corn, and Tomato Salsa

[ABOUT 6 CUPS]

The uncooked corn provides a nice crunch.

1 pint cherry tomatoes, stemmed and quartered

2 cups fresh or thawed frozen corn kernels

3 tablespoons fresh lime juice

1 tablespoon chopped fresh cilantro or flat-leaf parsley

Kosher salt and freshly ground pepper

1 ripe medium-size avocado

Combine the tomatoes, corn, lime juice, and cilantro in a nonaluminum container. Toss to combine and add salt and pepper to taste. Refrigerate, covered, for at least 1 hour and as long as 4 hours. Just before serving, peel, seed, and cube the avocado, and toss it with the rest of the ingredients.

NOTE: See page 22 for a neat method of cutting kernels from fresh corn.

Grilled Swordfish with Lime, Jalapeño, and Sour Cream Sauce

[4 SERVINGS]

Swordfish, with their graceful sail-like dorsal fins and dramatic swordlike bills, are a prized and elusive game fish in south Florida. Because they swim deep and are best caught at night, they're worth twice as many points as sailfish and marlin in the area's lucrative catch-and-release billfish tournaments. (The bill—the long, pointed snout—that the fish share is where Billy the Marlin, the mascot of the Florida Marlins baseball team, got his name.) Swordfish are caught commercially from long-line boats that drift heavy fishing line ten or more miles long. They are a prize catch for cooks, too. The firm, dense meat holds together beautifully on the grill, and the mild taste takes to any number of treatments. In this dish the fish gets a quick marinade and is served with a creamy, pleasantly zingy sauce. Have the butter in the pan, the jalapeños cut, and the lime juice squeezed before you begin grilling the fish so you can put the sauce together quickly. (Or make it ahead and reheat it.)

Alternatives: *salmon, bonito, shark, tuna, or kingfish steaks or fillets cut ¾ to 1 inch thick.*

4 6-ounce swordfish steaks, cut ¾ to 1 inch thick

2 tablespoons fresh lime juice

1 tablespoon soy sauce

1 tablespoon melted butter or olive oil

Kosher salt and freshly ground pepper

FOR THE SAUCE:

2 tablespoons unsalted butter

4 jalapeño peppers, seeded and cut into thin strips

¾ cup sour cream

1 tablespoon fresh lime juice

Fresh chives and lime wedges for garnish

Put the swordfish in a shallow nonaluminum pan. Mix the lime juice, soy sauce, and melted butter, and brush it onto both sides of the fish. Season with salt and pepper, and let stand for 10 minutes to absorb the flavors.

TO GRILL: Use indirect, medium heat (see page 100). Coat the grill rack with oil and, if adjustable, position it about 6 inches from the heat.

Grill the fish for about 8 minutes total, turning once and brushing it several times with the remaining lime juice mixture.

TO COOK INDOORS: Broil the fish about 6 inches from the heat source, turning once and basting several times, for about 6 minutes total.

While the fish is cooking, make the sauce: Melt the butter in a small saucepan over medium-low heat. Sauté the jalapeños, stirring, until just tender, about 2 minutes. Stir in the sour cream and leave the pan on the heat just until it's warmed through. (Don't let the sour cream boil, or it will curdle.) Remove the pan from the heat and stir in the lime juice and salt and pepper to taste. Spoon pools of sauce onto 4 dinner plates.

Remove the fish from the grill or broiler as soon as it is opaque throughout and yields easily when pierced with the tip of a sharp knife. Transfer to the plates, garnish with chives and lime wedges, and serve immediately.

PLANNING AHEAD: You can make the sauce anytime during the day the dish will be served and refrigerate it. Heat it through over low heat just before serving, taking care not to boil it.

Grilled Ginger-Pepper Salmon with Boniato Puree and Shallot Sauce

[6 SERVINGS]

Here's a sophisticated, wonderfully flavorful dish that will make your guests feel as though they're dining in a cutting-edge restaurant. The ginger-and-pepper-crusted salmon is served on a bed of softly sweet boniato puree that rests in a pool of buttery, tomato-flecked shallot and white wine sauce. (If you can't find boniatos, substitute potatoes.) The puree and sauce can be made several hours ahead and reheated, and you can have the ginger coating mixed and ready to go, keeping last-minute preparation to a minimum.

Salmon isn't native to south Florida waters, but it's readily available here as elsewhere in the country and takes beautifully to this four-star treatment. To keep it moist, remove it from the grill just before it seems done; it will finish cooking off the heat.

Alternatives: snapper, tuna or swordfish steaks or fillets.

FOR THE SAUCE:

4 tablespoons unsalted butter

1 shallot, peeled and finely chopped

1 garlic clove, peeled and minced

1 ripe tomato, peeled, seeded, and finely chopped

1 cup dry white wine

2 teaspoons fresh lime juice

½ cup chicken broth

Kosher salt and freshly ground pepper

FOR THE FISH:

3 tablespoons finely chopped fresh ginger

3 tablespoons coarsely ground pepper

1 tablespoon olive oil

6 6-ounce salmon fillets or steaks, cut about 1 inch thick

Kosher salt

Boniato Puree (page 218)

Snipped chives for garnish

To make the sauce, melt 1 tablespoon of the butter in a small, heavy saucepan over medium heat until foamy. Sauté the shallot, garlic, and tomato, stirring with a wooden spoon, until the shallot is translucent, about 3 minutes.

Add the wine and lime juice, and continue cooking over medium heat until reduced by half. Add the chicken broth and reduce again by half.

Add the remaining 3 tablespoons of butter and whisk until melted. Season to taste with salt and pepper. Keep the sauce warm over very low heat. (If making ahead, refrigerate it, covered, and warm over low heat before using.)

Mix the ginger, pepper, and oil together in a small bowl. Season the salmon with salt and coat on both sides with the ginger-pepper mixture. Prepare the puree. (If you make the Boniato Puree ahead, warm it in the microwave or in the top of a double boiler over low heat.)

TO GRILL: Use indirect, medium heat (see page 100). Coat the grill rack lightly with oil, and if adjustable, position it about 6 inches from the fire. Grill the salmon for about 4 minutes per side, turning once, until just cooked through.

TO COOK INDOORS: Broil about 6 inches from the heat source for about 4 minutes per side, turning once, until just cooked through.

Meanwhile, ladle pools of sauce onto 6 dinner plates and top each with a generous spoonful of the puree.

Transfer the salmon to the plates, garnish with the chives, and serve immediately.

Cashew-Crusted Pompano

[4 SERVINGS]

Pompano is prized for its distinctively delicate flavor and is usually sold with its silvery skin on so customers can be sure they aren't getting plaice or permit instead. Here, the fish gets a crusty topping of cashews, the sweet nut of the cashew apple tree. It is grown commercially in the West Indies and Brazil, and by hobbyists in south Florida.

Alternatives: snapper, John Dory, flounder, sole, lingcod, blackfish.

1 small garlic clove, peeled

½ cup unsalted cashews

2 tablespoons unsalted butter, softened

2 tablespoons plain dry bread crumbs

3 fresh basil leaves, coarsely chopped

Freshly ground pepper

Kosher salt

4 6-ounce pompano fillets

⅓ cup flour

4 tablespoons vegetable oil

Basil leaves for garnish

With the motor running, drop the garlic through the feeding tube of the food processor and process until chopped. Scrape down the sides, add the cashews, and pulse until the nuts are finely chopped but not pulverized. Add the butter, bread crumbs, basil, and a few grinds of pepper, and pulse until combined. (Or finely chop the nuts, garlic, and basil by hand, and stir together with the butter and bread crumbs.) Taste for seasoning, add salt if you like, and set aside.

With the tip of a sharp knife, score the skin side of the fillets with 3 shallow, diagonal cuts to keep them from curling.

Place the flour in a shallow dish. Season the fillets with salt and pepper, and coat them well on both sides with flour, shaking off the excess.

Preheat the broiler and lightly oil a baking sheet.

Heat the oil in a 12-inch skillet over high heat until shimmering. Add the fillets, skin-side down, and sauté, turning once, just until golden, about 3 minutes total. (The fish should not be cooked through.)

Transfer the fish to the baking sheet, skin side down, and spread the nut mixture over the top. Broil about 5 inches from the heat source until the top browns and the fillets are barely cooked through, about 3 minutes. Transfer to serving plates, garnish with basil, and serve immediately.

PLANNING AHEAD: You can make the nut topping a day or two ahead and refrigerate it, covered. Let it come to room temperature before using.

VARIATIONS: Macadamia nuts, pecans, and pistachios are good choices, too. Any leftover nuts freeze well.

Escovitch or Pescado en Escabeche (Pickled Fish)

[4 MAIN-DISH SERVINGS OR 8 APPETIZER SERVINGS]

Jamaicans call it escovitch; *to Cuban and other Spanish-speaking Caribbean cooks it's* pescado en escabeche, *pickled fish. Its name echoes its kinship to Latin American seviche (see page 37), but in this case the fish is cooked before it is covered with a vinegary marinade. Traditionally, pescado en escabeche (pes-CAH-doh en es-cah-BEH-cheh) is made in a crock and, preserved by its high acid content, is kept at room temperature. We like to use a glass baking dish, store it in the refrigerator, and serve it chilled. For the fullest flavor, make it a day or more ahead; it will keep well for at least two weeks. (The mango provides a wonderfully sweet contrast but holds up well for only a few days, so plan accordingly.) For a Jamaican accent, use the fresh ginger, allspice berries, and hot peppers. Serve with a green salad and crusty bread for a summer buffet. For appetizer portions, cut the sautéed fish into bite-sized pieces after it has cooled.*

Alternatives: swordfish, kingfish, bluefish, mackerel, tuna, mullet, and other dark-fleshed, slightly oily fish are traditional choices for the Hispanic version, while Jamaican cooks favor snapper. Almost any firm-fleshed fish will do, though, including grouper and scrod.

FOR THE FISH:

6 tablespoons olive oil

2 pounds fish fillets or steaks, cut ½ inch thick

Kosher salt and freshly ground pepper

½ cup flour

¼ cup fresh lime juice

Cayenne

6 garlic cloves, peeled and thinly sliced

2 carrots, peeled and cut into ¼-inch rounds

1 onion, peeled and thinly sliced

1 celery stalk, thinly sliced

1 large green bell pepper, cored, seeded, and thinly sliced

1 Scotch bonnet pepper or 4 jalapeño peppers, seeded and thinly sliced (optional)

½ cup imported black olives, pitted

FOR THE MARINADE:

1 cup white wine vinegar

½ cup dry white wine

½ cup water

12 whole peppercorns

12 whole coriander seeds or allspice berries

1½ inches fresh ginger, halved
lengthwise and thinly sliced
(optional)

TO FINISH THE DISH:

1 small ripe mango, cut into
½-inch dice (optional)

2 limes, thinly sliced

Cilantro or flat-leaf parsley for
garnish

Heat 3 tablespoons of the oil in a large skillet over medium-high heat.

Season the fish liberally with salt and pepper and dredge in the flour, shaking off the excess.

Sauté the fish, turning once, until nicely browned and just cooked through, about 5 minutes total.

Use a spatula to transfer the fish to a 9-by-13-inch glass baking dish. Sprinkle with the lime juice, dust lightly with cayenne, and set aside.

Heat the remaining 3 tablespoons of oil in the skillet over medium heat and sauté the garlic, carrots, onion, celery, bell pepper, and Scotch bonnet pepper for 3 or 4 minutes, until the onion is barely soft and the bell pepper and celery are bright green. Scrape the sautéed vegetables into the baking dish and spread over the fish along with the olives.

Combine the vinegar, wine, water, peppercorns, coriander seeds, and ginger in the skillet over high heat. Bring just to a boil, lower the heat, and simmer, covered, for 15 minutes.

Pour the marinade over the fish and arrange the diced mango and sliced lime on top. When the escovitch has cooled to room temperature, cover the dish with plastic wrap and refrigerate for at least 4 hours, and preferably overnight. Serve it chilled, garnished with cilantro.

Fresh shrimp should have little or no odor—especially no ammonia smell. The flesh should be pink or white with no yellowing at the edges or black spots; it should feel firm, not slimy or mushy, and fit tightly in the shell. (If you're allergic to sulfites, be advised that both fresh and frozen shrimp are typically treated with sulfites to keep the body fluids from darkening.)

Shrimp is sold by size, based on the number of shrimp per pound, from colossal (ten or fewer), jumbo (eleven to fifteen), extra-large (sixteen to twenty), and medium (twenty-one to thirty-five), all the way down to miniature (about one hundred). The bigger the shrimp, the higher the price per pound—but the less time required to peel and devein them.

To peel shrimp, start from the large end and pull the shell away from the body, leaving the tail on if you like. If you have a lot of shrimp, it can be a tedious job, and most markets will do it for you for an extra charge. Ask for the shells, though; they're great for enriching stock and will keep for several weeks in the freezer if you wrap them well.

The dark vein along the top of a shrimp is edible, and we don't think it's worth the bother to remove it from small and medium shrimp. The vein in larger shrimp contains grit; to remove it, make a shallow slit down the back of the shrimp and pull out the vein with the tip of a sharp knife. Then rinse the shrimp under cold running water.

Use fresh shrimp within a day. To store, rinse well under cold running water and put on ice, loosely covered with plastic wrap, in the coldest part of your refrigerator.

Shrimp Creole

[6 SERVINGS]

Mention Creole cooking and most people think of Louisiana, but Miami's cuisine is also enriched by this melding of African, French, Spanish, and indigenous American food ways. It's evident in dishes from Haiti as well as from Oriente, the easternmost province of Cuba, which was heavily influenced by French- and African-born settlers from Haiti.

Shrimp Creole, rich with tomatoes and the butter-sautéed "holy trinity" of celery, onion, and bell pepper, is a justly famous example of Creole cooking. The zesty sauce is even better if you make it a day ahead, and it takes just a few minutes to heat it and cook the shrimp. Serve it on a bed of fluffy white rice with a crisp green salad and crusty French bread for an easy-on-the-cook dinner party.

FOR THE SAUCE:

1 tablespoon unsalted butter

1 tablespoon vegetable oil

2 large onions, peeled and coarsely chopped

2 celery stalks, coarsely chopped

1 large green bell pepper, seeded, cored, and coarsely chopped

3 garlic cloves, peeled and minced

1 or 2 jalapeño peppers, seeded and minced

4 large tomatoes, peeled, seeded, and chopped, or two 14½-ounce cans low-sodium diced tomatoes

¼ cup dry white wine

¼ cup water

1 teaspoon sugar

1 teaspoon kosher salt

½ teaspoon freshly ground pepper

½ teaspoon chili powder

¼ teaspoon cayenne

2 lime slices

1 bay leaf

TO FINISH THE DISH:

2 pounds large fresh shrimp, peeled and deveined

Kosher salt and freshly ground pepper

2 tablespoons minced parsley plus more for garnish

4 to 5 cups hot cooked rice

Heat the butter and oil in a 12-inch skillet over medium heat. Sauté the onions, celery, bell pepper, garlic, and jalapeño, stirring often, just until soft, about 5 minutes. Stir in the tomatoes, wine, water, sugar, salt, pepper, chili powder, cayenne, lime slices, and bay leaf. Bring the sauce to a boil, lower the heat to a simmer, and let cook, uncovered, until slightly reduced, about 5 minutes.

Season the shrimp with salt and pepper. Remove the lime slices and bay leaf from the sauce and stir in the shrimp and parsley. Simmer just until the shrimp turn pink, about 3 minutes. Taste for seasoning and serve immediately over the rice.

Tips/Techniques: Cooking on Skewers

Food on a stick over a fire: It has a strong, almost primitive appeal—never mind that our cave-dwelling ancestors didn't bother with marinades and dipping sauces. Cooking on skewers has the practical advantage, too, of allowing you to grill small pieces of food that would otherwise fall through the grates. (A grill basket or a grate tray is another solution, but skewers are more fun.) Here are a few pointers:

- Load individual skewers with foods that cook in about the same length of time. If you want to combine longer-cooking vegetables like carrots with quick-cooking ones like tomatoes or mushrooms, parboil the carrots first to even out the timing. Put meat and quick-cooking vegetables on separate skewers.
- Don't pack the food tightly; leave a little space between each piece so it can cook evenly.
- Choose your weapon: Metal skewers are best for meat and other foods that require lengthy cooking. Wooden or bamboo ones are fine for vegetables and most seafood.
- To keep wooden or bamboo skewers from burning, soak them in water for at least thirty minutes before using. Add lime or lemon juice to the water to impart a little extra flavor to the food. And if you plan to use them often, soak a whole batch of skewers at once and store the extras, tightly wrapped, in the freezer. Using two wooden skewers for each kebab holds the food more securely and makes it easier to turn.

Gingered Shrimp and Star Fruit on a Stick

[4 SERVINGS]

On winter nights around the full moon, the bridges that connect Miami to Miami Beach and Key Biscayne are crowded with fishermen wielding lanterns and long-handled dip nets. The lantern light attracts the shrimp that are drifting on the tide just below the surface and is reflected back in their tiny, luminescent green eyes. On a good night, especially after a cold snap (we're talking 40 degrees here), a dip-netter can scoop up his five-gallon limit in short order and, though it's not strictly legal, might be found selling the shrimp the next day for a few dollars a pound from the back of a truck on a city street.

Chances are you buy your shrimp from more conventional sources for a lot more money. Here's a dish that is well worth the premium you pay for jumbo shrimp. The sweet and tangy marinade turns into a dandy dipping sauce, and star-shaped slices of carambola look sensational. If you can't find carambola (star fruit), substitute 1½-inch chunks of fresh pineapple.

16 fresh jumbo shrimp

FOR THE MARINADE:

6 tablespoons fresh lime juice

3 tablespoons olive oil

2 tablespoons orange marmalade

1 garlic clove, peeled and minced

1 teaspoon grated lime zest

1 teaspoon grated fresh ginger

1 teaspoon kosher salt

1 teaspoon freshly ground pepper

½ teaspoon red pepper flakes

TO FINISH THE DISH:

3 or 4 ripe carambola (star fruit)

8 12-inch wooden skewers, soaked in water

Following the top curve of the shrimp, cut through the shells with kitchen shears. Remove the veins, leaving the shells attached. Rinse the shrimp under cold running water and set aside to drain on paper towels.

Combine the lime juice, olive oil, marmalade, garlic, lime zest, ginger, salt, pepper, and pepper flakes in a self-sealing food storage bag. Squeeze it to dissolve the marmalade and mix the ingredients.

Add the shrimp, seal the bag, and turn to distribute the marinade. Let the shrimp marinate at room temperature for 20 minutes or in the refrigerator for up to 2 hours, turning it several times. (Don't let it go longer, or the lime juice will "cook" the shrimp and make it mushy.) When you remove the shrimp from the bag, reserve the marinade.

Cut the carambola into ½-inch slices (you'll need 16 pieces). Using 2 skewers for each kebab, thread on the carambola alternately with the shrimp, curving the shrimp into a tight C and inserting the skewers about 1 inch apart, with one just above the tail and the other in the thickest part of the shrimp.

TO GRILL: Use indirect, medium heat (see page 100). Coat the grill rack with oil and position it 4 to 6 inches from the fire. Grill the kebabs, turning frequently, for 6 to 8 minutes, until the shrimp is just opaque.

TO COOK INDOORS: Broil the kebabs 4 to 6 inches from the heat source, turning frequently, until the shrimp is just opaque, 6 to 8 inches.

While the shrimp is cooking, place the remaining marinade into a small saucepan, bring to a boil over high heat, and simmer, covered, for 3 minutes.

Serve the shrimp immediately and let your guests peel their own. Serve the marinade as a dipping sauce on the side.

NOTE: Leaving the shells on keeps the shrimp from drying out or curling up tightly during cooking.

Paella Marina

[6 TO 8 SERVINGS]

Paella, a saffron-tinged Spanish rice dish beloved in Spanish-speaking Miami, is often made with chicken and pork as well as shellfish. This seafood version showcases Florida lobster, a clawless cousin of the Maine lobster. Technically it's a spiny lobster, a variety that's harvested in the Caribbean and off southern California, Mexico, Australia, New Zealand, and South Africa as well as south Florida. Nearly all the edible meat is in the tail, and frozen tails (labeled rock or sometimes African lobster) are widely available. If that's how you buy yours, let them thaw in the refrigerator before splitting them.

Paella is named for the broad, shallow, two-handled paellera *in which it is traditionally made. They're wonderful pans—great for stovetop or oven cooking and attractive enough to take to the table—but a large Dutch oven or ovenproof skillet will work fine. There's no substitute, though, for short-grain Valencia rice and real saffron if you want authentic texture, color, and taste.*

This recipe has a long list of ingredients, but that doesn't mean it takes a long time to make, especially if you do the preliminary cooking a few hours or even a day ahead as we've suggested.

6 to 8 ounces chorizo, peeled and cut into ¼-inch slices

3 tablespoons olive oil

1 pound medium shrimp, peeled

4 Florida (spiny or rock) lobster tails, split lengthwise (see Note)

1 pound grouper or other firm, mild fish, cut into 1-inch cubes

Kosher salt and freshly ground pepper

1 large onion, peeled and chopped

4 garlic cloves, peeled and minced

1 2-ounce jar pimentos, drained and diced (optional)

1 large tomato, peeled, seeded, and diced (or 1 cup low-sodium canned diced tomatoes)

3 cups short-grain (Valencia) rice

3 cups chicken broth

12 ounces beer

½ cup dry white wine

2 bay leaves

1 teaspoon saffron threads in 1 tablespoon hot water

18 clams (the smallest available, such as cherrystone or little-neck), scrubbed

1 10-ounce package tiny frozen peas

Chopped parsley for garnish

Heat a paella pan, a 5-quart ovenproof skillet or casserole, or a large, flat-bottomed wok over medium-high heat. Sauté the chorizo, stirring occasionally, until browned and crisp, about 8 minutes. Set aside on paper towels to drain, and wipe out the pan.

Heat the oil over medium heat. Season the shrimp, lobster, and grouper well with salt and pepper. Sauté them, turning often, until barely opaque, about 3 minutes, and set aside. (The chorizo and seafood can be refrigerated at this point for up to 24 hours.)

Add the onion, garlic, and pimentos to the pan and sauté until the onion is soft, about 5 minutes. Stir in the tomato and cook for 3 minutes. (The vegetables can be refrigerated at this point for up to 24 hours. Reheat in the pan before continuing with the recipe.)

Stir the rice into the vegetable mixture and sauté for 3 minutes. Add the broth, beer, wine, bay leaves, 1 teaspoon of salt, and ¼ teaspoon of pepper. Bring the liquid to a boil, lower to a simmer, and let cook, uncovered, for 5 minutes without stirring.

Preheat the oven to 350 degrees.

Stir the saffron and hot water into the rice mixture and simmer for 2 minutes without stirring.

Remove the pan from the heat and add the chorizo, shrimp, lobster, and fish, burying them in the rice. Arrange the clams on top, pressing them into the rice.

Cover the pan loosely with foil and bake for 15 minutes, until the rice and seafood are completely cooked. Remove the pan from the oven, sprinkle the peas over the paella, cover it again, and let stand for 5 or 10 minutes.

Remove and discard the bay leaves and any unopened clams. Garnish with parsley and serve immediately.

VARIATIONS:
- For extra flavor, simmer the chicken broth with the shrimp shells, covered, for 15 minutes. Strain the broth and discard the shells.
- You can substitute 2 additional cups of chicken broth or 1 cup each clam juice and water for the beer and wine.

NOTE: To split the lobster, cut through the top and bottom shells with kitchen shears and slice through the meat with a large chef's knife.

Stone Crabs

Transplanted northerners wistful for the crunch of leaves underfoot and the crisp scent of fall in the air have one major consolation in Miami: stone crabs. October 15 marks the beginning of the seven-month stone crab season and releases pent-up lust for the succulent crustaceans. Seafood markets count on selling out of stone crab claws as fast as they get them in from the Florida Keys, and diners think nothing of waiting an hour or more for a table at south Florida's most venerable restaurant, Joe's Stone Crab, in Miami Beach. (Joe's, managed by the great-grandson of founder Joe Weiss, closes for the summer shortly after the stone crab season ends in mid-May.)

Stone crab meat is sweet, to be sure, but its popularity has as much to do with its beauty as its taste: Beneath the sunset-hued shell, the snowy white meat is tipped with black and edged with pink and gold. (Chilean stone crab is available off-season, even at some Miami restaurants, but to real purists the replacement doesn't measure up.)

Stone crabs are a uniquely renewable resource: Once caught in a trap and hauled to the surface, they sacrifice just one of their two claws to the fisherman and are thrown back to live another day. New claws (called retreads) grow in 18 months or so, and the cycle can be repeated three or four times with a single crab. The meat is highly perishable and sticks to the shell if frozen, so it is cooked and iced down as soon as it is landed.

Some chefs incorporate stone crabs into elaborate dishes, but that's gilding the lily as far as we're concerned. It is best served simply, chilled and cracked, with drawn butter or a mustard sauce. Here's all you need to know:

WHERE TO GET THEM: Stone crabs are air-shipped on ice around the country and are available in season at well-stocked seafood markets in many major cities. You can also order them directly from Joe's (1-800-780-2722 or, locally, 305-673-9035) or Francesca's Favorites (1-800-865-2722). They're priced according to the number of crab claws per pound, ranging from jumbo (2 per pound) and large (6 per pound) down to small (10 to 12 per pound). Figure on 4 large claws per person.

HOW TO STORE THEM: They should be stored on ice in the coldest part of your refrigerator for no more than two or three days.

HOW TO PREPARE THEM: Just before serving, put several claws at a time in a sturdy plastic bag, and crack them at the joints with a mallet. Remove the shell and the moveable pincer.

Leave the meat attached to the remaining pincer, which makes a good handle for dipping. Pile the claws on a platter and serve the dipping sauce in individual bowls.

WHAT TO SERVE WITH THEM: Despite the upscale price (expect to pay upwards of $25 per pound if you order them by phone), stone crab is a down-home sort of dish well matched by hash browns, coleslaw (try our Green Papaya and Red Pepper Slaw on page 79), Orange-Horseradish-Mustard Sauce (page 268), and, of course, Key Lime Pie (page 301).

On the Side

VEGETABLES

Boniato Puree

Calabaza Gratin

Stuffed Chayote

Malanga Soufflé

Crispy Jerk-Fried Onion Rings

Fried Ripe Plantains (Maduros)

Twice-Fried Green Plantains (Tostones)

Tropical Chips

Yuca with Mojo Criollo (Creole-Style Citrus-Garlic Sauce)

GRAINS, RICE, AND BEANS

Grit Sticks

Tropical Couscous

Caribbean Rice

Coconut-Orange Rice

Rice with Coconut Milk

Yellow Rice with Corn

Wild Rice with Mango and Pecans

Caribbean Pigeon Peas and Rice

Cuban-Style Black Beans

POTATOES

Bogotá-Style Potatoes

Ecuadoran Potato and Cheese Patties

Mashed Potatoes with Roasted Corn and Scallions

$\mathcal{V}$egetables

Carole lugged along a suitcase packed with boniatos and malangas when she flew to Baltimore to teach a cooking class not long ago, only to discover that she could have bought them at the local Safeway. Then Kathy spotted plantains next to the bananas at Logli's supermarket in Rockford, Illinois, where her father-in-law shops. That's when we knew tropical produce had gone mainstream.

If you grew up on boiled yuca and fried plantains, it's a welcome development, but if you didn't, it may leave you feeling out of the loop. Don't worry; the recipes and tips in this chapter—and in the Ingredients Guide on page 3—will put you right out there on the crest of the trend. You'll shop with confidence for tropical vegetables. You'll find them easy to prepare; after all, you peel a potato the same way whether it's called a boniato or an Idaho. And you'll discover what a treat they are to eat.

Even if chayote and calabaza have yet to make their way to a supermarket near you, there are lots of must-try recipes on the pages ahead—Latin American potato and cheese dishes, Caribbean rice and bean combinations, and sensational jerk-fried onion rings among them. All in all, it's a collection of side dishes worth putting front and center on your dinner table.

Boniato Puree

[6 TO 8 SERVINGS]

Boniato, an ivory-fleshed tropical sweet potato (see page 3), has a delicate sweetness that makes this puree an intriguing substitute for mashed potatoes, especially with a salty meat like baked ham. Boniato is drier than regular potatoes and requires more liquid to produce a moist puree.

> 2 pounds boniato, peeled and cut into 1-inch
>   chunks (see Note)
> Kosher salt
> ½ cup sour cream
> ½ to ¾ cup chicken broth
> 2 tablespoons unsalted butter (optional)
> Freshly ground pepper

Combine the boniatos, 1 teaspoon of salt, and water to cover in a large saucepan. Bring to a boil, lower the heat, and simmer, covered, until tender, 15 to 20 minutes.

Drain off the water and shake the boniatos in the hot pan to evaporate as much of the moisture as possible.

Mash the boniatos or put them through a ricer. Add the sour cream, chicken broth, butter, and pepper to taste, and beat until smooth. Taste for seasoning and texture, and add salt or broth if you like. Serve hot.

PLANNING AHEAD: The puree can be made in advance and reheated in a microwave oven or in the top of a double boiler.

VARIATION: You can substitute regular sweet potatoes or white potatoes, or a combination of the two, for the boniatos; use ¼ cup of broth to start and add more as needed.

NOTE: Boniatos oxidize and turn gray quickly, so cover them with water as soon as they're peeled; some cooks even peel them under running water.

Calabaza Gratin

[4 SERVINGS]

Calabaza, or West Indian pumpkin (see page 4), has a lovely pumpkinlike flavor but a sometimes watery texture that works best when combined with other ingredients, as in this creamy gratin. Queso blanco (also called queso fresco) is a fresh cheese that's usually associated with Mexican cooking, but it is popular with Miami's many South American and Central American natives, too. Grated Muenster is a good substitute in this recipe.

2 pounds calabaza

¼ cup flour

2 tablespoons unsalted butter

1 garlic clove, peeled and minced

2 tablespoons minced fresh parsley

½ cup (2 ounces) crumbled queso blanco or grated Muenster cheese

1½ teaspoons kosher salt

1⅓ cups half-and-half or milk

Preheat the oven to 325 degrees.

Remove the seeds and stringy fiber from the calabaza. Working carefully with a very sharp knife, cut off the tough outer skin and cut the orange flesh into 1-inch cubes. Toss the cubes with the flour, coating them evenly.

Grease a 2-quart gratin pan or casserole with 1 tablespoon of the butter and scatter the garlic in the bottom of the pan.

Add the calabaza in an even layer and sprinkle on the parsley, cheese, and salt. Pour on the half-and-half, barely covering the squash, and dot the top with the remaining 1 tablespoon of butter.

Bake for about 30 minutes, until the top is browned and the squash is tender.

VARIATIONS: If you can't find calabaza, substitute Hubbard, butternut, or other winter squash.

Stuffed Chayote

[8 SERVINGS]

Chayote, a member of the squash family (see page 5), is made for stuffing. Its firm, pale green skin makes a lovely receptacle, and its mild flesh mixes nicely with just about anything. (The soft seed has an almondlike taste and can be chopped and added to the mix.) Here it is combined with tomato, onion, garlic, and fresh peppers in a savory side dish. To turn it into a main course, add crabmeat, shrimp, browned ground beef, cooked black beans, or diced cheese. Or stuff the chayote with leftover Picadillo (page 148) and bake as directed.

4 medium-sized chayote

Kosher salt

1 to 2 tablespoons olive oil

½ cup finely chopped onion

¼ cup finely chopped red or green
    bell pepper

1 or 2 jalapeño peppers, seeded
    and minced

1 garlic clove, peeled and minced

1 medium-sized tomato, peeled,
    seeded, and chopped

2 tablespoons minced fresh parsley

1 teaspoon minced fresh oregano
    leaves or ½ teaspoon dry,
    crumbled

¼ cup dry bread crumbs

Freshly ground pepper

½ cup freshly grated Parmesan
    cheese

Cut the chayotes in half lengthwise and place in a saucepan with water to cover and 1 teaspoon of salt. Bring to a boil, lower the heat, and simmer, covered, until the skin is barely tender, about 15 minutes.

Drain the chayotes and let cool. Use a spoon to scoop out the flesh and seed, leaving a shell about ¼ inch thick. Coarsely chop the flesh and seed, and set aside.

Preheat the oven to 350 degrees. Lightly oil a baking sheet or dish large enough to hold the chayotes.

Heat the oil in a skillet over medium heat. Sauté the onion, bell pepper, jalapeño, and garlic until soft, about 5 minutes. Stir in the tomato, parsley, oregano, and reserved chayote, and cook for 5 more minutes. Stir in the bread crumbs and season with salt and pepper to taste.

Sprinkle the reserved chayote shells with salt and pepper, and mound the stuffing mixture in them. Place in the baking dish and sprinkle with the Parmesan.

Bake for 25 to 30 minutes, until the cheese is lightly browned and the chayote shells are tender.

PLANNING AHEAD: You can stuff the chayotes several hours ahead and refrigerate them, covered. Let them come to room temperature before baking or add about 10 minutes to the cooking time.

Malanga Soufflé

[4 SERVINGS]

Malanga, an earthy tropical root vegetable (see page 7), goes uptown in this elegant dish, its softly sweet, nutty flavor complemented by Parmesan cheese and ham. Despite its haute cuisine cachet, a soufflé is simple to make: You just fold beaten egg whites into a base mixture and bake it. The heat of the oven expands the air trapped in the egg whites, making the soufflé rise. (By the same token, it begins to fall as the air cools, so it needs to go straight from the oven to the table.) Mashed malanga makes a relatively heavy base, so this soufflé doesn't rise as high as some, but it still has a lovely light texture. The recipe works well with mashed potatoes, too.

½ pound malanga

Kosher salt

1 tablespoon unsalted butter, softened

2 tablespoons toasted bread crumbs

4 eggs, separated, plus 1 egg white

⅛ teaspoon freshly grated nutmeg

½ teaspoon paprika

Pinch of cayenne

⅓ cup half-and-half or milk

¼ cup diced ham (optional)

1 cup freshly grated Parmesan or Gruyère cheese, or a combination of the two

Peel the malanga and cut it into chunks. Put in a saucepan with 1 teaspoon of salt and water to cover, and bring it to a boil. Lower the heat and simmer briskly, covered, until the malanga is tender, about 20 minutes.

Meanwhile, coat a 4-cup soufflé dish or round, straight-sided baking dish with the butter and sprinkle with the bread crumbs. Place on a baking sheet and set in the refrigerator.

Preheat the oven to 400 degrees. Place one oven rack in the center position. Put the other rack at the bottom or remove it so the rising soufflé doesn't bump into it.

Beat the 4 egg yolks in a small bowl and stir in ¾ teaspoon of salt, the nutmeg, paprika, and cayenne. Set aside.

As soon as the malanga is tender, drain well and put through a potato ricer or food mill, or mash with a potato masher. Scrape it into a large bowl, add the half-and-half, and stir to combine. Add the egg yolk mixture and ham, and mix well.

In a large glass, ceramic, or stainless steel bowl, beat the 5 egg whites with a pinch of salt until fairly stiff but not dry.

Using a wire whisk, beat about one-third of the egg whites into the malanga mixture to lighten it. With a rubber spatula, fold in the remaining egg whites along with ¾ cup of the grated cheese, just until combined.

Spoon the mixture into the prepared dish and sprinkle with the remaining ¼ cup of cheese. Place in the oven and lower the heat to 375 degrees. Bake the soufflé until puffed, set, and golden, 25 to 30 minutes. Test for doneness by sliding a skewer at a 45-degree angle from the edge of the soufflé into the center. If wet particles cling to it, the soufflé will be creamy; if it comes out clean, the soufflé will be drier but will hold its puff longer.

Serve immediately: Slide 2 serving spoons, back to back, into the center of the soufflé and pull it apart. Make sure each serving includes a portion of both the crust and the soft interior.

PLANNING AHEAD: The soufflé can be combined up to 2 hours before baking and refrigerated. Allow an extra 10 minutes or so for it to bake.

NOTES:
- If any yolk or grease gets into the egg whites, they won't beat as high as they should.
- An aluminum bowl is not good for beating eggs because it can turn them gray; plastic is best avoided, too, because it retains grease easily.
- Work quickly once the malanga is cooked; it hardens as it cools.

Crispy Jerk-Fried Onion Rings

[4 SERVINGS]

Jerk seasoning gives these onion rings punch as well as crunch—a delightful indulgence that's well worth the effort and calories. Deep-frying isn't complicated, but it requires concentration (see page 28). Have everything—onions, coating mixture, draining pan—set out before you begin, and if you have kids, keep them out of the kitchen until you're done. Then pile the onion rings atop Macho Steak (page 133) or simple grilled burgers for a showstopping presentation.

> 2 medium-large onions, peeled
>
> Milk
>
> 1 cup flour
>
> 1 tablespoon cornstarch
>
> 3 tablespoons Jerk Seasoning (page 99)
>   or a commercial jerk blend
>
> Vegetable oil
>
> Kosher salt

Slice the onions into thin rings. (Use a mandoline, or the slicing attachment of a food processor if you have one.) Pile the rings in a bowl and add milk to cover them. Cover the bowl and refrigerate for at least 1 hour.

Drain the onions well, spread them on a baking sheet, and refrigerate while making the coating mixture.

Stir together the flour, cornstarch, and Jerk Seasoning in a large bowl.

Heat 2 to 3 inches of oil to 360 degrees in a deep fryer or a suitable pan (see page 28). If you don't have a deep-frying thermometer, check the temperature by dipping a wooden spoon handle into the oil; brisk bubbles will spring up around it when the oil is hot enough.

Line a baking sheet with several layers of paper towels and set it on the counter near the stove. Heat the oven to 200 degrees. Remove the onions from the refrigerator and set them on the counter near the stove, with the bowl of coating mix nearby.

Using tongs, scoop up a small handful of onion rings, dip them in the coating mix, shake off the excess, and release them gently into the hot oil. (Bring them right down to the surface of the oil first; don't drop them from above or the oil will splatter.)

Fry the onion rings, turning once, until golden brown, about 45 seconds. Transfer to the baking sheet to drain and put in the oven to keep warm. Let the oil return to 360 degrees between batches. Serve warm.

VARIATION: Use the same coating and deep-frying technique for thin-cut, homemade french fries or jicama fries.

NOTES:
- Soaking the onions in milk helps the coating to adhere.
- Most deep-frying is done at 370 to 375 degrees, but because onions contain a lot of sugar that can easily burn, 360 degrees is best here.
- Frying the onions in small portions keeps the oil temperature from dropping too low, which would make them greasy and soggy.

Fried Ripe Plantains (Maduros)

[8 SERVINGS]

Plantains, a big sister to the banana (see page 9), are widely used and loved by Latin American and Caribbean natives, but especially by Cubans. In pre-Castro days, Maria Lluria de O'Higgins writes in A Taste of Old Cuba, *a non-Cuban on the island who had thoroughly adopted native ways was considered* aplatanado, *literally "banana-ized." In Miami's Cuban restaurants it's a rare meal that isn't accompanied by fried plantains. In these* maduros *(mah-DURE-ose), their sweetness is intensified as they caramelize in the pan, making them a wonderful accompaniment to roasts. Make sure the plantains are black-ripe; they'll look as if they're ready to be pitched out. Don't worry, though; they'll hold their shape and deliver a marvelous taste.*

4 very ripe plantains (the skin should be black)
Vegetable oil

Peel the plantains (the skin should come off easily, like a banana's) and cut into ½-inch-thick diagonal slices.

Heat ½ inch of oil in a large skillet over medium-high heat and spread several layers of paper towels on the counter.

Working in batches, fry the plantains in a single layer until deep golden brown, about 3 minutes per side. As they fry, you may need to move them around a bit with a spatula to prevent sticking. Transfer to the paper towels to drain. Serve immediately.

VARIATION: Though not traditional, frying the plantains in a fifty-fifty combination of vegetable oil and unsalted butter adds a nice flavor.

Twice-Fried Green Plantains
(Tostones)

[6 SERVINGS]

If your roast pork isn't served with maduros *at a Cuban restaurant in Miami, chances are it will come with* tostones *(tose-TONE-ase), made with green plantains. They're wonderfully crisp outside thanks to the double frying, and they have a potatolike interior and taste. If there's a Latin market in your area, you may be able to buy a* tostonera, *a hinged wooden press that makes quick work of flattening the plantain slices after the first frying. If not, console yourself with the knowledge that the best Cuban cooks swear by hand-pressing. (Brown paper bags were once used for blotting and pressing the slices, but they're chemically treated these days and no longer considered safe.) Be sure to consult the Ingredient Guide for instructions on peeling green plantains, and note that you can refrigerate or even freeze the once-fried slices ahead of time to cut down on last-minute preparation.*

> 2 cups water
> Kosher salt
> 3 green plantains, peeled (see page 9)
> Vegetable oil

Combine the water and 2 teaspoons of salt in a bowl. Cut the plantains into ½-inch slices and soak in the salt water for 10 minutes. Blot between layers of paper towels and dry thoroughly.

Heat 1 inch of oil in a large, deep frying pan over medium-high heat and spread several layers of paper towels on the counter nearby. To check the oil temperature, insert a wooden spoon; bubbles will immediately spring up around it when the oil is hot enough.

Working in batches to avoid crowding the pan, fry the plantains until tender but not crisp, about 2 minutes per side. With a slotted spoon, transfer to the paper towels to drain in a single layer. When all the slices are fried, remove the pan from the heat.

Place several more layers of paper towels over the plantain slices and flatten them one by one with the heel of your hand to a thickness of about ¼ inch. (At this point the slices can be kept at room temperature for up to 2 hours, refrigerated for several days, or frozen for several weeks. Bring them to room temperature before proceeding.)

Return the skillet to medium-high heat and reheat the oil, checking the temperature as described above. Fry the plantain slices again until crisp and golden brown, about 3 to 4 minutes on each side. Drain on paper towels, sprinkle with salt, and serve immediately, or hold in a 200-degree oven for up to 30 minutes.

VARIATIONS:

⇒ Drizzle the *tostones* with a mixture of ¼ cup of olive oil and 2 crushed garlic cloves before serving.

⇒ Semi-ripe plantains aren't suitable for *tostones* but are good sliced and fried once for 3 or 4 minutes per side.

Tropical Chips

It may not occur to you to make potato chips from scratch, but chips made from green plantains (called *mariquitas*), boniato, malanga, and yuca are a deliciously different story and are well worth the effort. Here's how to make them: Peel the vegetables (we know plantains are a fruit, but they're used as a vegetable here), slice them thinly with a mandoline slicer or the thin slicing blade of a food processor, and then soak in ice water. (You can prepare them to this point up to several hours ahead of time.)

Heat 2 or 3 inches of peanut oil to 375 degrees in a deep, heavy pan or use a deep fryer and follow the manufacturer's instructions. (For more on deep frying, see page 28.)

Dry the vegetable slices well with paper towels and fry them in small batches until crisp and golden brown, about 2 minutes.

Remove with a slotted spoon and let drain on paper towels. Allow the oil to reheat to 375 degrees between batches.

Sprinkle the chips with salt or Jerk Seasoning (page 99) to taste and serve warm. One pound of fresh vegetables will give you about 4 servings.

Yuca with Mojo Criollo
(Creole-Style Citrus-Garlic Sauce)

[6 SERVINGS]

Yuca, a starchy tropical root vegetable, lends itself to a whole host of treatments (see page 10) but is best known and most loved in Miami in this form. Yuca con Mojo, as it appears on Cuban restaurant menus, is an essential and evocative element of many traditional Cuban meals, especially Nochebuena, *the Christmas Eve feast (see page 154). Even if it doesn't conjure images of home and hearth for you, you can appreciate the play of the creamy yuca against the tangy garlic sauce. The yuca is often served swimming in the sauce, but you can still enjoy the lively flavor if you employ a more measured hand.*

2½ pounds yuca

2 teaspoons kosher salt

½ to 1 cup Mojo Criollo (recipe follows)

Chopped parsley for garnish

Cut the yuca into 4-inch sections and use a paring knife to cut a ⅛-inch-deep slit down the length of each piece. With the tip of the knife, pry off the brown skin and pink underlayer, leaving the snowy white flesh. Cut each piece in half lengthwise and remove the fibrous cord that runs down the middle.

Cut the yuca into chunks and place in a saucepan with the salt and water to cover. Bring to a boil, lower the heat, and simmer, covered, until tender, about 20 minutes. (Check just as you would potatoes, with the tip of a knife; the yuca is done when it can be pierced easily but is still whole.)

Drain the yuca, transfer it to a serving bowl, pour on the mojo, and serve immediately.

VARIATIONS:

- Malanga, especially the yellow variety, is often served this way, too. Simply peel the malanga (no cord to remove) and proceed as directed.
- Many supermarkets with a Hispanic clientele carry frozen yuca, peeled and ready to cook. It's a good substitute for fresh and should be prepared according to package directions.

Mojo Criollo (Creole-Style Citrus-Garlic Sauce)

[ABOUT 1⅔ CUPS]

Mojo—pronounced MO-ho, from the Spanish verb mojar (to wet)—*is used in various forms in Puerto Rico, the Dominican Republic, and elsewhere in the Caribbean. In Miami you're most likely to encounter it something like this, bathing a batch of boiled yuca or malanga, or used as a marinade or sauce for poultry or pork. Lard was the original fat of choice, but even the most traditional Cuban cooks use olive oil or vegetable oil today. Bottled mojo is available in supermarkets with a Hispanic clientele, but it doesn't compare to homemade. A mortar and pestle is the traditional tool for mashing the garlic and salt, and if you have one, by all means use it.*

8 to 10 garlic cloves

1 teaspoon kosher salt

½ teaspoon ground cumin

1 teaspoon freshly ground
  pepper

1 medium onion, peeled
  and thinly sliced

½ cup olive or vegetable
  oil

1 cup sour orange juice or
  ½ cup each lime and
  regular orange juice

Working on a piece of parchment or wax paper, crush the garlic cloves with the side of a French chef's knife and remove the papery skin. Add the salt and mash the garlic into a paste with the tines of a fork.

Scrape the mixture into a saucepan and add the cumin, pepper, onion, and oil. Heat over low heat, stirring often, until the onion is soft, 8 to 10 minutes.

Add the sour orange juice, raise the heat to medium, and bring to a simmer. Serve immediately, hold it at room temperature for up to 2 hours, or refrigerate, covered, for up to 2 days. (If using as a marinade, let cool to room temperature first.)

Grains, Rice, and Beans

Of Cornmeal, Grits, and Masa Harina

Corn, that most American of grains, is believed to have originated in Mexico and was cultivated by indigenous people in both North America and South America before Columbus's arrival. It's no wonder, then, that dried, ground corn is cooked in a multitude of ways in Miami—stewed with okra and called *coocoo* by Barbados natives, kneaded and fried into tortillas in Mexican homes, cooked up as grits by Miamians with southern roots, to name just a few. They're not all using quite the same ingredient, though. Here's the difference:

If you dry corn and grind it, you get cornmeal—white or yellow depending on the variety of corn; fine, medium, or coarse depending on the grind. If you add water (three to five parts to one part cornmeal) and cook it, you get cornmeal mush. And if you're Italian, you call it polenta.

If you dry corn, soak it in lime or lye water to remove the outer skin from the kernel (at which point it's called hominy), dry it again, and then grind it, you get hominy grits. If you cook it with water (in about the same proportions as cornmeal), you still have grits—the kind served for breakfast with ham and eggs.

If you dry corn, boil it in lime water to remove the outer skin, and grind it, you get fresh *masa*, used to make tamales. If you dry the *masa*, you get *masa harina* (literally "dough flour") for either tortillas or arepas, depending on the variety of corn. Because the corn is cooked before it is turned into flour, Elisabeth Lambert Ortiz notes in *The Book of Latin American Cooking*, there's no such thing as a raw tortilla—only an unbaked one.

Grit Sticks

[6 TO 8 SERVINGS]

True grits lovers are born, not made—born, that is, into grits-eating families. Not many of us reared elsewhere share southerners' passion for them. These fried grit sticks, though, are hard for anyone to resist—crunchy outside, sweet and buttery inside, and positively addictive. (They're still very good, though not as rich, without the butter and olive oil.) If you're a grits devotee, you can dispense with the frying and enjoy this tasty batch straight up as cooked grits. Starting the grits with the water rather than stirring it in once the water is boiling is the secret to lump-free cooking (it works for polenta, too). Note that you need to plan ahead for grit sticks; they should be served freshly fried but need to chill first.

8 cups cold water

3 cups hominy grits

1 teaspoon kosher salt

½ teaspoon freshly ground pepper

Dash of freshly ground nutmeg

3 tablespoons unsalted butter (optional)

3 tablespoons extra-virgin olive oil (optional)

Peanut or vegetable oil

Combine the water and 2 cups of the grits in a large saucepan and bring to a boil over high heat. Turn the heat to medium-low and simmer, uncovered, for 20 to 30 minutes, stirring often with a wooden spoon. The grits are done when they come away from the sides of the pan when stirred and the spoon stays upright in the center when you let go of it.

Remove the pan from the heat and stir in the salt, pepper, nutmeg, butter, and olive oil.

Lightly oil a 9-inch square pan and scrape the grits into it, smoothing the top. Cover the pan and refrigerate for at least 3 hours and as long as 3 days. (If you're pressed for time, you can chill the grits in the freezer in under an hour.)

TO DEEP-FRY: Turn the chilled grits out onto a cutting board, and cut into sticks 2¼ inches long and ¾ inch wide. (You'll have 48.) Place the remaining 1 cup of dry grits in a shallow dish and roll the grit sticks in them to coat.

Heat 2 or 3 inches of peanut oil to 375 degrees in a deep fryer or a suitable pan (see page 28). Working in batches to avoid crowding the pan, fry the grit sticks until light golden brown,

3 or 4 minutes. Remove with a slotted spoon, drain on paper towels, and keep warm in a 200-degree oven until you're done. Serve immediately.

TO PANFRY: Cut the chilled grits into larger shapes—4½ by 1½ inch sticks, for example, or triangles as described below. Fry in ½ inch of olive oil or a mixture of olive oil and butter over medium-high heat, turning once, until golden brown, 3 or 4 minutes per side.

TO GRILL: Cut the chilled grits into 4½-inch squares and cut each square into 2 triangles. Brush with olive oil and grill over a medium fire, turning once, until lightly browned and crisp, 2 to 3 minutes per side.

VARIATIONS:

For a sharper flavor, omit the butter and stir in ½ cup of freshly grated Parmesan.

Although they would technically be "mush" sticks, not grit sticks, these can be made with medium- or fine-grind cornmeal, too.

Tropical Couscous

[8 SERVINGS]

You don't have to be a chef to practice fusion cooking. You do it in your own kitchen every time you combine elements from disparate cuisines. This couscous—the starch of choice in North Africa, made from semolina wheat—is a case in point. Rehydrated in orange juice and studded with fresh orange and papaya, it's right at home on the Miami table—great at room temperature as a side dish or chilled as a salad.

2¼ cups fresh orange juice

1 teaspoon ground cumin

1 teaspoon kosher salt

1 10-ounce box plain, instant couscous

2 tablespoons olive oil

2 tablespoons soy sauce

2 tablespoons fresh lime juice

1 teaspoon grated fresh ginger

1 small, ripe papaya

1 orange

¼ cup chopped fresh cilantro or flat-leaf parsley

Combine the orange juice, cumin, and salt in a saucepan and bring to a boil. Remove the pan from the heat and stir in the couscous. Set aside, covered, for 5 minutes.

Spoon the rehydrated couscous into a large bowl and stir in the oil, soy sauce, lime juice, and ginger. While the mixture cools slightly, peel and dice the papaya, and peel and section the orange, cutting each section into ½-inch slices. Stir the fruit into the couscous along with the cilantro. Serve at room temperature or chilled.

PLANNING AHEAD: If you're going to make this ahead of time and chill it, refrigerate the couscous mixture and the fruit separately, and combine them just before serving.

VARIATIONS: Fresh mango or pineapple is a good substitute for the papaya.

Rice flourished in Spain before Columbus's time and in Africa before the slave trade took hold, so two major groups of people brought a taste for the grain to the New World. And over the centuries, rice became a mainstay of diets throughout the Caribbean and Latin America. Against that backdrop, a single statistic makes clear what a cultural crossroads Miami has become: While Americans as a whole eat an average of 20 pounds of rice per person each year, Miamians eat 100 pounds of it, according to industry estimates.

The region makes a small contribution to the nation's rice stores, too: Two hours north of Miami, on the southeast shore of Lake Okeechobee, rice is a rotation crop for sugarcane growers. The fields are flooded every three years to kill pests and give the soil a rest from the demands of sugarcane. The rice planted in its place actually improves the soil by removing excess phosphorus and gives the growers a second cash crop.

Caribbean Rice

[4 SERVINGS]

Sauté a little onion and garlic, add a little allspice and cinnamon, and you've turned plain rice into a taste sensation. Allspice is the berry of the pimiento tree, the source of the wood that stokes the fires of authentic Jamaican jerk pits (see page 98). The evergreen trees grew on the island when Columbus first set foot there in 1494, and Jamaica remains the world's largest producer of allspice—so named because it tastes like a combination of cinnamon, nutmeg, and cloves. This rice dish makes a lively accompaniment to almost any meal and turns into a fine main dish salad with the addition of cooked poultry, meat, or beans, and a splash of oil and vinegar.

1 to 2 tablespoons unsalted butter or vegetable oil

½ cup finely chopped onion

4 scallions, trimmed and thinly sliced

1 garlic clove, peeled and minced

1 cup long-grain white rice

1 teaspoon ground allspice

½ teaspoon ground cinnamon

½ teaspoon freshly ground pepper

2 cups chicken or vegetable broth

1 sprig fresh thyme or parsley

½ to 1 teaspoon kosher salt

Chopped fresh parsley for garnish

Melt the butter in a saucepan over medium heat and sauté the onion, scallions, and garlic until soft, about 5 minutes. Add the rice, allspice, cinnamon, and pepper, and stir to coat the rice well. Add the broth and thyme. Taste the broth and add salt.

Bring to a boil over high heat, turn the heat to medium-low, and simmer, covered, for 18 to 20 minutes, until the liquid is absorbed and the rice is fluffy and dry. Remove the thyme sprig, garnish with chopped parsley, and serve.

PLANNING AHEAD: You can cook the rice early in the day, store it, covered, in the refrigerator, and reheat it in the microwave just before serving.

VARIATION: To substitute brown rice, increase the liquid and cooking time according to package directions.

Coconut-Orange Rice

[4 SERVINGS]

Coconuts grow all over the tropical and subtropical world, and they're very much a part of Miami's history. The area that is now Miami Beach was a coconut plantation in the early years of this century. When that venture failed, the plantation's owner, John Collins, turned to development and forged a city. Miami Beach's Collins Avenue, lined with hotels and high-rises, is named for him. On the other hand, Coconut Grove, one of Miami's oldest communities and most popular tourist destinations, had only two coconut palm trees to its name when it was founded in the 1880s, historian Arva Moore Parks writes in Miami: The Magic City. *Years later civic boosters went on a planting binge to make The Grove live up to its name.*

Some supermarkets and most health food stores carry unsweetened coconut. Don't substitute the sweetened variety; it would be too cloying here. If that's your only option, omit the coconut and enjoy the delicate citrus taste and red pepper accent on their own.

1 to 2 tablespoons butter or vegetable oil

½ cup finely chopped onion

1 cup long-grain white rice

¼ teaspoon crushed red pepper flakes

2 cups chicken or vegetable broth

1 tablespoon fresh lime juice

2 teaspoons freshly grated orange zest

½ to 1 teaspoon kosher salt

¼ cup toasted unsweetened coconut (see Note)

Melt the butter in a saucepan over medium heat and sauté the onion until soft, about 5 minutes. Add the rice and pepper flakes, and stir to coat the rice. Add the broth, lime juice, and orange zest. Taste the broth and add salt.

Bring to a boil over high heat, turn to medium-low, and simmer, covered, for 18 to 20 minutes, until the liquid is absorbed and the rice is fluffy and dry. Spoon the rice into a serving dish, garnish with the coconut, and serve.

PLANNING AHEAD: You can cook the rice and toast the coconut ahead of time; reheat the rice and garnish it just before serving.

NOTE: To toast flaked or grated coconut, spread on a cookie sheet and bake in a 350-degree oven for about 5 minutes, until lightly browned.

Rice with Coconut Milk

[8 SERVINGS]

The idea of cooking rice in coconut milk comes from Brazil and coastal Colombia, and this decidedly sweet dish is a fine accompaniment for baked ham or roast pork or beef. A traditional recipe would use all coconut milk, but we like to combine it with broth for a lighter dish. With the raisins, it will remind you of a light-textured rice pudding with a savory edge.

Coconut milk, by the way, is not the liquid you hear sloshing around inside a fresh coconut; that's coconut water, sometimes called juice. The "milk" is made by mixing and then straining grated coconut meat and water, and it's available canned in the Latin or Asian section of well-stocked supermarkets. Regular long-grain rice will work here, but short-grain produces a nicer texture.

> 2 tablespoons vegetable oil
> ½ cup minced onion
> 2 cups short-grain (Valencia) rice
> 1 cup raisins (optional)
> 2 cups unsweetened coconut milk (see Notes)
> 2 cups chicken or vegetable broth
> 1 to 2 teaspoons kosher salt

Heat the oil in a large saucepan over medium heat and sauté the onion until soft, about 5 minutes. Add the rice and raisins, and stir well to coat.

Add the coconut milk and broth. Taste the liquid and add salt.

Bring to a boil over high heat, turn to low, and simmer, covered, for 20 to 25 minutes, until the rice is tender and dry. If the coconut milk has formed a skin on top, stir it in with a fork. Serve hot.

PLANNING AHEAD: You can make and refrigerate the rice ahead of time and reheat it in the microwave just before serving.

NOTES:
- Make sure the onion is finely minced; the dominant taste should be coconut.
- Make sure the coconut milk is marked "unsweetened." If you find it in a 14-ounce can, just add 2 tablespoons of water to make 2 cups.

Yellow Rice with Corn

[6 SERVINGS]

Reddish annatto seeds (achiote in Spanish) come from a small tropical tree, and the pre-Columbian Indians of the Caribbean used them to make body paint, according to scholar and cookbook author Jessica B. Harris in Sky Juice and Flying Fish. *Harris speculates that black slaves and their descendants began tinting lard and later cooking oil with annatto as a replacement for the reddish-hued palm oil of West Africa. Annatto oil is also used in Latin America and the Spanish-speaking Caribbean, which makes one wonder if it was developed as an inexpensive way of creating a saffronlike tint. In any event, annatto produces vivid orange-yellow rice that looks and tastes great with corn in this dish. (Bijol is a commercial blend of annatto and food coloring.)*

1 to 2 tablespoons vegetable oil
½ cup diced onion
½ teaspoon ground annatto or Bijol (see Note)
1½ cups long-grain white rice
1 teaspoon ground cumin
½ teaspoon ground cinnamon
1 teaspoon kosher salt
1 cup fresh or thawed frozen corn kernels

Heat the oil in a large saucepan over medium heat and sauté the onion until soft, about 5 minutes. Add the annatto and rice, and cook, stirring constantly, for 1 minute, until the rice is thoroughly coated with oil and coloring. Stir in the cumin, cinnamon, and salt.

Add 3 cups of water, raise the heat to high, and bring to a boil. Turn to medium-low and simmer, covered, for 18 to 20 minutes, until the rice is fluffy and dry.

Remove the pan from the heat, stir in the corn, and set aside, covered, for 5 minutes, until the corn is heated through. Serve hot.

PLANNING AHEAD: You can make and refrigerate the rice ahead of time and reheat it in the microwave just before serving.

NOTE: If you can find whole annatto seeds, you can make your own annatto oil: Heat 1 cup of vegetable or olive oil in a heavy saucepan over medium heat. Add ¼ cup of annatto seeds and keep just below a boil for 5 minutes. Remove from the heat and let stand until the oil turns a deep orange color, about 1 hour. Strain the oil into a small jar and discard the seeds. The oil will keep for several months in a closed jar in the refrigerator. Use anytime you'd like to brighten up rice or even dough. A little goes a long way: 1 tablespoon is enough to color 1½ to 2 cups of uncooked rice. Substitute 1 tablespoon of this for the oil and ground annatto in the recipe. If you can't find annatto or Bijol, use packaged yellow rice or simply leave it white—it will taste just as good.

Wild Rice with Mango and Pecans

[6 SERVINGS]

It's a long way by any measure from the marshy lake shores of northern Wisconsin, where wild rice clings to slender stalks of grass in the cool early fall, to the backyards of Miami, where mangos hang heavy from sometimes towering trees in the sweltering midsummer. Results like this, though, make it worth the trip: The nutty, deep brown wild rice and sweet peach-colored mango look and taste great together.

Wild rice is the seed of an aquatic grass, not a true rice, and was so precious to the Ojibwa Indians that they battled other tribes for control of upper midwestern ricing grounds. Nearly two centuries later, it is still precious—and pricey—though it's more often harvested by machine than from canoes. It's hard to give exact water ratios and cooking times; wild rice expands about three times in volume and cooks in 35 to 60 minutes, depending on the type. Use the package directions as a guide. This dish is a wonderful accompaniment for Roast Duckling (page 128) or Roast Chicken (112) and makes an elegant vegetarian entree or cold salad.

1 cup wild rice

3 to 5 cups water (see introduction)

1 teaspoon kosher salt

1 small bay leaf

1 to 2 tablespoons unsalted butter or vegetable oil

1 large shallot, peeled and minced (see Note)

½ cup pecan pieces

1 teaspoon ground cumin

A dash or two of Caribbean hot sauce or Tabasco

1 ripe mango, peeled, seeded, and diced (about 1 cup)

2 tablespoons chopped fresh parsley

Put the rice in a colander and rinse under cold running water. Combine in a saucepan with the water, salt, and bay leaf, and bring to a boil over high heat. Turn the heat to low, and simmer, covered, for 35 to 60 minutes, checking occasionally and adding more water if necessary.

Meanwhile, melt the butter in a small pan over low heat and sauté the shallot until soft, about 3 minutes. Stir in the pecans, cumin, and hot sauce, and set the pan aside off the heat.

When the rice grains are plump but still whole and slightly firm to the bite, drain any water remaining in the pan and discard the bay leaf. Shake the rice around in the hot pan to evaporate the remaining moisture.

Stir the shallot mixture into the rice. Add the mango and parsley, and toss to combine. Serve hot, at room temperature, or chilled.

PLANNING AHEAD: You can cook the rice ahead of time and combine it with the shallots, but add the mango and parsley just before serving.

VARIATION: You can make the wild rice go further by using half the amount and combining it with 1½ cups of cooked brown or white rice.

NOTE: Shallots, which have a mild onion-garlic flavor, can burn easily and should always be cooked over low heat.

In Any Language, It's Beans and Rice

Most Miami Cubans cook black beans with white rice and call it *moros y cristianos,* but those from eastern Cuba use red beans and call it *congri.* Nicaraguans also combine red beans and rice, but they cook them separately first, use a slightly different bean, and call it *gallo pinto.* Jamaicans use red beans as well but add hot peppers and call the dish rice and peas—similar but not identical to the *riz et pois* served by Haitians. In Puerto Rican homes the beans are pigeon peas and the name is *arroz con gandules.* These are not by any means all the nuances of bean cuisine in Miami, but you get the idea.

Beans are an age-old protein source, cultivated by the Incas and Aztecs in pre-conquest Latin America and by African slaves in the seventeenth-century Caribbean. And over the centuries each country has made them its own. Understanding such distinctions has been a key to success for the nation's largest Hispanic-owned company, Goya Foods. Before micromarketing was a buzzword, Goya was building its customer base by paying close attention to where newly arrived Latin and Caribbean immigrants settled, and selling neighborhood stores the kinds of beans, rice, flour, and spices that the newcomers preferred. Before it registered with the community at large, Goya figured out in the mid-1980s that Little Havana, Miami's original Cuban enclave, was assuming a new identity as Cubans moved to the suburbs and Nicaraguans, Colombians, and Hondurans took their place. Among the evidence: Black-bean sales dropped, and the small red beans needed for *gallo pinto* were in demand.

Caribbean Pigeon Peas and Rice

[6 TO 8 SERVINGS]

Here is our interpretation of a Caribbean-style beans and rice dish using pigeon peas, also known as Congo peas, gunga peas, gungoo peas, and gandules, and favored by Dominicans, Puerto Ricans, and Bahamians. (The Bahamas are actually in the Atlantic, not the Caribbean, but they're a cultural part of the region and of Miami.) This goes beautifully with roast pork and is hearty enough to be a meal in itself when served with a salad. Omit the bacon, sauté the vegetables in oil, and the vegetarians in your life will love it, too.

8 ounces dried pigeon peas or *gandules* (about 1 cup) (see Variations)

4 slices bacon, thinly sliced

1 large onion, peeled and diced

1 large green bell pepper, seeded, cored, and diced

½ Scotch bonnet chile or 2 or 3 jalapeño peppers, seeded and minced

3 garlic cloves, peeled and minced

2 tomatoes, peeled, seeded, and diced, or 1 cup low-sodium canned diced tomatoes

½ teaspoon dry-leaf oregano, crumbled

½ teaspoon ground cumin

1 teaspoon salt

½ teaspoon freshly ground pepper

1½ cups uncooked long-grain white rice

Rinse the peas and discard any impurities. Soak in water to cover for 4 hours or as long as overnight.

Drain the peas and combine them with about 8 cups of water in a large, heavy Dutch oven or saucepan. Bring to a boil over high heat, turn to medium-low, and let simmer, uncovered, until just tender, about 1 hour.

Meanwhile, brown the bacon in a skillet over medium heat. Add the onion, bell pepper, Scotch bonnet pepper, and garlic, and sauté until the onion is soft, about 5 minutes. Stir in the tomatoes, oregano, and cumin, and set aside off the heat.

When the peas are done, drain them and reserve 3 cups of the cooking water.

Return the peas to the pot along with the onion mixture, reserved cooking water, and salt and pepper. Bring to a boil over high heat. Add the rice, turn the heat to low, and simmer, covered, until the liquid is absorbed and the rice is tender. Serve hot.

PLANNING AHEAD: This is one of those dishes that improves with age; it can be made up to 2 or 3 days ahead and reheated.

VARIATIONS:

- Frozen pigeon peas (labeled *gandules verdes*) are sometimes available and are a good shortcut. Cook a 14-ounce package in 4 cups of water for 15 minutes and pick up the recipe at the point where you drain them and reserve the cooking water. Don't bother with canned pigeon peas; they're too mushy.
- Black-eyed peas are the next best thing if you can't find pigeon peas at all.
- For *moros y cristianos* (Moors and Christians)—the Cuban dish named in honor of Spain's expulsion of the dark-skinned Moors in 1492—substitute black beans for the pigeon peas and omit the Scotch bonnet pepper.
- Among the virtually endless variations on this theme, you can add 1 teaspoon of capers and 4 chopped green olives along with the tomatoes, or substitute unsweetened coconut milk for some or all of the 3 cups of cooking water.

Cuban-Style Black Beans

[6 TO 8 SERVINGS]

If Cuban Miami has a signature dish, it's black beans, frijoles negros, *an essential element of traditional meals, especially on festive occasions like Christmas Eve* (Nochebuena, *page 154). Visitors to Miami can't help but encounter black beans at Cuban restaurants, where they're served at breakfast or lunch with white rice, fried eggs, and Fried Ripe Plantains (page 226), and at dinner with white rice and just about everything. (See the* moros y cristianos *variation in the Caribbean Pigeon Peas and Rice recipe on page 244 for another favorite version.) There's no absolute agreement among Cuban cooks on just what should go into the pot with the beans. Some add a ham hock, some add cilantro, and some wouldn't think of adding sugar. Consistency is another debatable point—thick and creamy or thin and souplike? It depends on whom you ask.*

This relatively understated version is the way we like them best, with a hint of sweetness complementing the mellow flavor of the sofrito (sautéed onion, green bell pepper, and garlic). *As you'll note, black beans are cooked in their soaking liquid to preserve as much flavor and color as possible. If you leave all the liquid in the bean pot after the initial cooking, you'll have black bean soup. Black beans are even better the second day; Juanita Plana, a well-known Miami caterer, likes to serve leftovers with cilantro and sliced onion as a cold salad.*

1 pound dry black beans (2¼ cups)	1 teaspoon ground cumin
2 tablespoons plus ¼ cup (optional) olive oil	1 teaspoon dry-leaf oregano, crumbled
2 large yellow onions, peeled and finely chopped	1 bay leaf
2 green bell peppers, seeded, cored, and finely chopped	1½ teaspoons brown sugar
3 garlic cloves, peeled and minced	2 to 3 teaspoons salt
	1 tablespoon red wine vinegar
	½ teaspoon freshly ground pepper

Rinse the black beans and discard any impurities. Put in a large, heavy pot with 6 cups of water and let soak for 4 hours or as long as overnight.

Bring the beans to a boil over high heat, turn to low, and let simmer, uncovered, until barely tender, about 30 minutes. As they cook, skim off any foam that forms on the surface.

Meanwhile, heat the 2 tablespoons of oil in a skillet over medium heat and sauté the onions, bell peppers, and garlic until soft, about 5 minutes. Stir in the cumin and oregano, cook 1 more minute, and set aside off the heat.

Set a colander in a heavy bowl to catch the cooking liquid and drain the beans. Return them to the pot, along with 3 cups of the liquid. Add the onion mixture, bay leaf, and sugar, and bring to a boil. Lower the heat and simmer, covered, for 30 minutes. Season with salt and cook, covered, until the beans are soft, about 30 minutes longer.

Remove the bay leaf and stir in the vinegar, pepper, and the remaining ¼ cup oil. Serve hot over white rice.

VARIATIONS:

- For additional flavor elements, add 4 dashes of Caribbean hot sauce or Tabasco with the sautéed vegetables and/or 1 tablespoon of dark rum or dry sherry during the last 5 minutes of cooking.
- For a creamier consistency, scoop out 1 cup of the finished beans, puree them in a food processor or blender, and return to the pot.
- For a shortcut version, add three 15½-ounce cans of black beans to the sautéed onion mixture after you've added the cumin and oregano. (Drain the beans or not, depending on the consistency you prefer.) Stir in the vinegar, sugar, and salt to taste, and simmer for 5 minutes.
- As noted above, leaving all the cooking liquid in the pot produces a nice batch of black bean soup. Serve it garnished with diced onion and tomato, and, for a Tex-Mex touch, a dollop of sour cream.

Potatoes

Potatoes, along with corn, tomatoes, hot chiles, and chocolate, were the New World's gift to the old—culinary treasures that European explorers carried home in place of the spices and gold they sought. Potatoes are native to the Peruvian Andes and were cultivated by the Incas. Spanish explorers introduced them to Europe in the 1500s, but, like tomatoes, they were slow to gain acceptance. Both are members of the nightshade family and were thought to be poisonous. (The small green fruits that sometimes develop from potato blossoms are poisonous but not, of course, the underground tubers.) Scotsman Sir Walter Scott and a Belgian named André Parmentier are variously credited with dispelling the fears and popularizing potatoes in Europe. Irish immigrants introduced the potato to North America in the early 1700s, and the rest, as Ronald McDonald would say, is history.

Bogotá-Style Potatoes

The Andes Mountains, where potatoes originated, cut a swath along the Pacific coast of South America, from Venezuela and Colombia in the north to the tip of Chile in the south. Naturally enough, potatoes are a staple throughout the region. And because all roads in this part of the world lead to Miami, we're learning new ways with the familiar spud. This rich and savory Colombian dish makes an excellent accompaniment to grilled meats.

6 large baking potatoes (about 3 pounds)

Kosher salt

2 tablespoons unsalted butter

1 large onion, peeled and finely chopped

3 tomatoes, peeled, seeded, and coarsely chopped

½ Scotch bonnet or 2 or 3 jalapeño peppers, seeded and minced

⅔ cup heavy cream or half-and-half

Freshly ground pepper

8 ounces Muenster cheese, grated (about 2 cups) (see Note)

Peel and quarter the potatoes and place in a saucepan with water to cover and 2 teaspoons of salt. Bring to a boil, lower the heat, and simmer, covered, for 15 to 20 minutes, until they can be pierced easily with a knife but are still firm.

While the potatoes are cooking, melt the butter in a saucepan over medium heat and sauté the onion until soft, about 5 minutes. Add the tomatoes and peppers, and cook for 5 more minutes. Stir in the cream, season to taste with salt and pepper, and set the mixture aside off the heat.

When the potatoes are done, reheat the cream mixture to just below a simmer and stir in the cheese until melted and smooth.

Drain the potatoes well, transfer to a serving dish, and pour on the sauce. Serve immediately.

NOTE: Don't add the cheese until you're ready to use the sauce, or it will become stringy.

Ecuadoran Potato and Cheese Patties

[6 SERVINGS]

Barbara Estrada, an Illinois-born friend, makes these for her husband when he's homesick for his native Ecuador, where they're called llapingachos *(yah-pin-GAH-chose). She serves them plain as a side dish, with avocado slices as an appetizer, or topped with a fried egg as a main dish. They're also lovely with sautéed chopped tomatoes and onions. You can omit the butter and sauté the onion in a tablespoon of vegetable oil for a less rich but still very good result.*

> 2 pounds baking potatoes
>
> Kosher salt
>
> 4 tablespoons unsalted butter
>
> 1 large onion, peeled and finely chopped
>
> ½ cup minced cilantro or flat-leaf parsley
>
> Freshly ground pepper
>
> 6 ounces Muenster cheese, grated (about 1½ cups)
>
> Vegetable oil

Peel and quarter the potatoes and place them in a saucepan with water to cover and 2 teaspoons of salt. Bring to a boil, lower the heat, and simmer, covered, until they can be pierced easily with a knife but are still firm, 15 to 20 minutes.

While the potatoes are cooking, heat 1 tablespoon of the butter in a skillet over medium heat and sauté the onions until soft, about 5 minutes. Set aside.

Drain the potatoes well and shake them around in the hot pan to evaporate as much moisture as possible. Put them through a ricer or food mill, or mash them well with a potato masher. Stir in the remaining 3 tablespoons of butter, the sautéed onions, the cilantro, and salt and pepper to taste.

When cool enough to handle, shape the potato mixture into 12 balls about the size of golf balls. Poke a deep hole in each ball with your finger and fill it with about 1 tablespoon of the cheese. (It will be easier to do if you wad the cheese into a ball first.) Carefully seal the hole closed and gently flatten the ball into a patty. (You don't want the cheese to leak out in the pan.)

Heat a thin layer of oil in a large nonstick skillet over medium heat. (Or use a griddle if you have one and sauté them all at once.) Working in batches, sauté the patties, turning once, until golden brown, 3 to 4 minutes per side. Coat the pan again with oil as necessary and keep the finished ones warm on a baking sheet in a 200-degree oven. Serve immediately.

VARIATION: For a quick alternative, stir the cheese into the mashed potatoes along with the onion and cilantro, scrape the mixture into a buttered baking dish, and brown under the broiler.

Mashed Potatoes with Roasted Corn and Scallions

[4 SERVINGS]

Fresh-roasted sweet corn, tangy scallions, creamy mashed potatoes—what a terrific combination! You may want to make a double batch because everyone is sure to want seconds. If they're available, yellow-fleshed Yukon Gold or Yellow Finn potatoes are especially pretty in this dish. A potato masher certainly does the job, and some people swear by a potato ricer. But if you have a food mill, try running the hot potatoes through it; it produces wonderfully fluffy results. (A food processor is out, of course; it will turn the potatoes to glue.)

2 pounds Yukon Gold or other
   medium-starch potatoes

Kosher salt

1½ cups kernels from fresh sweet
   corn (2 ears) (see Variation)

2 to 4 tablespoons unsalted butter
   (optional)

1 to 1⅓ cups buttermilk

3 scallions, trimmed and thinly
   sliced

Freshly ground pepper (preferably
   white)

Peel the potatoes, halve or quarter them if large, and place in a saucepan with water to cover and 2 teaspoons of salt. Bring to a boil, lower the heat, and simmer, covered, until they can be pierced easily with a knife but are still firm, 15 to 20 minutes.

Heat a nonstick skillet over medium-high heat and dry-sauté the corn, stirring occasionally, until lightly browned, about 5 minutes.

While the potatoes are cooking, heat the butter and buttermilk in a saucepan or in the microwave on medium heat until the butter is melted.

Drain the potatoes well and shake them around in the hot pan to evaporate as much moisture as possible. Mash them thoroughly, drizzling and beating in the buttermilk mixture as you work. When the potatoes are light and fluffy, stir in the reserved corn, scallions, and salt and pepper to taste. Serve immediately.

VARIATION: If fresh corn isn't available, use frozen kernels; let them thaw and drain on several layers of paper towels before roasting.

Salsas, Chutneys, and Sauces

Tropical Sunrise Salsa

Grilled Pineapple and Avocado Salsa

Orange and Roasted Red Pepper Salsa

Fresh Tomato Salsa

Corn and Black Bean Salsa

Pikliz (Haitian-Style Hot Vegetable Relish)

Tropical Fruit Curry

Green Mango Chutney

Gingered Banana Chutney

Papaya–Three Pepper Chutney

Carambola-Cranberry Sauce

Orange-Horseradish-Mustard Sauce

Hot Orange Sauce

Creamy Mango Sauce

 We're grilling and broiling more and panfrying less these days, and that means we need to be more imaginative than Grandma was when it comes to dressing up a piece of chicken, meat, or fish. If there is no frying pan, there are no pan juices and browned bits to deglaze and turn into a sauce or gravy. What to do? Explore the possibilities of salsas and chutneys.

Whether fresh, like Orange and Roasted Red Pepper Salsa, or cooked, like Gingered Banana Chutney, they add as much moisture, more color, and far fewer calories than a pan sauce—and no fat. (Be sure to check out the salsas listed with Main Courses, too; though we've paired them with particular dishes, they will go just as well with many others.)

If made with vinegar, a chutney will keep for months and improve with age—a lovely holiday gift from your kitchen. Speaking of holidays, no matter what else is on your Thanksgiving or Christmas dinner menu, be sure to include Carambola-Cranberry Sauce. Garnished with golden, star-shaped slices of carambola, it's the most festive relish we know.

Tropical Sunrise Salsa

[ABOUT 2½ CUPS]

This light, fresh-tasting salsa has the gorgeous pink, salmon, and yellow hues of the dawn sky over Biscayne Bay. (For spectacular south Florida sunsets, you need to go to Key West, where there's nothing but ocean between you and the sun, and watching it set from Mallory Square is a communal rite.) Canned pineapple will do in a pinch, but there's really no substitute for the intense sweetness and edge of fresh fruit. Basil seems just the right herb here, but fresh mint would be a nice alternative. This is a fine accompaniment for simple grilled or broiled chicken or fish.

½ ripe papaya (about ½ pound), seeded, skinned, and cut into small dice

½ ripe mango, seeded, skinned, and cut into small dice

½ cup diced fresh pineapple

1 medium cucumber, peeled, seeded, and cut into small dice

1 or 2 jalapeño peppers, stemmed, seeded, and minced

4 scallions, trimmed and thinly sliced

2 to 4 tablespoons finely chopped fresh basil

2 tablespoons fresh lime juice

Kosher salt and pepper to taste

Combine the papaya, mango, pineapple, cucumber, jalapeños, scallions, basil, and lime juice in a small glass bowl. Toss gently just to combine. Serve immediately or refrigerate, covered, for up to 1 hour. (If making further ahead of time than that, add the papaya and pineapple just before serving; otherwise, they'll make the salsa watery.)

Grilled Pineapple and Avocado Salsa

[ABOUT 3½ CUPS]

You probably associate pineapples with Hawaii, but the fruit originated in South America, and pineapple plantations once covered huge swaths of modern-day Miami. Grilling or broiling the pineapple caramelizes some of its sugars and adds an irresistible flavor and color to this salsa, with avocado providing a mellow counterpoint. Serve the leftover half pineapple grilled or broiled as a side dish or dessert at another meal.

½ ripe pineapple, peeled and sliced into 1-inch rounds

Vegetable oil

Kosher salt and freshly ground pepper

½ ripe Florida avocado or 1 California avocado

2 tablespoons fresh lime juice

½ cup diced Vidalia or other sweet onion, or 6 to 8 scallions, trimmed and thinly sliced

½ yellow or green bell pepper, seeded and diced

1 to 2 jalapeño peppers, seeded and minced

2 tablespoons chopped cilantro or flat-leaf parsley

Brush the pineapple slices with oil, and season with salt and pepper.

TO GRILL: Use indirect, medium heat (see page 100). Grill the pineapple about 5 inches from the fire until lightly caramelized, 8 to 10 minutes per side.

TO COOK INDOORS: Position an oven rack so the pineapple will be about 5 inches from the heat source. Broil for 8 to 10 minutes per side, until lightly caramelized. Or arrange the slices on a grill pan and grill over high heat.

Set the pineapple aside to cool.

Cut the avocado into ¼-inch dice and combine in a small glass bowl with the lime juice, onion, bell pepper, jalapeños, and cilantro.

Trim away and discard the tough core from the cooled pineapple slices and cut into ¼-inch dice. Add to the avocado mixture, toss gently to combine, and season to taste with salt and pepper. Serve immediately or refrigerate. The salsa will keep well for up to 2 days.

Orange and Roasted Red Pepper Salsa

[ABOUT 2½ CUPS]

This brightly flavored and colored salsa turns the simplest grilled meat or fish into a company meal. Florida's commercial orange-growing region is at the center of the state, but plenty of Miamians have backyard orange trees and the fruit figures large in local lore. The story goes that a bouquet of orange blossoms persuaded railroad magnate Henry Flagler to extend his Florida East Coast Railway to south Florida, the event that led to the incorporation of Miami in 1896. After a hard freeze devastated the central Florida citrus crop in the winter of 1894–95, Julia Tuttle sent the blossoms north to Flagler in St. Augustine as proof that frost-free Miami was fertile territory for growers and shippers. Whether or not the flowers were the deciding factor, Tuttle, the "mother of Miami," got her wish, and this frontier settlement became a city. And not incidentally, the land she owned at the mouth of the Miami River became much more valuable.

> 2 oranges
> 2 red bell peppers, roasted, peeled, seeded,
>   and diced (see page 190)
> 1 or 2 jalapeño peppers, seeded and minced
> ½ cup diced red onion
> 2 tablespoons chopped fresh cilantro or flat-leaf parsley
> 1 tablespoon fresh lime juice
> Kosher salt and freshly ground pepper

Working with 1 orange at a time, cut off both ends with a sharp paring knife and set it flat on a work surface. Slice down along the curve of the orange, cutting away the peel and bitter white pith. Hold the peeled fruit over a bowl to catch the juice and slice between the membranes to remove each segment. Cut the segments into ½-inch slices.

Combine the orange slices and juice, bell peppers, jalapeños, onion, cilantro, and lime juice in a small glass bowl. Toss gently to combine and season to taste with salt and pepper. Serve immediately or refrigerate. The salsa will keep well for up to 2 days.

Fresh Tomato Salsa

[ABOUT 4 CUPS]

As with most things, fresh is best when it comes to tomato salsa. If your jalapeños are on the mild side, you may want to add extra.

4 large tomatoes, seeded and diced

¼ cup chopped onion

¼ cup chopped cilantro or flat-leaf parsley

1 or 2 garlic cloves, peeled and minced

2 or more jalapeño peppers, minced

1 tablespoon extra-virgin olive oil

1 tablespoon fresh lime juice

Kosher salt and freshly ground pepper

Combine the tomatoes, onion, cilantro, garlic, jalapeños, oil, and lime juice in a nonaluminum bowl. Taste for seasoning, and add salt and pepper if you like. Refrigerate, covered, for at least 1 hour before serving so the flavors can blend. It will keep for a few days.

Corn and Black Bean Salsa

[ABOUT 4 CUPS]

This crisp, colorful salsa couldn't be easier to make. It's terrific with seafood or as a dip with corn chips.

2 cups fresh corn kernels (see Note and Variation)

1½ cups Basic Black Beans (page 19) or one 15½-ounce can, rinsed and drained

1 small red bell pepper, seeded and diced

2 jalapeño peppers, seeded and diced

¼ cup chopped cilantro or flat-leaf parsley

1 bunch scallions, trimmed and thinly sliced

1 tablespoon fresh lime juice

½ teaspoon ground cumin

Kosher salt to taste

Stir together the corn, beans, bell and jalapeño peppers, cilantro, scallions, lime juice, cumin, and salt to taste in a small glass or plastic bowl.

Cover tightly and refrigerate for at least 1 hour so the flavors can blend. It will keep well for up to 2 days.

VARIATION: You can use frozen or drained canned corn kernels in place of fresh corn. There is no need to cook them.

NOTE: See page 22 for a neat way to cut kernels from a corn cob.

Pikliz (Haitian-Style Hot Vegetable Relish)

[ABOUT 4 CUPS]

In one of those great Miami melting pot innovations, Haitian-born educator Gepsie Mettelus serves pikliz (pick-LEEZ) on hamburgers. Her recipe takes advantage of American convenience foods but is true to the fiery spirit of the island original. Make your first batch with jalapeños and then decide if you can handle hotter peppers.

1 10-ounce package grated vegetables for coleslaw

1 10-ounce package frozen mixed vegetables

1 large onion, peeled and diced

10 to 12 small hot peppers, seeded and diced

10 to 12 whole cloves (see Note)

4 to 6 whole garlic cloves, peeled (see Note)

1 cup cider vinegar

1 cup sour orange juice (or ½ cup each lime and regular orange juice)

½ teaspoon kosher salt

Combine the coleslaw mix, mixed vegetables, onion, peppers, cloves, garlic, vinegar, sour orange juice, and salt in a large, lidded, nonaluminum container. Refrigerate for at least 1 day before using. It will keep indefinitely in the refrigerator.

NOTE: Wrapping the cloves and garlic in a piece of cheese cloth will save you from biting into them.

Tropical Fruit Curry

[ABOUT 3 CUPS]

Serve this sweet and lively curry as a sauce with grilled or broiled meat, chicken, or fish, as a side dish over rice, or as a main dish combined with sautéed shrimp. Curry powder is a blend of spices that typically includes cardamom, cinnamon, cloves, coriander, cumin, fenugreek, mace, nutmeg, pepper, and turmeric. If your curry powder is more than a couple of months old, it's time to buy a new jar. If you like it hot, look for a Madras blend. When adding curry powder to any dish, it's important to sauté it to release its full flavor.

½ medium papaya, pared, seeded, and cut into small dice

½ medium mango, pared, seeded, and cut into small dice

1 cup diced pineapple (preferably fresh)

1 medium banana, peeled, quartered lengthwise, and cut into ¼-inch slices

2 tablespoons fresh lime juice

2 tablespoons vegetable oil

1 large onion, peeled and thinly sliced

1 garlic clove, peeled and minced

1 tablespoon curry powder

½ teaspoon ground cumin

½ teaspoon ground allspice

½ cup unsweetened coconut milk

½ cup raisins

2 teaspoons grated fresh ginger

1 teaspoon kosher salt

½ teaspoon freshly ground pepper

Toss the papaya, mango, pineapple, and banana with the lime juice and set aside.

Heat the oil in a saucepan over medium heat and sauté the onion and garlic until soft, about 5 minutes.

Stir in the curry powder, cumin, and allspice, and sauté for 1 minute.

Add the coconut milk, raisins, ginger, salt, and pepper, and simmer for 5 minutes.

Stir in the reserved fruit and simmer for about 5 minutes to blend the flavors. Adjust the seasoning if necessary and serve hot or at room temperature.

Green Mango Chutney

[ABOUT 4 CUPS]

Like curry, chutney is an East Indian contribution to the Caribbean pantry. Preserved by vinegar, this one has a robust flavor that improves with age. It will keep in the refrigerator for up to six months and makes a great gift from your kitchen. Serve it with any roast or grilled meat, or mix a few tablespoons of it with sour cream or mayonnaise for a fabulous chicken salad dressing.

3 cups cider vinegar

1 cup fresh orange juice

2 large unripe mangos, halved, pitted, peeled, and diced (see Variations)

2 cups dark brown sugar

2 tablespoons tamarind juice or pulp, or 2 teaspoons each lime juice, molasses, and Worcestershire sauce

2 teaspoons minced fresh ginger

1 garlic clove, peeled and minced

1 cup minced onion

½ teaspoon red pepper flakes

1 teaspoon ground cinnamon

4 whole allspice berries

1 teaspoon ground nutmeg

1 cup raisins

Kosher salt and freshly ground pepper

Bring the vinegar and orange juice to a boil in a large saucepan. Add the mangos and simmer, covered, for 15 minutes.

Stir in the brown sugar, tamarind, ginger, garlic, onion, pepper flakes, cinnamon, allspice, and nutmeg. Bring back to a boil, lower the heat, and simmer, uncovered, for 20 minutes.

Stir in the raisins and simmer about 15 minutes more, until the mixture is thick and jam-like.

Remove from the heat, taste for seasoning, and add salt and pepper if you like. Spoon into screw-top jars, let cool before capping them, and refrigerate.

VARIATIONS: Tart green mango is our first choice for this dish, but if ripe mango is all you can find, use it. Unripe papaya is another alternative. You might also like to add 2 diced carambolas or firm bananas along with the raisins.

Gingered Banana Chutney

[ABOUT 2 CUPS]

Fresh ginger, jalapeño pepper, and cayenne add a pleasing bite to this savory chutney. It is especially good with roast pork or ham.

1 cup white vinegar

½ cup brown sugar

1 cup fresh orange juice

3 cups diced ripe bananas (about 5 medium bananas)

1 tablespoon grated fresh ginger

1 jalapeño pepper, seeded and minced

½ cup raisins

4 whole allspice berries

1 teaspoon kosher salt

½ teaspoon ground cinnamon

½ teaspoon ground nutmeg

½ teaspoon freshly ground pepper

⅛ teaspoon cayenne

Bring the vinegar to a boil over high heat in a large nonaluminum saucepan. Stir in the sugar and orange juice, and return just to a boil. Turn the heat to medium-low and simmer for 10 minutes.

Stir in the bananas, ginger, jalapeño, raisins, allspice, salt, cinnamon, nutmeg, pepper, and cayenne. Return to a simmer and cook, stirring frequently, until thickened, 20 to 30 minutes. Let the chutney cool to room temperature and remove the allspice berries before serving.

PLANNING AHEAD: The chutney can be stored, tightly covered, in the refrigerator for up to 6 months.

Papaya–Three Pepper Chutney

[ABOUT 2 CUPS]

Papaya has a perfumy sweetness that marries well with the bell peppers and jalapeño peppers in this colorful chutney. There is no vinegar to preserve it, so plan to use it within two or three days. It goes especially well with roast chicken.

1 medium or ½ large ripe papaya
   (12 to 14 ounces)

2 red bell peppers

1 green bell pepper

1 to 3 jalapeño peppers

¼ cup finely chopped red onion

1 tablespoon grated fresh ginger

⅓ cup honey

2 tablespoons fresh lemon juice

½ teaspoon kosher salt

Freshly ground pepper

Peel and seed the papaya and cut it into ½-inch cubes. Seed the bell peppers and jalapeños, and slice into julienne strips.

Stir together the papaya, bell peppers, jalapeños, onion, ginger, honey, lemon juice, salt, and pepper to taste in a large nonaluminum saucepan. Bring just to a boil over high heat. Turn the heat to medium-low and simmer, stirring occasionally, until thickened, 10 to 15 minutes. Let the chutney cool to room temperature before serving.

VARIATION: Use green rather than ripe papaya for a more piquant flavor.

NOTE: Coat the inside of your measuring cup with vegetable oil spray before pouring in the honey, and it will slip out cleanly.

Carambola-Cranberry Sauce

[ABOUT 3 CUPS]

This cranberry sauce is filled with tangy bits of carambola and garnished with star-shaped slices of the golden fruit—a wonderfully festive dish for a holiday table. The timing couldn't be better: Carambolas (see page 5) are available from late summer to early spring but are at their best in November and December. The choice of fruit is ideal, too: Carambola keeps its bright color and crisp texture when sliced and develops an assertive, almost quincelike flavor when cooked. If the ones you find at the store are green around the edges, leave them at room temperature to ripen. If they're a bit overripe and brown on the ridges, trim away the discoloration with a paring knife.

> 2 ripe carambolas
> 1 cup fresh orange juice
> 1 cup sugar
> 1 12-ounce bag cranberries, rinsed and picked over
> 1 tablespoon grated fresh ginger

Cut one of the carambolas in half crosswise and set half of it aside. Cut the remaining fruit into ½-inch slices, remove the seeds, and cut into dice.

Combine the orange juice and sugar in a heavy saucepan and bring to a boil, stirring until the sugar dissolves. Reduce the heat and simmer for 5 minutes.

Stir in the cranberries, ginger, and diced carambola. Simmer, stirring occasionally, until the berries begin to pop, about 8 minutes. Set aside to cool and pour into a serving dish.

Cut the reserved carambola into ¼-inch slices, and arrange them on top of the sauce. Serve chilled or at room temperature.

PLANNING AHEAD: You can make the sauce up to three days before serving.

VARIATION: For a deeper red color and a more complex flavor, substitute dry red wine for all or part of the orange juice.

NOTES:

- Buy extra bags of cranberries when they're abundant at holiday time and keep them in your freezer for use throughout the year. They'll keep up to a year and can be used without defrosting.
- Take the cranberries off the heat when they begin to pop; otherwise, they'll get mushy and bitter.

Orange-Horseradish-Mustard Sauce

[ABOUT 2 CUPS]

We created this zingy sauce to serve with stone crab claws (page 213), but it's a taste bud–tingling accompaniment for shrimp and other seafood, too.

> 1 cup orange marmalade
> ¼ cup Dijon mustard
> ¼ cup prepared horseradish
> ½ cup mayonnaise

Combine the marmalade, mustard, horseradish, and mayonnaise in a small bowl and mix well with a fork. Serve immediately or refrigerate for up to 2 days. (It begins losing its punch after that.)

Hot Orange Sauce

[ABOUT 1½ CUPS]

Here's a variation on the same theme that is terrific with roast or grilled meat or chicken.

1 cup orange marmalade
¼ cup fresh orange juice
2 teaspoons grated fresh ginger
1 teaspoon prepared horseradish
½ teaspoon hot pepper sauce

Combine the marmalade, orange juice, ginger, horseradish, and pepper sauce in a small bowl and mix well with a fork. Serve immediately or refrigerate for up to 2 days.

Creamy Mango Sauce

[ABOUT 1½ CUPS]

This smooth, sweet sauce has a tangy edge and a soft peach color that goes beautifully with seafood. Try it with papaya instead of mango or, for a hotter version, stir in minced jalapeño with the salt and pepper.

1 ripe mango, peeled and pitted, or 1 cup mango puree

½ cup sour cream or plain yogurt

2 tablespoons fresh lime juice

1 teaspoon grated fresh ginger

¼ teaspoon ground cumin

¼ teaspoon hot pepper sauce (optional)

Kosher salt and freshly ground pepper

Cut the mango into chunks. Combine it in a food processor or blender with the sour cream, lime juice, ginger, cumin, and pepper sauce, and process until smooth. Season to taste with salt and pepper. Serve immediately or refrigerate for up to 1 week.

Desserts

Carambola Upside-Down Cake

Warm Calabaza Spice Cake with Browned Butter–Rum Glaze

Roasted Plantain Cake with Toasted Coconut Topping

Chocolate-Pecan Torte with Chocolate Glaze

Couldn't-Be-Easier Key Lime Cake

Tres Leches
(Nicaraguan Three-Milk Cake)

Piña Colada Cheesecake

Tangy Lemon Tart with Sugary Almond Crust

Guava Linzertorte

Free-Form Mango Tart

Chocolate Key Lime Tart

Key Lime Pie

Mango Margarita Pie with Gingersnap Crust

Orange-Almond Biscotti

Chocolate-Coconut Tuiles

Easy Coconut Flan

Creamy Rice Pudding with a Hint of Lime

Individual Chocolate–Cuban Coffee Soufflés

Oranges in Red Wine

Orange-Marinated Strawberries

Lemon Sorbet with Variations

Sugar Syrup

Mango Madness: Mango Ice Cream and Mango Ice

Bananas in Rum Caramel over Vanilla Ice Cream

Banana-Papaya Batidos
with Variations

Cuban Coffee Sauce

Chunky Mango Sauce

Passion Fruit Sauce

In a place where voluptuous mangos, lush papayas, and succulent citrus are as close as the backyard, it's easy to understand why tropical fruit takes center stage at dessert. It's an embarrassment of riches, really. We're overwhelmed by overactive fruit trees the way northern gardeners are undone by bumper crops of zucchini. It's not uncommon to find a stack of star-shaped carambola, yours for the taking, next to the office coffeepot in the fall or to be sent home with a bag of Key limes after dinner at a friend's house in the winter. The truth is that we consider this bounty our due for enduring the months of sultry weather that make it possible. The price for being able to plant a papaya seed in your yard one summer and have a ten-foot tree the next is not being able to turn off your air-conditioning before Thanksgiving!

Thanks to modern shipping and storage methods, you can explore the tropical harvest almost anywhere these days. Begin by taking home some of those exotic fruits you see in your produce department. It's often love at first bite for peach-pineapple-like mango; others, like perfumy papaya, can be an acquired taste. The only way to find your favorites is to try them for yourself, and our Ingredients Guide (page 3) will help you make your choices.

Tropical fruit isn't the whole story of Miami desserts, of course. Sugar is also a part of our Caribbean inheritance and our everyday life. If you need an energy boost while driving in rush hour, chances are you can find a vendor at a busy intersection selling bags of fresh-cut sugarcane. Sugar has been a mainstay of Caribbean economic and culinary life for hundreds of years. In her book A *Taste of Old Cuba,* Maria Lluria de O'Higgins recalls that eating sugar was considered an act of patriotism in the post–World War I Cuba of her childhood. "It is not uncommon, still," she writes, "to hear a Cuban of my generation say, '*Dos para mi y tres para Cuba*' ('Two for me and three for Cuba'), while pouring five heaping teaspoons of sugar into a cup of *café con leche* [coffee with milk]."

It's not surprising, then, that Caribbean and Latin American desserts are known for their intense sweetness. A sliver of Nicaraguan Tres Leches cake or Cuban flan is enough to satisfy the keenest sweet tooth. So is a modest piece of our Chocolate-Pecan Torte with Chocolate Glaze or Mango Margarita Pie. Miamians are as fitness and fat conscious as most Americans. Perhaps even more so, given our climate: It's simply too hot here to hide extra pounds behind bulky sweaters most of the time. But we are no more immune to the soul-satisfying pleasure of beautifully crafted sweets.

Baking doesn't leave you nearly as much room for improvisation as other kinds of cooking; a cake or cookie recipe is essentially a chemical formula, and if you tinker too much with the ingredients or proportions, it won't turn out well. That's why it's important to read the recipe all the way through before beginning, and to measure accurately as you go along. Here are a few other tips and tricks of the trade:

- In general, ingredients should be at room temperature. That means you should take out refrigerated items such as eggs about an hour before using them. If you need to separate eggs, though, it's easier when they're cold. Butter that is to be cut into pastry dough is another exception to the room-temperature rule; it should be chilled to ensure a flaky crust.

- If you have only one set of measuring spoons, treat yourself to a second one so you don't have to stop to wash the spoons in the middle of a recipe.

- Unless otherwise specified, bake cakes in the center of the oven, and pies and tarts in the lower third. (Being closer to the heating element helps crisp the bottom of the crust.) If you need to rearrange the racks, do so before turning on the oven.

- A large mesh strainer is a great tool for sifting. Set it in a mixing bowl, measure the ingredients into it, and tap it gently to sift them.

- Pay attention to the difference between "1 cup flour, sifted," which is measured and then sifted, and "1 cup sifted flour," which is sifted and then measured. Why sift at all? It incorporates air into the flour and lightens the final product.

- Unless otherwise specified, use large eggs.

- Unsalted butter is the best choice for baking as well as cooking. It allows you more control over the amount of salt in the finished dish, and because salt acts as a preservative, it tends to be fresher than salted. It also has a lower water content.

- Don't use salted butter to grease a pan; the salt can cause the cake to stick. To flour a greased pan, spoon in about 1 tablespoon of flour, tilt the pan back and forth until it is completely coated, and tap the excess flour into the wastebasket.

- Cake flour is milled from softer wheat than all-purpose flour and produces more tender baked goods. The two are not interchangeable, so don't substitute one for the other.

- The acid in cultured dairy products such as buttermilk, sour cream, and yogurt is used to activate the baking soda in some recipes. Here is how to make a substitute for 1 cup of buttermilk: Pour 1 tablespoon of vinegar or lemon juice into a measuring cup and add enough regular milk to make 1 cup. Let stand for 10 minutes before using. If you add 3 tablespoons of melted butter to the mixture, you'll have a sour cream substitute.

- Baking powder loses its oomph over time, so buy it in small quantities. To check for potency, dissolve a teaspoon of it in hot water; it should bubble briskly.

- Unsweetened chocolate is 100 percent chocolate "liquor," the substance that remains after most of the cocoa butter is extracted from processed cocoa beans. Bittersweet and the slightly sweeter semisweet chocolate are made from chocolate liquor, sugar, vanillin, and an emulsifier called lecithin. They can be used interchangeably. After chocolate liquor is dried and ground, it's called cocoa powder; Dutch-process cocoa has the smoothest taste and darkest color because it is treated with alkali to reduce its acidity.

- The best chocolate to use in baking is the one that tastes best to you out of hand. The ingredient list on the package is another good guide; chocolate liquor should be the first one listed. Callebaut, El Rey, Nestlé, Tobler, Valrhona, and Van Leer are among the brands known for pure, high-quality chocolate.

- To melt chocolate, chop it first and use a double boiler or a microwave, following the manufacturer's instructions; direct heat can easily scorch it, ruining its flavor and texture. Be sure your utensils are dry and the container is uncovered, because a few drops of water or condensation can make chocolate "seize," hardening and losing its sheen. (Larger amounts of liquid don't have the same ruinous effect.) To salvage seized chocolate, try stirring in 1 teaspoon of vegetable oil per ounce of chocolate; it doesn't always work, but it's worth a try.

- Vanilla comes from vanilla beans, which in turn come from *Vanilla planifolia,* the only member of the orchid family that produces an edible fruit. Buy pure vanilla extract; the imitation kind is made from byproducts of papermaking and, not surprisingly, has a bitter aftertaste.

Carambola Upside-Down Cake

[8 SERVINGS]

Star-shaped carambola slices glistening with buttery syrup crown this spectacular-looking dessert. The fruit's mildly sweet, slightly citric flavor works well with the orange-tinged cake, inspired by a creation of Disney Institute chef Mario Martinez. An upside-down cake traditionally is baked in a cast-iron skillet, but a cake pan works just as well and produces straight rather than slanted sides. The cake is best served warm. If you make it ahead of time, cool it in the pan and rewarm it in a 350-degree oven for about 10 minutes before inverting it onto a serving platter.

FOR THE TOPPING:

3 large or 4 medium carambolas

4 tablespoons unsalted butter

¾ cup light brown sugar

½ cup coarsely chopped pecans

FOR THE CAKE:

1½ cups sifted cake flour

2½ teaspoons baking powder

½ teaspoon salt

5⅓ tablespoons unsalted butter, at room temperature

½ cup sugar

2 eggs

1 teaspoon vanilla extract

½ cup fresh orange juice

Cut the carambolas into ½-inch crosswise slices and remove and discard the seeds.

Melt the butter over low heat in a 9- or 10-inch ovenproof skillet or round cake pan. Stir in the brown sugar until it dissolves.

Remove the pan from the heat and arrange the carambola slices over the bottom. Scatter the pecans between the slices and set the pan aside.

Preheat the oven to 350 degrees.

Sift the flour, baking powder, and salt together in a small bowl.

In the bowl of an electric mixer, beat the butter at low speed until smooth. Increase the speed to medium, add the sugar, and beat for 2 minutes, until fluffy. Beat in the eggs, one at a time, and the vanilla extract.

Turn the mixer speed to low and add the flour mixture alternately with the orange juice in 3 additions, beating until well incorporated.

Scrape the batter into the prepared pan and bake for 30 to 45 minutes, until the cake is golden brown and has begun to pull away from the sides of the pan.

Let the cake cool for a few minutes on a rack and run a small knife around the edges of the pan to loosen it. Protecting your hands with pot holders, invert the cake onto a serving platter and scrape out any fruit or syrup that clings to the pan. Serve warm.

VARIATIONS: Although it won't have the same eye-catching appearance, the cake will taste great made with sliced ripe mango, papaya, or, of course, pineapple. Walnuts, almonds, or macadamia nuts can be used in place of the pecans.

Warm Calabaza Spice Cake with Browned Butter–Rum Glaze

[14 TO 16 SERVINGS]

This exceptionally moist and flavorful spice cake is made with calabaza (see page 4), a Caribbean squash that is also known as West Indian pumpkin. If it's not available, substitute Hubbard or other hard-shelled squash, or save a step and use 1 cup of plain canned pumpkin. The simple glaze is a winner, too—one you'll want to use on other cakes and cookies.

1 pound calabaza or other hard-shelled squash

½ cup sour cream

2¼ cups sifted cake flour

1 tablespoon baking powder

1 teaspoon baking soda

½ teaspoon salt

2 teaspoons ground cinnamon

½ teaspoon ground ginger

½ teaspoon ground allspice

½ teaspoon freshly grated or ground nutmeg

¼ teaspoon ground cloves

½ cup coarsely chopped walnuts or pecans

½ cup raisins

8 tablespoons (1 stick) unsalted butter, at room temperature

½ cup granulated sugar

1 cup firmly packed light brown sugar

3 eggs

1 teaspoon vanilla extract

2 tablespoons dark rum

Browned Butter–Rum Glaze (recipe follows)

Scrape the seeds and fiber from the calabaza and cut it into chunks. Steam over boiling water for 20 to 25 minutes or microwave, covered with plastic wrap, at full power for 8 to 10 minutes, until tender. Set aside to cool.

Preheat the oven to 350 degrees. Butter and flour a 9- or 10-inch Bundt or tube pan.

Scrape out the flesh of the calabaza; you should have 1 cup. Combine with the sour cream in a blender or food processor and process until smooth. Set aside.

Sift the flour, baking powder, baking soda, salt, cinnamon, ginger, allspice, nutmeg, and cloves together into a bowl. Add the walnuts and raisins, and toss to coat. (This keeps them from sinking to the bottom of the cake.) Set aside.

Beat the butter at low speed in the large bowl of an electric mixer until creamy. Add the granulated and brown sugars, and blend well. Increase the speed to medium-high and add the eggs, one at a time, beating well after each addition. Beat in the vanilla extract and rum.

Turn the mixer speed to low and beat in the flour mixture alternately with the calabaza mixture in 3 additions.

Scrape the batter into the prepared pan and bake for 45 to 50 minutes, until it has pulled away slightly from the sides of the pan and a cake tester inserted in the center comes out clean and dry.

Let the cake cool on a rack in the pan for 10 minutes. Invert it onto a second rack, remove the pan, and let cool for 15 or 20 minutes more, until set but still warm. Drizzle on the glaze, let it harden for a few minutes, and serve.

Browned Butter–Rum Glaze:

1 tablespoon unsalted butter

¾ cup sifted confectioners' sugar

½ teaspoon vanilla extract

1 to 2 tablespoons dark rum

Melt the butter in a small saucepan over low heat and let sizzle until golden brown, about 1 minute. (Be careful not to burn it.)

Remove the pan from the heat and stir in the sugar and vanilla extract with a wooden spoon. Slowly add the rum, still stirring, until the glaze is thin enough to pour.

Pour the glaze over the cake and let drizzle down the sides.

Roasted Plantain Cake with Toasted Coconut Topping

[14 TO 16 SERVINGS]

Roasting intensifies the natural sweetness of plantains (page 9), those oversized cooking bananas that aren't ripe until their skins turn black. Once roasted, they make a fine dessert on their own sprinkled with brown sugar or spooned over ice cream. If you can't find ripe plantains, buy yellow (mid-ripe) ones and enclose them in a paper bag for several days to speed up the process. Regular bananas, ripe but not black, work well here, too. The toasted coconut and pecan topping tastes as good as it looks and makes this cake a fast seller at bake sales. We like to serve it with vanilla or coconut ice cream.

FOR THE CAKE:

3 large black-ripe plantains or
   5 medium-size ripe bananas

2¼ cups sifted cake flour

1 tablespoon baking powder

½ teaspoon baking soda

½ teaspoon salt

8 tablespoons (1 stick) unsalted
   butter, at room temperature

1¼ cups sugar

2 eggs

2 tablespoons banana liqueur or
   dark rum

1 teaspoon vanilla extract

1 cup coarsely chopped walnuts

FOR THE TOPPING:

2½ tablespoons unsalted butter,
   cut into small pieces and
   chilled

¼ cup firmly packed brown sugar

1 tablespoon flour

1 cup shredded sweetened coconut

½ cup coarsely chopped walnuts

Up to a day before making the cake, roast the plantains: Place them in a foil-lined baking dish, prick the skin to let steam escape, and bake in a preheated 350-degree oven for 35 minutes, until soft and juicy. Or prick the skin and microwave them on full power for about 5 minutes. Set aside to cool, and if not using immediately, refrigerate them.

Preheat the oven to 350 degrees. Lightly butter and flour a 9-by-13-inch cake pan or a 10-inch angel food pan. (If using the tube pan, cut a parchment paper liner for the bottom.)

Remove the roasted plantains from their skins and puree in a food processor or blender. You should have about 1½ cups.

Sift the flour, baking powder, baking soda, and salt together into a bowl. Set aside.

Beat the butter at low speed with an electric mixer until creamy. Add the sugar and mix well. Add the pureed plantain and mix until well incorporated. Increase the mixer speed to medium-high and add the eggs, one at a time, beating well after each addition. Beat in the liqueur and vanilla extract.

Turn the mixer speed to low and slowly add the dry ingredients, beating until well incorporated. Increase the speed to high and beat for 2 minutes. Stir in the walnuts.

Scrape the batter into the prepared pan and bake for 25 minutes.

Meanwhile, combine the butter, brown sugar, flour, coconut, and nuts for the topping in a small bowl and mix with your fingers until crumbly.

Remove the partially baked cake from the oven and scatter the topping over it. Bake for 15 to 20 minutes more, until the topping is golden brown and a cake tester inserted in the center of the cake comes out clean.

Cool the cake on a rack. If using an angel food pan, unmold it onto a second rack and reverse it onto a serving plate so the topping is on top. Cut and serve.

Chocolate-Pecan Torte
with Chocolate Glaze

[8 TO 10 SERVINGS]

No celebration of New World cuisine would be complete without chocolate, that most ambrosial of gifts from the Americas. We so strongly associate it with dessert that it's surprising to learn chocolate was served only as a drink until well into the nineteenth century. The word comes from xocolatl, Aztec for "bitter water," and the unsweetened beverage the Aztecs made from cocoa beans was bitter indeed. They considered it an aphrodisiac and reserved it for royalty. Legend has it that the Aztec ruler Montezuma drank fifty goblets of chocolate a day, which, if true, would make him the greatest chocoholic (not to mention stud!) of all time.

This intensely chocolate cake couldn't be richer—or simpler to make. There is only one bowl to wash. Because it's flourless, this small cake would be a welcome addition to a Passover menu.

FOR THE CAKE:

4 ounces semisweet chocolate, coarsely chopped

1¾ cups pecans

½ cup plus 2 tablespoons sugar

8 tablespoons (1 stick) unsalted butter, at room temperature

3 eggs

FOR THE GLAZE:

6 ounces semisweet chocolate, coarsely chopped

6 tablespoons butter

1 teaspoon light corn syrup

20 pecan halves

Preheat the oven to 375 degrees. Butter an 8-inch cake pan. Cut out a circle of parchment or wax paper to fit the bottom of the pan. Insert the paper and butter it, too.

Melt the chocolate in the top of a double boiler or in the microwave. Set aside to cool slightly.

IN A FOOD PROCESSOR: Combine the nuts and 2 tablespoons of the sugar in the food processor and pulse until the nuts are finely ground. Scrape them onto a piece of wax paper. Combine the butter and the remaining ½ cup of sugar in the processor and process until well blended. Add the melted chocolate and eggs, and process until smooth. Add the nuts and pulse just until well blended.

WITH AN ELECTRIC MIXER: First grind the nuts finely in a nut grinder and set them aside. Beat the softened butter and the sugar on medium speed until light and creamy. Add the eggs one by one, beating well after each addition. Turn the beater speed to low and add the chocolate and nuts, beating just until incorporated.

Scrape the batter into the prepared pan and bake for 25 to 30 minutes, or until a crust forms on the top. Set aside on a rack to cool for about 20 minutes.

To make the glaze, heat the chocolate, butter, and corn syrup in a small, heavy saucepan over low heat, stirring frequently, until the chocolate is almost melted. Remove from the heat to finish melting, stirring once or twice. (Don't whisk or beat the glaze; you don't want air bubbles marring the finish.) Set aside for a few minutes to cool and thicken slightly.

Invert the cake onto a cake rack placed over a baking pan and remove the paper. Reserve ¼ cup of the glaze and pour the rest onto the middle of the cake. Tilt the plate so the glaze covers the top and runs down the sides; smooth the sides if necessary with a metal cake spatula dipped in hot water.

Dip one end of each pecan into the reserved glaze. Place on a baking sheet and refrigerate for a few minutes, until the glaze is set. Arrange the pecans around the edge of the cake with the chocolate coating to the outside. Transfer the cake to a serving plate.

PLANNING AHEAD: You can bake the torte up to 2 days ahead and glaze it up to 1 day ahead. The unglazed torte freezes beautifully, too, for up to 1 month.

NOTES:
- Food processor blades are hard to scrape, so use this trick to get all the batter into the pan: Remove the processor bowl from the machine and insert your finger in the shaft to hold the blade in place. Pour as much of the batter as possible into the pan. Return the processor bowl to the machine, lock the cover in place, and run the processor for a few seconds to let centrifugal force pull the batter off the blade. Remove the cover and blade, and scrape the batter off the sides of the bowl and into the pan.
- Here is how professionals line a round pan with parchment paper: Cut a square of paper a little larger than the pan. Fold it in half, then quarters, eighths (you'll have a triangle), and finally sixteenths. Press the triangle against the bottom of the pan with the long point at the center and cut the paper even with the edge of the pan. When you unfold it, you'll have a circle that's just the right size.

Couldn't-Be-Easier Key Lime Cake

[14 TO 16 SERVINGS]

Key limes have a tarter, more acidic flavor than Persian limes, but either one will work well in this simple and luscious dessert. It's a shortcut variation on the East 62nd Street Lemon Cake created by "queen of cakes" Maida Heatter, the most distinguished—and delightful—member of the Miami culinary community.

This cake will keep nicely for several days in the refrigerator and is actually better the second day. Whipped cream and thin strips of lime zest make a pretty garnish. Cake mix recipes like this one are immensely popular with readers of the Miami Herald's food section but have been known to trip up cooks who think they're supposed to mix the cake according to package directions first. Don't make that mistake; dump the dry mix into the bowl, throw out the box, and proceed as directed below.

FOR THE CAKE:

1 yellow cake mix (2-layer size)

8 ounces plain yogurt or sour
  cream

3 eggs

⅓ cup vegetable oil

¼ cup fresh lime juice

1 tablespoon grated lime zest

FOR THE GLAZE:

½ cup fresh lime juice

¾ cup sugar

FOR SERVING:

¼ cup confectioners' sugar

Preheat the oven to 350 degrees. Butter and flour a 9- or 10-inch Bundt or other tube pan.

To make the cake, combine the cake mix, yogurt, eggs, vegetable oil, lime juice, and zest in a mixing bowl. Beat on low speed with an electric mixer until combined. Increase the speed to medium and beat for 2 minutes.

Scrape the batter into the prepared pan and bake for 40 to 45 minutes, until the cake pulls away slightly from the sides of the pan and a cake tester inserted in the center comes out clean and dry.

While the cake is baking, make the glaze: Combine the lime juice and sugar in a small saucepan and heat over low heat until the sugar dissolves.

Set the cake, still in the pan, on a cooling rack. Poke tiny holes in the cake with a thin skewer or cake tester and brush with half the glaze.

Let the cake cool in the pan for 10 minutes, then invert it onto a second rack. (Put wax paper under the rack to catch drips.) Poke the top and sides of the cake all over with the skewer and brush on the rest of the glaze.

Just before serving, sift the confectioners' sugar over the top of the cake.

Tres Leches
(Nicaraguan Three-Milk Cake)

[15 TO 20 SERVINGS]

Tres Leches is the tiramisu of Miami restaurant menus—an extremely sweet, rich, and ubiquitous dessert. Though Nicaraguan in origin, it's served at Cuban, Peruvian, and just about every other kind of Latin American restaurant in town. It's a sponge cake soaked in three "milks"—evaporated, sweetened condensed, and fresh cream. It's usually topped by a meringue that requires about 30 minutes of cooking. Some home cooks substitute marshmallow cream as a shortcut, but we much prefer the simple whipped cream topping below. Stabilized by the corn syrup and powdered sugar, it holds up well for several hours and has a lovely, light texture and taste. Though not as overwhelmingly sweet as some versions, this Tres Leches is still very rich and is best cut in small portions. You can make the cake ahead and freeze it, and add the topping at serving time.

FOR THE CAKE:

1 tablespoon unsalted butter

1½ cups all-purpose flour

1 teaspoon baking powder

¼ teaspoon salt

5 eggs, separated

1 cup sugar

½ teaspoon vanilla extract

¼ cup milk

FOR THE THREE MILKS:

1 14-ounce can sweetened
  condensed milk

1 5-ounce can evaporated milk

1 cup heavy cream

1 tablespoon dark rum

1 teaspoon vanilla extract

FOR THE TOPPING:

1 cup heavy cream, chilled

1 teaspoon vanilla extract

1 tablespoon light corn syrup

¼ cup confectioners' sugar

To make the cake, preheat the oven to 350 degrees. Butter and flour a 9-by-13-inch cake pan.

Sift the flour, baking powder, and salt together in a small bowl and set aside.

In the bowl of an electric mixer, beat the egg yolks on high speed until very thick, about 3 minutes. Add ¾ cup of the sugar and beat for 2 minutes more, until the mixture is pale, thick, and creamy. Beat in the vanilla extract and milk.

Sift the flour mixture onto the batter and gently fold it in.

Wash and dry the beaters well and beat the egg whites in another bowl until soft peaks form. Add the remaining ¼ cup of sugar and beat the whites until stiff, shiny peaks form.

Stir ⅓ of the whites into the batter to lighten it, and gently fold in the rest.

Pour the batter into the prepared pan and tap the pan on the counter to level the mixture. Bake for about 35 minutes, until the top of the cake springs back when touched lightly, or a cake tester inserted in the center comes out clean and dry.

Wash and dry the beaters and mixing bowl, and set them in the freezer.

Set the cake on a rack to cool in the pan for 10 minutes. Meanwhile, stir the condensed milk, evaporated milk, cream, rum, and vanilla extract together.

Invert the cake onto a deep rectangular serving dish or leave it in the pan. Poke it all over with a cake tester or a thin skewer. Slowly spoon the milk mixture over it, allowing it to soak in before adding more. Set the cake aside.

To make the topping, combine the cream, vanilla, corn syrup, and sugar in the cold mixing bowl. Beat until the cream is thick enough to hold soft peaks. (Take care not to overbeat.)

Spoon up any excess milk mixture and pour it over the cake again. Spread the whipped cream on top, and if the cake is on a platter, spread it on the sides. Refrigerate the cake for at least 2 hours and serve cold.

Piña Colada Cheesecake

[12 SERVINGS]

If you enjoy sipping a piña colada, you're sure to love this scrumptious cheesecake. From the coconut in the crust to the pineapple juice in the topping, it's a showstopping dessert. Coconut cream, a concentrated version of sweetened coconut milk, contributes to the rich flavor and texture of the filling. Look for it where cocktail mixes are stocked in your supermarket or liquor store. (Coco Lopez is one popular brand.)

FOR THE CRUST:

1 cup graham cracker crumbs (see Notes)

¼ cup shredded sweetened coconut

3 tablespoons sugar

5 tablespoons unsalted butter, melted

FOR THE TOPPING:

½ cup sour cream

3 tablespoons sugar

FOR THE FILLING:

1½ pounds cream cheese, at room temperature

½ cup sugar

1 cup sour cream

1 cup coconut cream

2 tablespoons dark rum

1 teaspoon vanilla extract

4 eggs, lightly beaten

1 8-ounce can crushed pineapple

Position one of the oven racks in the center and spread a piece of aluminum foil on it to catch drips. Preheat the oven to 350 degrees.

Stir the graham cracker crumbs, coconut, and sugar into the melted butter. Press the mixture across the bottom and ¾ of the way up the sides of a 9-inch springform pan. Bake the crust for about 10 minutes, until firm and lightly browned, and set aside on a rack to cool.

To make the filling, mix the cream cheese and sugar together in a food processor or with an electric mixer. Add the sour cream, coconut cream, rum, and vanilla extract, and beat well. Add the eggs and beat just until combined, scraping down the sides once or twice.

Drain the pineapple, pressing it to extract as much juice as possible. Reserve 2 tablespoons of the juice and stir the pineapple into the cream cheese mixture.

Scrape the filling into the prepared crust. Bake the cheesecake for about 1 hour, until the edges are set but the center still moves slightly when you shake the pan.

Meanwhile, make the topping by stirring together the sour cream, sugar, and the reserved 2 tablespoons of pineapple juice.

When the cheesecake is ready, remove it from the oven and raise the temperature to 400 degrees. Spread the topping over the cake. Bake the cheesecake for 5 more minutes, until the topping has set and lost its gloss.

Turn off the oven, open the oven door, and let the cake cool to room temperature on the oven rack, about 1 hour. (Cooling it slowly reduces the chances that the top will crack, but if pressed for time, you can cool it on a rack out of the oven.)

Run a thin metal spatula or knife around the sides of the pan to loosen the cheesecake. Cover with foil or plastic wrap and refrigerate until thoroughly chilled, at least 4 hours.

Just before serving, remove the sides of the pan and cut the cake with a thin knife, rinsing the blade with hot water and wiping it off between slices.

NOTES:

- You can buy ready-made graham cracker crumbs or make your own; about 15 cracker squares yields 1 cup. Pulse the crackers in a food processor or seal them in a sturdy plastic bag and roll over them with a rolling pin until finely crushed by not pulverized. Vanilla wafers or gingersnaps (about 15 cookies per cup) would be a nice alternative in this recipe.
- Coconut is the perfect addition here, but with other pies consider adding ground nuts, grated citrus zest, or spices that complement the filling. Or consider making the crust with chocolate wafers.
- If you find it hard to spread the crumb mixture evenly in the pan, try pressing it on with the bottom and sides of a drinking glass or custard cup.
- The eggs are added to the filling mixture last to prevent too much air from being beaten into them; otherwise, the cheesecake will rise dramatically in the oven—and fall just as dramatically when it cools.
- If you plan to bring a cheesecake to a friend's house, cut out a circle of cardboard the same size as the bottom of your springform pan, cover it with aluminum foil, and insert it in the pan in place of the bottom before baking the cake. That way you won't need to worry about retrieving the rest of your pan.
- An 18-inch length of unflavored dental floss, held taut, is another good tool for cutting cheesecake—as long as you're cutting it in the kitchen and not at the table!

It's no wonder the Queen of Hearts liked to make tarts—they're so much prettier than pies. There's no top crust to hide the beauty of the filling, and the fluted edge sets it off like a picture frame. Freezing the unbaked shell, as we describe in the recipes that follow, means you don't need to bother with pie weights to keep those delicate edges from collapsing in the oven. If you don't have a tart pan, you can get one from a kitchenware store or mail-order outlet for as little as $5; be sure it has a removable bottom.

Tangy Lemon Tart with Sugary Almond Crust

[8 TO 10 SERVINGS]

We're not sure which we like better, the feathery light, intensely lemony filling or the sweet, crunchy crust. We are sure, though, that they're a winning combination. The filling holds up well, and the tart can be made a day ahead.

FOR THE CRUST:

⅓ cup slivered almonds

2½ tablespoons sugar

1 tablespoon grated lemon zest

¾ cup all-purpose flour

½ teaspoon salt

6 tablespoons (¾ stick) unsalted butter, cut into small pieces and frozen (see Notes)

1 egg yolk

1 tablespoon ice water

FOR THE FILLING:

1½ cups sugar

3 tablespoons cornstarch

6 eggs

1 cup fresh lemon juice

1 tablespoon grated lemon zest

4 tablespoons (½ stick) unsalted butter, cut into small pieces

½ cup heavy cream

Toasted sliced almonds and confectioners' sugar for garnish

To make the crust, combine the almonds, sugar, and lemon zest in a food processor and process until finely ground. Add the flour and salt, and pulse to combine. With the motor running, drop the butter pieces down the feeding tube and pulse until the largest pieces are the size of small peas. Whisk together the egg yolk and water, and add it to the flour mixture, pulsing until it begins coming together. (To make the crust by hand, grind or pound the almonds as fine as possible and mix the dough with a pastry blender.) Press the dough into a ball, flatten into a disk, wrap in plastic, and refrigerate for at least 30 minutes.

Lightly butter a 9- or 9½-inch tart pan with a removable bottom.

On a lightly floured surface, roll out the dough into a circle about 13 inches in diameter. Fit it into the prepared pan, letting the extra dough drape over the edges. Roll across the top of the pan with a rolling pin to cut off the excess.

Place the pan in the freezer until the crust is frozen solid, at least 30 minutes. (If you plan to freeze it longer, wrap it in foil.)

Preheat the oven to 375 degrees.

Line the frozen tart shell with heavy-duty aluminum foil and immediately place it in the oven. Bake until lightly colored, about 20 minutes.

Cool the shell on a rack for about 10 minutes, remove the foil, and bake until golden, 5 to 10 minutes. Set aside on a rack to cool completely.

While the shell is baking, begin making the filling: Mix the sugar and cornstarch together in a nonaluminum saucepan and whisk in the eggs one at a time. Add the lemon juice and zest, and whisk until well blended. Heat over low heat, stirring constantly with a wooden spoon, until the mixture is thick and translucent, about 10 minutes. Remove from the heat and whisk in the butter until melted. Let cool to room temperature and refrigerate until chilled, about 1 hour.

To assemble the tart, whip the cream until it holds soft peaks and gently fold into the lemon custard. Spoon the filling into the cooled tart shell, smooth the top, and refrigerate until serving time.

Remove the outer ring from the pan and slide the tart off the pan bottom and onto a serving platter. Garnish with almonds and a dusting of confectioners' sugar, and serve.

NOTES:

- Rather than cut up the butter for the crust, you can freeze it whole and grate it into the flour using the large holes of a box grater.
- To remove the outer ring from the pan when a tart is finished, set the pan on a small can. The ring should fall away easily, but if it doesn't, you'll have both hands to free it.

Guava Linzertorte

[8 TO 10 SERVINGS]

Guava jelly takes the place of the usual raspberry jam in this linzertorte, a lattice-topped tart named for its place of origin, Linzer, Austria. The jelly (not to be confused with canned guava paste) has a seductive, almost honeylike sweetness and color that go beautifully with the rich walnut crust. Look for it among the jams and jellies in specialty shops or in supermarkets with a Latin or Caribbean clientele. (If you can't find it, raspberry, apricot, peach, or black currant preserves will produce a delectable, if not tropical, result.) This is a recipe to save for a day when you have time to enjoy baking—and time to savor the fruits of your labors with someone special over a cup of coffee or tea.

FOR THE CRUST:

1½ cups all-purpose flour

1 teaspoon ground cinnamon

½ teaspoon salt

8 tablespoons (1 stick) unsalted
   butter, cut into small pieces
   and frozen

¾ cup sugar

2 cups walnut pieces, finely ground

2 egg yolks

Finely grated zest of 1 lemon

FOR THE FILLING:

2 teaspoons fresh lemon juice

1 cup guava jelly

Confectioners' sugar for garnish

To make the crust, combine the flour, cinnamon and salt in a food processor and pulse to combine. With the motor running, drop the butter pieces down the feeding tube and pulse until the largest pieces are the size of small peas. Add the sugar and ground nuts, and pulse to combine. Add the egg yolks and lemon zest, and pulse just until the dough comes together. (Or mix by hand using a pastry blender.)

Turn the dough out onto a piece of wax paper and divide into thirds. Form ⅓ into a disc and the remaining ⅔ into a second disk. Cover with plastic wrap and refrigerate for 1 hour. (If you have to refrigerate it longer, let the dough sit at room temperature for 15 minutes before rolling it out.)

Preheat the oven to 400 degrees. Lightly butter a 9- or 9½-inch tart pan with a removable bottom.

Unwrap the larger piece of dough and press it evenly over the bottom and sides of the prepared pan with your fingers. Bake for about 15 minutes, just until it begins to color.

Meanwhile, roll out the smaller piece of dough between 2 sheets of wax paper into a circle about 12 inches across and refrigerate it.

Set the baked shell aside on a rack to cool for a few minutes. Lower the oven temperature to 350 degrees.

Stir the lemon juice into the jelly and spread evenly over the shell.

Remove the top piece of wax paper from the remaining dough and use a sharp knife or kitchen shears to cut the dough and bottom piece of wax paper into strips about ¾ inch wide.

Starting in the middle of the tart, place a strip of dough over the jelly and peel off the wax paper. Repeat, arranging strips of dough about ½ inch apart across the top of the tart. Arrange a second layer perpendicular to the first, forming a lattice pattern, and trim the ends of the strips by pressing them against the edge of the pan. (For a more finished look, you can roll leftover dough into small balls and use them to fill in empty spaces around the edge of the tart.)

Bake the tart until the crust is golden and the jelly is bubbling, about 40 minutes.

Let cool completely on a rack. Poke a small knife around the edge of the pan to make sure the crust isn't sticking and remove the tart pan ring. Slide the tart off the pan bottom and onto a serving platter. Sprinkle with confectioners' sugar, and serve.

Free-Form Mango Tart

[8 TO 10 SERVINGS]

It's the rare Miamian who doesn't have a mango tree down the street, if not in the backyard, so there's no such thing as too many mango recipes when the season rolls around in midsummer. (Believe it or not, the fruit can be a lawn maintenance nightmare if you have a big, prolific tree.) This simple and yummy tart goes together easily, but you could make it even easier by substituting a sheet of frozen puff pastry for the homemade dough. Either way, it's best eaten the day it's made.

The same is true of the Tarte Tatin variation, which was inspired by a dessert that Allen Susser serves at his award-winning Miami restaurant, Chef Allen's. In the 1980s, Allen, Norman Van Aken, Mark Militello, Robbin Haas, and Douglas Rodriguez were known as the Mango Gang, a group of cutting-edge chefs who put Miami on the culinary map with their New World cuisine.

FOR THE CRUST:

1 cup all-purpose flour

¼ cup yellow cornmeal

1 teaspoon sugar

½ teaspoon salt

7 tablespoons unsalted butter, cut into small pieces and frozen

3 tablespoons sour cream or plain yogurt

⅓ cup ice water

FOR THE FILLING:

2 ripe mangos, peeled, pitted, and sliced

2 tablespoons sugar

1 tablespoon unsalted butter

FOR THE GLAZE:

¼ cup guava jelly or apricot preserves

1 tablespoon water

To make the dough, measure the flour, cornmeal, sugar, and salt into the bowl of a food processor and pulse to combine. With the motor running, drop the butter pieces down the feeding tube and pulse until the largest pieces are the size of small peas. Stir the sour cream and ice water together. Add to the processor, 1 tablespoon at a time, pulsing between each addition, until the dough begins to clump. (Or mix by hand using a pastry blender.)

Wrap the dough in plastic wrap, pat into a disc, and refrigerate for at least 1 hour.

Preheat the oven to 400 degrees.

Cut a piece of parchment paper the length of a baking sheet and set on a work surface. Roll the dough out on the parchment in a circle about 12 inches in diameter. Slide the parchment, dough and all, onto a baking sheet.

Arrange the mango slices on the dough, overlapping slightly and leaving a 2- to 3-inch border all the way around. Sprinkle the fruit with 1 tablespoon of the sugar and dot with the butter. Fold the edges of the dough up over the filling, letting the dough pleat as you work your way around the circle. Brush the exposed dough with water and sprinkle with the remaining 1 tablespoon of sugar.

Bake the tart for 35 to 40 minutes, or until the pastry is golden and crisp.

Meanwhile, melt the jelly over low heat in a small saucepan and stir in the water. Set aside.

Let the tart cool on the pan for 10 minutes. Slip a wide spatula under it and slide onto a cooling rack. Brush the glaze on the fruit. Serve the tart warm or at room temperature.

VARIATION: Classic French Tarte Tatin (named for the Tatin sisters who created it) is made with apples, but mangos are an exotic substitute. Make the dough as directed above and chill it. Combine ½ cup of sugar and 2 tablespoons of butter in a 9- or 10-inch cast-iron skillet or cake pan. Caramelize over low heat and set aside. Roll the dough into a 10-inch circle. Arrange the mango slices over the caramel in the pan and top with the dough, tucking the edges under if necessary. Bake in a 400-degree oven for about 25 minutes, until the crust is lightly browned. Let the tart cool on a rack for 5 minutes before inverting onto a serving plate. (If some of the mangos stick to the pan, just scrape them off and arrange them on top of the tart.)

Chocolate Key Lime Tart

[8 TO 10 SERVINGS]

The meeting of the sweet-tart lime filling and the rich chocolate topping in this gorgeous tart is a sensory delight. The cachet surrounding small, seedy, yellow-skinned Key limes stems in part from the fact that they can be hard to find. They're mainly a backyard crop in south Florida, and most of those sold in supermarkets here and elsewhere in the country are imported from the Caribbean and Central America. Key limes are more acidic than the larger, seedless, green Persian limes and have a tart aftertaste. It is a fairly subtle distinction once the juice is mixed into the filling, and you'll have a delightful dessert whichever kind you use. In a variation on this theme, Chef Dawn Sieber of the Atlantic's Edge restaurant at Cheeca Lodge in the Florida Keys coats the bottom of a baked tart shell with chocolate and lets it dry before pouring in the filling.

FOR THE CRUST:

1 cup all-purpose flour

2 tablespoons sugar

½ teaspoon salt

8 tablespoons (1 stick) unsalted butter, cut into small pieces and frozen

1 egg yolk

1 tablespoon ice water

½ teaspoon vanilla extract

FOR THE FILLING:

1 14-ounce can sweetened condensed milk

3 egg yolks, slightly beaten

½ cup fresh Key or Persian lime juice

½ teaspoon grated lime zest

FOR THE TOPPING:

6 ounces semisweet chocolate, finely chopped

¾ cup half-and-half

To make the crust, combine the flour, sugar, and salt in a food processor and pulse to combine. With the motor running, drop the butter pieces down the feeding tube and pulse until the largest pieces are the size of small peas.

Add the egg yolk, water, and vanilla extract, and pulse for a few seconds until the dough begins to clump. (Or cut the butter into the dry ingredients by hand and stir in the liquids.)

Handling the dough as little as possible, pat it into a disc, wrap in plastic wrap, and refrigerate for at least 1 hour.

Lightly butter a 9- or 9½-inch tart pan with a removable bottom.

Roll out the dough on a lightly floured surface into a circle about 13 inches in diameter. Fit into the prepared pan, letting the extra dough hang over the edge. Roll across the top of the pan with a rolling pin to cut off the excess. Place the pan in the freezer until the crust is frozen solid, at least 30 minutes. (If you plan to freeze it longer, wrap it in foil.)

Preheat the oven to 375 degrees.

Line the frozen tart shell with heavy-duty aluminum foil and immediately place it in the oven. Bake until lightly colored, about 20 minutes.

Cool the shell on a rack for about 10 minutes, remove the foil, and bake until golden, 5 to 10 minutes. Set aside on a rack to cool completely.

To make the filling, whisk the milk, egg yolks, lime juice, and zest together.

Preheat the oven to 350 degrees.

Pour the filling into the cooled shell and bake until the filling is set, 10 to 12 minutes. Let cool on a wire rack, then refrigerate until thoroughly chilled, about 2 hours.

To make the topping, bring the chocolate and half-and-half to a boil in a small saucepan over high heat, stirring constantly. Lower the heat and simmer, still stirring, until the chocolate melts completely. Set aside to cool slightly.

Pour the chocolate mixture over the chilled tart, tilting the pan to spread it evenly. Refrigerate for up to 4 hours before serving.

PLANNING AHEAD: The unbaked tart shell can be frozen, well wrapped, for a month. You can bake the shell a day ahead and store it at room temperature.

NOTE: This dough contains a lot of butter, which means it will be very hard when you take it from the refrigerator, so beat it with your rolling pin a few times to get it going. The high butter and sugar content also means it softens quickly, so work fast. For easier handling, roll it out between 2 sheets of plastic wrap or parchment paper. Remove the top sheet, turn the dough over into the pan, and remove the second sheet.

Key Lime Pie

Mention "Miami" and "dessert" in the same sentence, and most people think of Key lime pie. There was even an effort in the state legislature a few years ago to have it declared the official Florida pie. (The bill passed the House but not the Senate—blocked, perhaps, by pecan pie enthusiasts from north Florida, which despite its name is a much more southern place than south Florida.) Given that Key limes were cultivated in the Florida Keys as early as 1835 and that canned milk was much more readily available there than fresh until the 1930s, it makes sense that enterprising cooks began combining the two. (Some sources suggest that they were inspired by a "Lemon Magic" pie recipe featured on cans of Eagle Brand Condensed Milk.)

Key lime pie can be made with a graham cracker or pastry crust and topped with meringue, whipped cream, or nothing at all. The one thing it can't be is green: The lime, its juice, and the filling they make are naturally pale yellow, and anything else smacks of colorization. The filling doesn't need to be cooked in order to thicken; the acid in the lime juice accomplishes that by causing the proteins in the egg yolks and milk to bond. However, baking the pie briefly gives it a slightly firmer texture and eliminates any concerns about eating raw eggs.

4 eggs, separated

1 14-ounce can sweetened condensed milk

½ cup fresh Key lime juice

1 9-inch graham cracker pie shell (homemade or purchased)

½ teaspoon cream of tartar

¼ cup sugar

Preheat the oven to 350 degrees.

Beat the egg yolks in a large bowl until light in color. Add the condensed milk and lime juice, and beat until thickened, about 2 minutes.

Pour the mixture into the pie shell and bake for 12 to 15 minutes, until set.

Meanwhile, beat the egg whites until foamy, add the cream of tartar, and beat until soft peaks form. Add the sugar and beat until stiff.

Remove the pie from the oven and raise the temperature to 450 degrees.

Spread the meringue over the pie, making sure to seal it to the edges of the crust all the way around. Bake for about 5 minutes, until the meringue is lightly golden.

Let the pie cool to room temperature on a rack and refrigerate until chilled.

VARIATIONS:

- Use Persian lime juice if Key limes aren't available.
- Omit the meringue if you like and serve the chilled pie with sweetened whipped cream.

Mango Margarita Pie
with Gingersnap Crust

[8 TO 10 SERVINGS]

Tequila and orange liqueur give a kick to this light-as-air pie, and a spicy gingersnap crust sets off the sweet-tart filling. It takes time to make, but it's sure to win you raves. This is like an old-fashioned chiffon pie with one difference: Because it's no longer considered advisable to eat raw eggs, you beat the egg whites and sugar while heating, like a seven-minute frosting, before adding them to the filling. You can make the crust a day ahead and complete the pie several hours before serving. If fresh mango is available, see page 7 for pointers on removing the flesh. If it isn't, look for frozen mango puree among the Latin products in your grocer's freezer case.

FOR THE CRUST:

1¼ cups gingersnap cookie crumbs
(about 20 cookies)

5 tablespoons unsalted butter,
softened

3 tablespoons sugar

FOR THE FILLING:

2 envelopes unflavored gelatin

½ cup fresh lime juice

4 eggs, separated

1 cup pureed ripe mango
(1 medium mango)

¼ cup tequila

3 tablespoons orange liqueur

1 cup sugar

1 cup heavy cream

Paper-thin mango and lime slices
for garnish

Preheat the oven to 350 degrees.

To make the crust, combine the crumbs, butter, and sugar in a 9½-inch pie plate. Mix well with your hands and press the mixture up the sides of the pan. Bake until lightly browned, 8 to 10 minutes, and set aside on a rack to cool.

To make the filling, stir the gelatin, lime juice, and egg yolks together in a small saucepan and let stand for a few minutes to soften the gelatin. Cook over low heat, stirring constantly with a wooden spoon, for about 5 minutes, until the gelatin melts and the mixture thickens slightly. Don't let it boil.

Stir the gelatin mixture, mango, tequila, and liqueur together in a large bowl. Refrigerate for about 1 hour, stirring often, until it has the consistency of unbeaten egg whites. (If it thickens too much, set over a bowl of hot water and whisk to thin it.)

Meanwhile, put the egg whites in a nonaluminum saucepan over low heat—or in a double boiler over rapidly boiling water—and beat at low speed with a handheld electric mixer or a whisk until foamy. Turn the speed to high and gradually add the sugar, beating until the mixture holds stiff peaks, 6 to 8 minutes with an electric mixer. Set aside to cool.

Beat the cream until stiff. Fold the cream and the cooled egg white mixture into the mango mixture. Pour into the prepared pie crust, mounding it at the center.

Refrigerate the pie until set, about 1 hour. Just before serving, overlap mango slices around the edge of the pie and arrange lime slices in a decorative pattern in the center.

VARIATIONS:

➡ If you'd rather not cook with alcohol, substitute orange juice for the tequila and orange liqueur.

➡ To make mango mousse, puree the mango with 2 tablespoons of lime juice. Beat the egg whites and ½ cup of sugar over low heat as described above. Beat 1 cup of heavy cream until stiff and fold into the mango puree along with the egg white mixture.

Orange-Almond Biscotti

[ABOUT 3 DOZEN]

These twice-baked Italian cookies are almost as refreshing as a freshly squeezed glass of orange juice. Biscotti are made for dunking—in a cup of espresso or a glass of sherry, port, or vin santo— but these are also great for crunching with a bowl of orange sorbet. They freeze beautifully and make a fine gift from your kitchen, so think about making a double batch. Grinding the nuts with some of the dry ingredients is a trick we learned from Maida Heatter.

1 cup whole blanched almonds

Zest of 1 brightly colored orange, removed in strips with a zester or vegetable peeler

¾ cup sugar

2½ cups all-purpose flour

1 teaspoon baking powder

½ teaspoon baking soda

½ teaspoon salt

1 teaspoon ground cinnamon

3 eggs

2 tablespoons orange liqueur

1 teaspoon vanilla extract

Preheat the oven to 350 degrees.

Spread the almonds on a baking sheet and toast until golden brown, about 8 minutes. When cool enough to handle, chop coarsely, then set aside.

Line the baking sheet with parchment paper or coat lightly with vegetable oil spray.

Combine the orange zest and 2 tablespoons of the sugar in a food processor and process until finely ground. Leave the mixture in the food processor.

Sift the remaining sugar, flour, baking powder, baking soda, salt, and cinnamon together into a large bowl.

Scoop ½ cup of the dry ingredients and ½ cup of the toasted almonds into the food processor and process until the nuts are finely ground. Stir the mixture into the dry ingredients along with the remaining almonds.

In a small bowl, beat the eggs with the orange liqueur and vanilla extract. Stir the mixture into the dry ingredients until well blended.

Divide the dough in two and pat each half into a log about 12 inches long and 1½ inches wide. Place the dough logs about 3 inches apart on the prepared baking sheet. Bake until golden brown, about 30 minutes.

Remove the pan from the oven and let the dough cool for 10 minutes. Lower the oven temperature to 325 degrees.

Transfer the dough logs to a cutting board. Use a serrated knife to cut them on the diagonal into ½-inch slices. Lay the slices flat on the baking sheet and return to the oven. Bake, turning once, until lightly browned, about 7 minutes per side.

Let the cookies cool completely on wire racks and store in an airtight container. They'll keep at room temperature for 2 weeks or in the freezer for 2 months.

VARIATIONS:

➡ Add ½ cup of shredded sweetened coconut to the dough if you like.

➡ Pecans, walnuts, or macadamia nuts can be used in place of almonds.

➡ You can dress up the biscotti by brushing half of each cooled cookie with melted semisweet or milk chocolate.

NOTES:

• If the dough sticks to your hands, dampen them with cold water. Don't dust the dough with flour, or the cookies may become heavy and tough.

• To refresh the flavor of less-than-fresh biscotti, heat them in a 300-degree oven for 10 minutes.

Chocolate-Coconut Tuiles

[ABOUT 1 DOZEN]

Tuiles—French for "tiles"—are thin, curved cookies named for their resemblance to roof tiles, like the dusky orange ones that grace Mediterranean-style homes in Coral Gables, one of Miami's oldest suburbs. The architecture of the drier, cooler Mediterranean region isn't particularly well suited to subtropical Miami, but it was in keeping with developer George Merrick's dream of Coral Gables as an American Riviera. Merrick was the most visionary of the developers who gave Greater Miami its shape during a feverish 1920s land boom. He plowed $100 million in profits back into the project and hired famed orator William Jennings Bryant to promote Coral Gables, only to be left penniless by the devastating 1926 hurricane. Coral Gables, with its red clay "tuiles," survived and eventually thrived.

Back to edible tuiles: These simple, delicate cookies are a fine accompaniment for Coconut Sorbet (page 317, see the Variation), Oranges in Red Wine (page 314), or, for a triple dose of chocolate, Individual Chocolate–Cuban Coffee Soufflés (page 312). The recipe is adapted from one in Michel Richard's Home Cooking with a French Accent.

> 1½ cups shredded sweetened coconut
>
> 1½ teaspoons light corn syrup
>
> 1½ teaspoons unsalted butter, cut into small pieces
>
> ¼ teaspoon vanilla extract
>
> 8 ounces bittersweet chocolate, finely chopped
>
> Confectioners' sugar or unsweetened cocoa

Preheat the oven to 350 degrees.

Combine the coconut, corn syrup, butter, and vanilla extract on a baking sheet. Toss to combine and spread in a thin layer. Bake until the coconut is lightly toasted, about 15 minutes, stirring occasionally.

Meanwhile, melt the chocolate in the top of a double boiler or the microwave.

Line 2 baking sheets with parchment paper or wax paper.

Stir the toasted coconut mixture into the melted chocolate. Spoon a tablespoon of it onto one of the baking sheets and use the back of a spoon or a small spatula to spread it into a circle about 2½ inches in diameter and ⅛ inch thick. Repeat with the remaining chocolate, spacing the circles about ½ inch apart.

Let sit at room temperature until no longer sticky, about 5 minutes. Cover with a second layer of parchment paper. Roll the paper loosely and gently into a tube shape, just enough to give the tuiles a slight curve, and refrigerate until very firm, about 1 hour.

Shortly before serving, carefully peel the tuiles from the paper and sift confectioners' sugar or cocoa over them. Store any extras in the refrigerator or freezer.

VARIATIONS: You can vary the size of the tuiles to suit your purpose or leave them flat and layer them with Tangy Lemon Tart filling (page 293) for a napoleonlike dessert.

Easy Coconut Flan

Flan—Spanish baked custard—is as common in Miami as it is in Madrid thanks to its popularity on Cuban restaurant menus. Sweetened condensed milk and canned coconut in syrup make this version intensely sweet and rich—and extremely easy to make. Don't be put off by the idea of caramelizing a pan; there's nothing complicated about it.

> 1 cup sugar
>
> ¼ cup water
>
> 4 eggs
>
> 1 14-ounce can sweetened condensed milk
>
> 1½ cups shredded coconut in syrup (see Note)
>
> 1 tablespoon fresh lime juice
>
> 2 tablespoons dark rum or 1 teaspoon vanilla extract
>
> Fresh papaya or mango slices for garnish (optional)

Bring the sugar and water to a boil in a heavy saucepan over low heat, swirling the pan until the sugar is dissolved and the mixture is perfectly clear. Raise the heat to high and boil the sugar mixture, without stirring, until the syrup turns a caramel color, 5 to 7 minutes. Watch it carefully; it can burn easily.

Carefully pour the caramel into a 9-inch round cake pan. Protecting your hands with mitts or pot holders, tilt and swirl the pan to coat the bottom and sides well with the caramel. Set aside to cool and harden.

Preheat the oven to 350 degrees. Put a tea kettle full of water on to boil.

Combine the eggs, milk, coconut in syrup, lime juice, and rum in a mixing bowl and beat well. Pour the mixture into the caramelized pan.

Set the caramelized pan inside a larger baking dish (a 9-by-13-inch pan works well) and place in the oven. Pour enough boiling water into the large pan to reach halfway up the sides of the smaller one.

Bake for 60 to 70 minutes, until a knife inserted in the center comes out clean. The custard should be set on the edges but still jiggly in the center. It will fully set as it cools.

Remove the flan from the hot-water bath and let cool to room temperature on a wire rack. Refrigerate, covered, for at least 4 hours to firm and chill.

Just before serving, run a small metal spatula around the sides of the pan and gently tip it from side to side to see if the custard is loose. If the caramel on the bottom is still hard, dip the pan in hot water to loosen it and test again. Invert the flan onto a rimmed platter, tapping gently on the bottom of the pan to release it. (Don't worry if a little caramel remains hardened on the pan.) Garnish with papaya slices if you like and serve.

PLANNING AHEAD: You can make the flan up to 2 days ahead.

VARIATION: You can make individual flans in six 3-ounce ramekins; shorten the baking time by about 20 minutes.

NOTE: Look for shredded coconut in syrup in 18-ounce cans in the Latin or canned fruit section of your supermarket. If you can't find it, substitute ½ cup of shredded sweetened coconut, chopped into shorter strands, and 1 cup of Sugar Syrup (see page 318).

Creamy Rice Pudding
with a Hint of Lime

[8 TO 10 SERVINGS]

Rice pudding spells comfort in many languages, from Yiddish to Swedish to Spanish. This delicately sweet lime-kissed version has a Cuban accent. It is sublime plain or can be dressed up in a host of ways, as suggested in Variations. Short-grain rice produces the creamiest texture, but if you can't find it, long-grain white rice will work.

1 cup short-grain (Valencia) rice	4 cups milk
½ teaspoon salt	1 teaspoon vanilla extract
½ to ⅔ cup sugar	2 tablespoons dark rum (optional)
Zest of 1 lime, removed in strips with a zester or vegetable peeler	

Combine the rice, salt, and 2 cups of water in a large, heavy saucepan over high heat. Bring just to a boil, turn the heat to low, and let simmer, covered, for 15 to 20 minutes, until most of the liquid is absorbed.

Stir in the sugar, lime zest, and milk, and raise the heat to medium-high. (Use the larger amount of sugar for more pronounced sweetness.) Bring the pudding just to a boil and turn the heat to low. Simmer, uncovered, stirring occasionally, for about 45 minutes, until the milk is absorbed, the rice is tender, and the pudding is thick.

Remove from the heat. Stir in the vanilla extract and rum if using. Remove the lime zest. Serve at room temperature or chilled.

VARIATIONS: For an even richer pudding, whip ½ cup of heavy cream and fold it into the cooled pudding. And for a different flavor accent, substitute lemon or orange zest or a stick of cinnamon for the lime zest.

Here is a mix-and-match list of possible additions to the finished pudding:

- 1 drained 8-ounce can crushed pineapple
- ¼ cup raisins plumped in the rum
- 1 cup diced fresh mango
- ¼ cup shredded sweetened coconut

Individual
Chocolate–Cuban Coffee Soufflés

[8 SERVINGS]

Café cubano, *the strong, sweet espresso sipped night and day at walk-up cafe windows and in offices and restaurants all over Miami, has been called the elixir of exile. Bustelo, Pilon, Goya, and other companies compete to roast blends of Arabica or Robusta beans that will satisfy Cuban-born customers, who believe they grew up on the best coffee in the world. Even Starbuck's felt compelled to create its own* café cubano *when it moved into the Miami market.*

If your store doesn't stock a Cuban-style blend, substitute any brand of espresso powder in this imaginative and impressive dessert, adapted from a recipe that Molly O'Neill featured in her New York Times Magazine *column a few years ago. (She credited it to the Gramercy Tavern.) The chocolate chunks in the center of each individual soufflé melt during baking and form a sauce when you cut the soufflé open.*

1 tablespoon unsalted butter

⅓ cup plus 1 tablespoon sugar

½ cup heavy cream

2 teaspoons instant Cuban coffee or espresso powder

2½ ounces unsweetened chocolate, chopped

10½ ounces semisweet chocolate:
  2½ ounces chopped and
  8 ounces cut into 8 chunks that are about 1 inch long, ½ inch thick, and ½ inch wide

2 egg yolks

5 egg whites

Confectioners' sugar

Preheat the oven to 425 degrees. Butter eight 3-ounce ramekins and dust lightly with 1 tablespoon of the sugar. Place on a baking sheet and set in the refrigerator.

Heat the cream in a small saucepan over low heat until steaming but not boiling. Stir in the coffee powder until dissolved. Remove the pan from the heat and stir in the chopped unsweetened and semisweet chocolate (not the chunks) until melted.

Whisk in the egg yolks, one at a time, and half of the ⅓ cup of sugar. Scrape the mixture into a large mixing bowl.

In another bowl, beat the egg whites until they hold soft peaks. Beat in the remaining sugar until stiff but not dry.

Using a rubber spatula, stir ⅓ of the egg whites into the chocolate mixture to lighten it. Gently fold in the remaining whites until well combined; don't worry if streaks remain.

Spoon the mixture into the chilled ramekins, filling them almost to the rim, and place a chunk of chocolate in the center of each one. Bake the soufflés, still on the baking sheet, for 7 to 10 minutes, until they puff up over the rim of the ramekins. Sift confectioners' sugar over the top of each one and serve immediately.

PLANNING AHEAD: You can make the chocolate soufflé base up to 2 days ahead and refrigerate with a piece of plastic wrap pressed against the surface to prevent a skin from forming. Rewarm in a double boiler before beating and folding in the egg whites.

NOTE: Chilling the molds helps the soufflés rise evenly.

Oranges in Red Wine

[6 SERVINGS]

This simple and addictively delicious Italian dessert is a great showcase for Florida oranges, a commodity so important (along with grapefruit) that we have a state Department of Citrus as well as a Department of Agriculture. From November to June each year, more oranges are harvested here than in any other part of the world except Brazil. Many aficionados consider Temples—a sweet, juicy, thin-skinned orange-tangerine cross—the best eating orange the state produces. Navel or Valencia oranges would also be good choices for this dish. Serve it with Orange-Almond Biscotti (page 305) for dunking in the sweet, spicy wine syrup.

¾ cup sugar

1 cup water

1 cup dry red wine

2 cloves

1 1-inch-long cinnamon stick

1 1-inch-long vanilla bean or 1 teaspoon vanilla extract

4 lemon slices

6 large oranges

Stir the sugar and water together in a saucepan until the sugar dissolves. Add the wine, cloves, cinnamon, vanilla bean, and lemon slices, and bring to a boil over high heat. Turn the heat to low and simmer, uncovered, for 15 minutes.

Meanwhile, cut both ends from each orange and stand flat on a cutting board. Cut down along the curve of fruit with a sharp paring knife, trimming away the peel and white pith. Slice the oranges into ¼-inch rounds and remove the seeds if necessary.

Arrange the orange slices in a refrigerator container and strain the hot wine syrup over them. Let cool to room temperature and refrigerate, covered, for at least 4 hours. To serve, divide the orange slices and syrup among 6 dessert bowls.

Orange-Marinated Strawberries

[8 SERVINGS]

Each winter, while the tourists head for the beaches to pick seashells, Miamians head for the fields to pick strawberries. The Redland, a farming region about an hour south of downtown, is dotted with "u-pic" and "let-us-pick-for-you" fields from December until April. The trip is an annual ritual for many of us—often capped with a thick strawberry milkshake at Burr's or a sticky bun at Knaus's, two of the best-known berry farms. These orange-kissed berries are lovely on their own or served with whipped cream or your favorite ice cream. Don't make them more than 30 minutes ahead, or the berries will lose color and texture.

2 quarts strawberries

2 tablespoons sugar

Grated zest of 1 orange

⅓ cup fresh orange juice

1 tablespoon orange liqueur

Wash and stem the berries and cut them in half lengthwise. Arrange in a single layer in a shallow pan.

Whisk the sugar, orange zest, juice, and liqueur together in a small bowl. Pour over the strawberries and let steep, covered, at room temperature for 30 minutes before serving.

NOTES:

- Before juicing citrus fruit, remove the zest with a vegetable peeler or citrus zester; well wrapped, it will keep in the freezer for up to 6 months.
- Don't buy strawberries that are white or green around the stem; that means they were picked unripe. Check the container for stains or wetness that indicate crushed or over-ripe berries. And if you have a choice, small strawberries are often more flavorful than large ones.

The Beach Boys may have sung about endless summer, but Miamians live it, from early May until late October or even November. Most Halloween nights, half the trick-or-treaters have pulled off their costumes by the time they reach your door because it's too darned hot. Needless to say, frozen desserts are especially welcome here. Many fine south Florida restaurants, such as Norman Van Aken's award-winning Norman's, serve rainbow-hued assortments of handmade tropical fruit sorbets, perhaps presented on an oversized white plate surrounded by slices of the fruit from which they were made.

Most sorbets have just three ingredients—sugar syrup for sweetness and texture, lemon or lime juice for acidity, and fruit juice or puree for flavor and color—and if you've never made one before, you'll be surprised at how easy it is. An ice cream maker produces the creamiest texture because it churns air into the frozen mixture, but you can make good sorbets using your food processor and freezer. The sweetness of the fruit can vary from batch to batch, so taste the mixture before you freeze it; it should be a little on the sweet side because it will lose some intensity once frozen. Sorbet is never as good as when it's freshly made, so plan to serve it the same day.

Lemon Sorbet with Variations

[ABOUT 1 QUART]

The fruit sorbets are wonderfully refreshing, and the coconut version is intensely rich. Add chocolate sauce, and you'll think you're eating a frozen Mounds bar.

> 1 cup fresh lemon juice
> 1⅓ cups Sugar Syrup (recipe follows)
> 1 cup water

Combine the lemon juice, syrup, and water. Taste for sweetness and add more syrup if necessary.

WITH AN ICE CREAM MAKER: Pour the mixture into the bowl of the ice cream maker and process according to the manufacturer's instructions.

WITH A FOOD PROCESSOR: Pour the mixture into ice cube trays or a 9-inch square cake pan and place in the freezer until almost frozen, 1 to 2 hours. Scrape the mixture into a processor and pulse until smooth. Return it to the trays or pan and freeze again until almost firm, 30 minutes to 1 hour. Process again.

Pack the sorbet into a freezer container and freeze until firm.

VARIATIONS:

- *Lime Sorbet:* use ¾ cup of fresh lime juice, ¼ cup of fresh lemon juice, 2 cups of Sugar Syrup, and 1 cup of water.
- *Passion Fruit Sorbet:* use 1 cup of passion fruit puree, 1 tablespoon of fresh lime juice, 2 cups of Sugar Syrup, and 1 cup of water.
- *Mango or Papaya Sorbet:* use 2 cups of mango or papaya puree, ¼ cup of fresh lime juice, and 1⅓ cups of Sugar Syrup.
- *Pink Grapefruit Sorbet:* use 2½ cups of fresh grapefruit juice, 2 tablespoons of Campari, and 1½ cups of Sugar Syrup.
- *Coconut Sorbet:* use one 14-ounce can of coconut milk, one 15-ounce can of coconut cream, 1 cup of grated sweetened coconut, 1 tablespoon of fresh lime juice, 1 teaspoon of vanilla extract, and a pinch of salt.
- *Piña Colada Sorbet:* make the Coconut Sorbet and replace ½ cup of the grated coconut with ½ cup of drained crushed pineapple.

Sugar Syrup

[ABOUT 3½ CUPS]

You can make a big batch of this and store it in the refrigerator for weeks.

2 cups water

2 cups sugar

Bring the water and sugar to a boil in a saucepan, stirring to dissolve the sugar. Boil for about 5 minutes. Set aside to cool to room temperature. Refrigerate to chill before using.

Mango Madness

These 2 frozen mango desserts couldn't be easier or tastier.

MANGO ICE CREAM: Stir 2 cups of partially pureed mango pulp into a quart of softened vanilla ice cream and freeze until firm. Makes about 1½ quarts.

MANGO ICE: Peel, seed, and slice 2 ripe mangos. Spread on a cookie sheet and freeze until firm. Store in a freezer bag until needed. Remove from the refrigerator for 5 minutes, puree in a food processor or blender until smooth, and serve. Makes about 1 quart.

Bananas in Rum Caramel over Vanilla Ice Cream

Hot, buttery rum sauce and cold, creamy ice cream are an irresistible combination. Igniting the rum burns off some of the alcohol—and impresses your guests if you do it at the table. Several hours or even days ahead of time, make the sauce up to the point where you would add the bananas, and refrigerate it. After dinner, reheat the sauce, slice the bananas, scoop the ice cream, and heat the rum. Bring them to the table along with the matches, and it's showtime!

4 firm, ripe bananas	1 tablespoon grated orange zest
6 tablespoons unsalted butter	¼ cup dark rum
¼ cup granulated sugar	Vanilla ice cream
⅓ cup fresh orange juice	Toasted sweetened coconut for garnish (optional)

Peel the bananas. Cut them in half lengthwise and then in quarters crosswise.

Melt the butter in a 12-inch skillet over low heat. Stir in the sugar, raise the heat to medium, and cook until the sugar caramelizes, about 5 minutes. Don't worry if the sugar and butter separate.

Slowly stir in the orange juice with a wooden spoon, watching out for splatters. Add the orange zest and stir until the caramel dissolves and the sauce comes together.

Add the bananas, cut side down, and cook, turning once, until hot.

Meanwhile, warm the rum over low heat in a metal soup ladle or small saucepan, and ignite it with a long wooden match. Pour the lit rum into the skillet and spoon the flaming sauce over the bananas. Shake the pan until the flames die.

Place a scoop of ice cream in the center of each of 4 dessert plates. Arrange the bananas around the ice cream, spoon the caramel sauce over it, and serve immediately.

VARIATION: You can substitute two black-ripe plantains for the bananas.

NOTE: When caramelizing sugar, cook it over low heat until it dissolves, or it may crystallize.

Banana-Papaya Batidos
with Variations

[2 SERVINGS]

Long before there were smoothies, there were batidos *(bah-TEE-dohs), blended fruit and milk drinks that have been providing frosty refreshment throughout Latin America and the Caribbean for decades. Batidos are served at lunch counters and juice stands all over Miami, in flavors as exotic as mamey and as familiar as banana. Made with ice rather than ice cream, they're a low-fat alternative to milk shakes, especially if you use skim milk. Here are a few of our favorite blends.*

1 cup peeled, seeded, and diced ripe papaya

½ cup diced ripe banana

1 cup milk

½ cup crushed ice

Combine the papaya, banana, milk, and ice in a blender and process just until smooth. Pour into 2 tall, chilled glasses and serve at once.

VARIATIONS:

- *Papaya-Mango:* use 1 cup of diced mango, 1 cup of diced papaya, 1½ cups of milk, and ½ cup of crushed ice.
- *Frozen Mango:* use 2 cups of diced frozen mango, 1½ cups of milk, and sugar to taste.
- *Guava:* use ½ cup of frozen unsweetened guava puree, 3 tablespoons of sugar, 1 cup of milk, and ½ cup of crushed ice.

Cuban Coffee Sauce

[ABOUT 2½ CUPS]

Making a dessert sauce is a quick, do-ahead way of putting your personal stamp on purchased pound cake or ice cream. Cuban Coffee Sauce is also great with warm chocolate cake, and Mango or Passion Fruit Sauce turns a tropical fruit salad into a refreshing dessert.

2 cups half-and-half

1 tablespoon instant Cuban coffee or espresso powder

4 egg yolks

¼ cup sugar

1 tablespoon coffee liqueur

Bring the half-and-half and coffee powder just to a boil in a large saucepan and set aside off the heat.

Whisk the egg yolks and sugar together in a mixing bowl until the sugar dissolves and the mixture is thick and pale yellow.

Slowly whisk the cream mixture into the yolks and pour it back into the saucepan. Cook without boiling over medium-low heat, stirring constantly with a wooden spoon, for about 7 minutes, until it smoothly coats the back of the spoon.

Strain the sauce into a storage container and stir in the coffee liqueur. Let cool to room temperature, then refrigerate. Serve cold. The sauce will keep for up to 1 week.

Chunky Mango Sauce

If you prefer a smooth sauce, puree both mangos.

2 ripe mangos, peeled and seeded

3 tablespoons fresh lime juice

3 to 5 tablespoons sugar

Fresh orange juice (optional)

Cut one of the mangos into ¼-inch dice. Chop the other one coarsely and puree in a food processor or blender. Add the lime juice and sugar to taste, and process until smooth. Thin the sauce with orange juice if necessary. Combine with the cubed mango in a storage container and chill. The sauce will keep for up to 1 week.

Passion Fruit Sauce

[ABOUT 2½ CUPS]

The seeds of the passion fruit add texture and a deeper flavor, but if you prefer a smooth sauce, strain it through a sieve.

> 6 ripe passion fruit or 1 cup thawed frozen puree
> ½ cup sugar
> ⅔ cup water
> 2 teaspoons fresh lime juice
> 2 tablespoons rum

Cut each passion fruit in half and scoop out the pulp and seeds with a teaspoon.

Combine the passion fruit pulp, sugar, water, and lime juice in a nonaluminum saucepan. Heat over low, stirring, until the sugar dissolves, about 2 minutes.

Remove the pan from the heat and stir in the rum. Cool the sauce to room temperature and refrigerate until chilled before serving. It will keep for up to 1 week.

Menu Suggestions and Wine Choices

People eat with their eyes first, so look for ways to balance color, texture, and taste on the plate. A soft main course such as steamed yellowtail, for example, is better matched by grainy couscous than smooth mashed potatoes. When you do serve mashed potatoes, a crisp green vegetable like asparagus provides nice contrasting color and crunch. And juxtaposing a spicy salsa against a sweetly glazed main dish is a great way to wake up those taste buds. Here are a few suggested menus to get you started, complete with wine recommendations by *Miami Herald* wine columnist Fred Tasker.

A loaf of bread, in some cases a salad, and a dessert are all that's needed to complete these meals.

Paella Marina (page 211)
Wine: This rich, multiflavored dish needs a full-flavored white wine such as viognier.

Orange-Tamarind Brisket with Boniato and Carrots (page 139)
Wine: Serve a juicy red Beaujolais with this long-simmered, pungently spiced meat.

Arroz con Pollo (page 115)
Wine: Match all these savory flavors with a big chardonnay, or, if you prefer red, a soft Chilean cabernet sauvignon/merlot blend.

Chicken and Black Bean Pot Pie with Cornmeal Crust (page 119)
Wine: The complex flavors call for a full-flavored wine with some acidity, such as a white chenin blanc or a red barbera.

Florida White Chili (page 61)
Wine: Try a spicy Argentine white torrontés.

Ajiaco Santafereno (Bogotá-Style Chicken and Potato Stew, page 59)
Wine: Serve a big, rich, dry, white sémillon.

Shrimp Creole (page 207)
Wine: The rich, varied flavors call for another full-flavored white—an Australian sémillon/chardonnay blend.

Grilled Gingered Shrimp and Spinach Salad (page 86)
Wine: Viognier would be nice with this mildly spicy dish.

Chicken, Orange, and Black Bean Salad (page 85)
Wine: The fruity flavors would be well matched by a fruity California chardonnay.

Full-Course Dinners

Cold Avocado and Cucumber Soup (page 44)
Garlicky Grilled Pork Tenderloin (page 160)
Papaya–Three Pepper Chutney (page 265)
Bogotá-Style Potatoes (page 248)
Mango Margarita Pie with Gingersnap Crust (page 303)
Wine: A soft merlot would go well with these savory, spicy flavors.

Scallop Seviche (page 37)
Cuban-Style Braised Chicken (page 108)
Sautéed carrots and snowpeas

Yuca with Mojo (page 229)
Easy Coconut Flan (page 309)
Wine: Argentine torrontés.

Cold Mango Soup with Raspberry Puree (page 45)
Oven-Steamed Yellowtail with Roasted Tomato Sauce (page 183)
Tropical Couscous (page 234)
Steamed asparagus or green beans
Oranges in Red Wine (page 314)
Wine: A light but high-acid white such as sauvignon blanc.

Florida Orange and Tomato Gazpacho (page 47)
Grouper with Malanga-Pecan Crust (page 186)
Tropical Fruit Curry (page 262)
Steamed green beans
Creamy Rice Pudding with a Hint of Lime (page 311)
Wine: A super-rich meal requires an equally rich chardonnay from California or Australia.

Ginger, Lime, and Calabaza Soup with Ginger Cream (page 51)
Jerk-Fried Snapper with Banana-Orange Rum Sauce (page 181)
Rice with Coconut Milk (page 238)
Steamed zucchini and carrots
Orange-Marinated Strawberries (page 315)
Wine: Gewürztraminer is perfect for this spicy, fruity, rich meal.

Green salad with Mango Vinaigrette (page 70)
Gaucho Grill (page 137)
Yellow Rice with Corn (page 239)
Sautéed sugarsnap peas
Lemon Sorbet (page 317) with Orange-Almond Biscotti (page 305)
Wine: Grilled red meat always goes well with cabernet sauvignon, or to be extra authentic, try the Argentine red sensation, malbec.

Potato and Black Bean Pancakes with Cilantro–Goat Cheese Sauce (page 24)
Romaine and Queso Blanco Salad (page 77)
Caribbean Rice (page 236)
Veal Chops with Silken Mango-Lime Sauce (page 153)
Bananas in Rum Caramel over Vanilla Ice Cream (page 320)
Wine: A crisp red such as a cabernet franc from France's Loire Valley.

Black Bean and White Corn Soup (page 53)
Rack of Lamb with Coriander Marinade (page 171)
Green Mango Chutney (page 263)
Mashed Potatoes with Roasted Corn and Scallions (page 251)
Individual Chocolate–Cuban Coffee Soufflés (page 312)
Wine: In Spain they would drink a deep, dark red Rioja; an American merlot would also be nice.

Green salad with Sunny Citrus Vinaigrette (page 69)
Roast Chicken with Savory Guava Glaze (page 112)
Wild Rice with Mango and Pecans (page 241)
Calabaza Gratin (page 219)
Chocolate-Pecan Torte with Chocolate Glaze (page 284)
Wine: Match these fruity, sweet-tart flavors with a white viognier or red pinot noir.

Spinach salad with Orange-Raspberry Vinaigrette (page 72)
Grilled Swordfish with Lime, Jalapeño, and Sour Cream Sauce (page 198)
Ecuadorian Potato and Cheese Patties (page 249)
Steamed green beans
Tangy Lemon Tart with Sugary Almond Crust (page 293)
Wine: This meaty fish needs a red wine, such as a sangiovese from California.

Calabaza, Sweet Potato, and Apple Bisque (page 49)
Grilled Whole Turkey with Mojo Marinade (page 125)
Malanga Soufflé (page 222)

Carambola-Cranberry Sauce (page 266)
Guava Linzertorte (page 295)
Wine: A white sémillon/chardonnay blend from Australia or a cabernet sauvignon/merlot blend from Chile.

Finger-Lickin' Red-Hot Jerk-Barbecued Ribs with Tropical Barbecued Sauce (page 161)
Green Papaya and Red Pepper Slaw (page 79)
Warm Yuca Salad (page 81)
Corn on the cob
Chocolate Key Lime Tart (page 299)
Wine: Four-alarm food calls for a sturdy, fruity red—zinfandel.

Cuban-Style Black Bean Soup (page 245, see Variations)
Corn, Chile, and Cheese Quesadillas (page 21) topped with Guacamole with Papaya and Avocado (page 16)
Passion Fruit Sorbet (page 317, see Variations) and fresh tropical fruits
Wine: A fruity white riesling from Germany or California.

Yuca Puffs (page 29)
Stuffed Chayote (page 220)
Rice, Bean, and Corn Salad with Jalapeño Dressing (page 82)
Couldn't-Be-Easier Key Lime Cake (page 286)
Wine: A potent Sancerre from France.

Hot and Tangy Black Bean Dip (page 18)
Guacamole with Papaya (page 16)
Orange and Roasted Red Pepper Salsa (page 258)

Tortilla chips
Conch Fritters (page 31)
Salt Cod Accras (Fritters) (page 33)
Jamaican-Style Beef Patties (page 26)
Wines: A safe way to handle a multi-flavor cocktail party is to put out bottles of white, rosé, and red and let your guests choose for themselves. An inexpensive selection would be a dry California rosé or cabernet and a Chilean cabernet sauvignon. A go-for-broke, all-French solution would be white and red burgundies and a potent rosé from Domaines Ott. If you prefer to serve a single wine, a rosé champagne, Spanish cava, or other sparkling wine could handle all the flavors. Count on about six glasses per bottle.

Mixed Drinks

Here are five popular tropical drinks. They will mix more smoothly if you substitute an equal amount of Sugar Syrup (page 318) for the sugar.

CUBA LIBRE (FREE CUBA): Combine 2 tablespoons of fresh lime juice, the zest of ½ lime, and 2 ounces of light or dark rum in a tall glass filled with ice cubes. Fill with 4 to 6 ounces of Coca-Cola and stir well. Garnish with lime wedges.

MOJITO: Place 2 fresh mint sprigs, the zest and juice of 1 lime, and 1 teaspoon of sugar in a tall glass. Blend with a long spoon, crushing the mint. Add 1½ ounces of white rum and ice cubes, and fill with club soda. Stir and add another sprig of mint. Stir again. Serve with a straw.

DAIQUIRI: Place 2 ounces of light rum, 1 tablespoon of sugar, the juice of ½ lime, and ½ cup of crushed ice in a blender and process on high for 10 to 20 seconds. Serve in a chilled cocktail glass. (Variation: Add ¼ cup of frozen fruit puree such as guava, passion fruit, mango, or pineapple to the blender.)

PIÑA COLADA: Place 2 ounces of pineapple juice, 2 ounces of light rum, 2 ounces of cream of coconut (Coco Lopez), and the juice of ½ lime in a blender and process on high for 1 minute. Pour into a chilled glass. Garnish with coconut shavings.

SANGRIA (4 SERVINGS): Pour 1 bottle of Spanish Rioja and 1 cup of club soda into a glass pitcher. Add 4 tablespoons of sugar or more to taste, the juice of 2 limes, 1 cup of drained fruit cocktail, slightly crushed, and 1 orange, seeded and sliced. Fill the pitcher with ice cubes and stir well. Pour into wineglasses and garnish with fruit slices.

Selected Bibliography

Anderson, Jean, and Barbara Deskins. *The Nutrition Bible*. New York: William Morrow, 1995.

Harris, Dunstan A. *Island Cooking: Recipes from the Caribbean*. Freedom, Calif.: The Crossing Press, 1988.

Harris, Jessica B. *Sky Juice and Flying Fish: Traditional Caribbean Cooking*. New York: Simon & Schuster, 1991.

Herbst, Sharon Tyler. *The New Food Lover's Companion*. New York: Barron's, 1995.

Idone, Christopher, and Helen McEachrane. *Cooking Caribe*. New York: Clarkson Potter, 1992.

Karoff, Barbara. *South American Cooking: Foods and Feasts from the New World*. Reading, Mass.: Addison-Wesley, 1989.

Lalbachan, Pamela. *The Complete Caribbean Cookbook*. Boston: Charles E. Tuttle, 1994.

McGee, Harold. *On Food and Cooking*. New York: Charles Scribner's Sons, 1984.

Merola, Tony. *Floribbean Flavors: A Reflection of Florida's New Cuisine*. Nashville, Tenn.: FRP, 1996.

O'Higgins, Maria Josefa Lluria de. *A Taste of Old Cuba*. New York: HarperCollins, 1994.

Ortiz, Elisabeth Lambert. *The Book of Latin American Cooking*. New York: Vintage Books, 1980.

———. *The Complete Book of Caribbean Cooking*. New York: Ballantine Books, 1973.

Parks, Arva Moore. *Miami: The Magic City*. Miami, Fla.: Centennial Press, 1991.

Portes, Alejandro, and Alex Stepick. *City on the Edge: The Transformation of Miami*. Berkeley, Calif.: University of California Press, 1993.

Presilla, Maricel E. *Celebrating Cuban Cuisine*. Privately printed, 1987.

———. *Feliz Nochebuena, Feliz Navidad: Christmas Feasts of the Hispanic Caribbean*. New York: Henry Holt, 1994.

Raichlen, Steven. *Miami Spice*. New York: Workman, 1993.

Randelman, Mary Urrutia, and Joan Schwartz. *Memories of a Cuban Kitchen*. New York: Macmillan, 1992.

Routhier, Nicole. *Nicole Routhier's Fruit Cookbook*. New York: Workman, 1996.

Schlesinger, Chris, and John Willoughby. *Thrill of the Grill*. New York: William Morrow, 1990.

Schneider, Elizabeth. *Uncommon Fruits & Vegetables*. New York: Harper and Row, 1986.

Valldejuli, Carmen Aboy. *Puerto Rican Cookery*. Gretna, La.: Pelican Publishing Company, 1975.

Walsh, Robb, and Jay McCarthy. *Traveling Jamaica with Knife, Fork & Spoon: A Righteous Guide to Jamaican Cookery*. Freedom, Calif.: The Crossing Press, 1995.

Willinsky, Helen. *Jerk: Barbecue from Jamaica*. Freedom, Calif.: The Crossing Press, 1990.

Acknowledgments

We would both like to thank our agent, Jane Dystel, and our editor, Beth Crossman, for seeing the possibilities of this book and helping us to realize them; Elaine Stone for her skillful recipe testing; *Miami Herald* wine columnist Fred Tasker for sharing his knowledge; Tony Merola, formerly of Brooks Tropicals, and the staff of the Florida Department of Agriculture for answering countless questions; chefs Robbin Haas, Mark Militello, Douglas Rodriquez, Allen Susser, Norman Van Aken, and author Steven Raichlen for helping to make Miami cuisine what it is today.

—C.K., K.M.

My personal thanks go to Judy Gordon, Wendy Nottoli, and George Emerson for their loyal friendship and thoughtful input; my friend and former partner in Bobbi & Carole's Cooking School, Bobbi Garber, who always encouraged me to write; the talented teachers who gave classes at the school: Giuliano Bugialli, Maida Heatter, Ken Hom, Jacques Pepin, Perla Meyers, Paula Wolfert, and others; Julia Child, that great lady of cuisine, who showed me through her television shows and books that anything is possible. I am also indebted to my friends Sissi Feltman, Lois Kaufman, and Madeleine Low, whose sense of stylish entertaining was an inspiration, and to my cousin Annette Freedland for sharing her love of cooking. My gratitude to Elizabeth Kuehner-Smith and the staff at *Wine News*; Caroline Kelm, the lovely lady of Ocean Reef Club; caterer Juanita Plana, my Cuban connection; my friend, Beth Weiner; my brother and sister-in-law, Shelby and Sharon Freedland, for their warm encouragement; and my sons-in-law, Mark Kramer and Roy Hirschhorn.

—C.K.

My personal thanks to my husband, John Dorschner, and our sons, Andrew and Peter, for their love and support; Mary Kennedy for her able assistance and good company; Mimi O'Higgins for introducing me to the world of cookbooks and Cuban cuisine; Susan Friedland and Jennifer Griffin for guiding and encouraging me along the way; and *Miami Herald* writers Nancy Ancrum, Marta Barber, Viviana Carballo, Howard Kleinberg, Lydia Martin, Gay Nemeti, Geoffrey Tomb, and Andres Viglucci for their fine and informative work. I'm also grateful for the encouragement I received from my mother, Edna Martin; my brother, Mike Martin; my sister, Polly Martin; my aunts, Thora Framsted, Doris Lindquist, Lillian Miller, and Clara Waldo; my mother-in-law, Nellie Dorschner; my sister-in-law, Mary Marts; and friends Margaria Fichtner, Maida Heatter, Colleen Hettich, Paula Musto, Maria Temkin, Elisa Turner, Kim Yerkes, Kathy Foster, Jackie Greenberg, Robin Dougherty, and Joan Chrissos.

—K.M.

Index

acid, 276, 316
Adobo Seasoning, 157
   Roast Pork Little Havana with, 155–57
   Roast Pork Loin and Bananas with Tropical Glaze, 158–59
Africa, 7, 89, 207, 234, 235, 239
Ajiaco Santafereno (Bogotá-Style Chicken and Potato Stew), 59–60
all-purpose flour, 276
allspice, 173
   Caribbean Rice, 236
almond(s):
   Orange-Almond Biscotti, 305–6
   Tangy Lemon Tart with Sugary Almond Crust, 293–94
Andes Mountains, 248
annatto seeds, 115, 117, 239
   Yellow Rice with Corn, 239–40
appetizer(s) and first course(s), 13–39
   about, 15
   Basic Black Beans, 19–20
   Caribbean-Style Crab Cakes, 38–39

Coconut Shrimp in Island-Spiced Batter, 35–36
Conch Fritters, 31–32
Corn, Chile, and Cheese Quesadillas, 21–22
Crispy Corn Pancakes, 23
Guacamole with Papaya, 16
Hot and Tangy Black Bean Dip, 18
Jamaican-Style Beef Patties, 26–27
Potato and Black Bean Pancakes with Cilantro–Goat Cheese Sauce, 24–25
Salt Cod Accras (Fritters), 33–34
Scallop Seviche, 37
Yuca Puffs, 29–30
Apple Bisque, Calabaza, Sweet Potato, and, 49–50
Arawak Indians, 7, 10, 59, 90, 98
Argentina, 137
Arroz con Pollo (Chicken with Yellow Rice), 115–17
   variations, 117
Arugula with Fat-Free Papaya-Mint Dressing, Baby Greens and, 75–76

avocado(s), 17, 135
   Avocado, Corn, and Tomato Salsa, 197
   Aztecs and, 17
   Caribbean Fajitas, 135–36
   Cold Avocado and Cucumber Soup, 44
   discoloration, 136
   Grilled Pineapple and Avocado Salsa, 257
   Grilled Tuna Steaks with Avocado, Corn, and Tomato Salsa, 196–97
   Guacamole with Papaya, 16
   preparation, 17
   types of, 17, 135
Avocado, Corn, and Tomato Salsa, 197
   Grilled Tuna Steaks with, 196–97
Aztecs, 5, 185, 242, 284
   avocados and, 17

Baby Greens and Arugula with Fat-Free Papaya-Mint Dressing, 75–76
Bahamas, 31, 243